NATIONAL MUSIC
AND OTHER ESSAYS

NATIONAL MUSIC

and Other Essays

RALPH VAUGHAN WILLIAMS

London
OXFORD UNIVERSITY PRESS
1963

Oxford University Press, Amen House, London E.C.4

GLASGOW NEW YORK TORONTO MELBOURNE WELLINGTON
BOMBAY CALCUTTA MADRAS KARACHI LAHORE DACCA
CAPE TOWN SALISBURY NAIROBI IBADAN ACCRA
KUALA LUMPUR HONG KONG

NATIONAL MUSIC
First edition 1934

SOME THOUGHTS ON
BEETHOVEN'S CHORAL SYMPHONY
with writings on other musical subjects
First edition 1953

THE MAKING OF MUSIC
First edition 1955

First issued in OXFORD PAPERBACKS 1963

*Printed in Great Britain by
Richard Clay and Company, Ltd.,
Bungay, Suffolk*

Preface

Ralph Vaughan Williams started writing about music with a number of articles for *The Vocalist* in 1902. The subjects he chose ranged from 'The School of English Music' to *Ein Heldenleben*; from 'The Soporific Finale' and 'Good Taste' to 'The words of Wagner's Music Dramas'. He enjoyed putting his thoughts into order, and he had a direct and personal manner of presenting what were sometimes provocative ideas.

His contributions on 'Conducting' and 'Fugue' to the 1904 edition of *Grove* were comprehensive studies of given subjects, and his preface to *The English Hymnal* of 1906 was a statement of what he had set out to do in his musical editorship and why it seemed necessary. After this he wrote occasional articles for *The R.C.M. Magazine* and rewrote, for publication in *The Music Student*, lectures on folk-song, the fruit of his study and of his experience in collecting and arranging. He also wrote on 'British music of the Tudor Period', 'The age of Purcell', 'British Music in the eighteenth and early nineteenth centuries' and on 'Dance Tunes'.

After the 1914–18 war he contributed a few articles to *Music and Letters* and the *Journal of the English Folk Song Society*. *National Music* was the first book he published. He gave this title to a course of lectures (the Mary Flexner lectures) given in October and November 1932 at Bryn Mawr College, Pennsylvania. In his preface he wrote:

I have kept the personal form of address to an audience, but have modified many of the sentences. I have omitted a little and added a little. I have also altered the order in some places and have divided the material into nine chapters instead of the original six lectures. The lectures when originally delivered had the great advantage of being illustrated by Mr. Horace Alwyne, F.R.M.C.M. (Pianoforte) and the Bryn Mawr students choir under the direction of Mr. Ernest Willoughby, A.R.C.M.

This last sentence is an important one, for the writer always believed that music is to be heard: he liked to allow his audience to listen to the musical point he was describing or explaining. If no pianist or choir were available he would use a record, would play or, if necessary, sing himself. His singing was rather a last-ditch measure and was apt to divert the audience from the subject they were supposed to be considering. He was never afraid of committing himself and perhaps one of the bravest things he ever did was, when giving the first of the Arnold Bax Memorial Lectures at Cork University, to choose as his subject the relationship between English and Irish folk-songs, proving that all the Irish folk-songs came from the English pale. The audience did not lynch him, but some of them would have liked to. This he knew and wickedly enjoyed, describing the operation as 'making them think'.

The lectures originally entitled *The Making of Music*, now reprinted in this volume, were also given in America, at Cornell University, where he spent the autumn of 1954 as visiting Professor, a time he enjoyed very much. The lively interest and friendliness of young musicians delighted him, though he was somewhat dismayed by the number of incipient composers and fledgling musicologists who attended these talks. This trip was not confined to the eastern States for, with the blessing of Professor Donald Grout, the head of the Music Department, Keith Falkner, who was then a professor at Cornell, arranged a tour which took him across the country, lecturing at the Universities of Michigan, Ann Arbor, Chicago, Bloomington, and the University of California at Los Angeles, as well as at the University of Toronto. At all these he spoke on the substance of music, the historic and national importance of folk-songs, and the composer's necessity to use the speech of his own country before he ventured to explore foreign languages. It was a distillation of a lifetime's thoughts on 'the great art which we all serve' as he once called music.

Most of his audiences were young, many of them exploring the newest techniques and having the confident assurance of youth that they come to break all bonds and bring truth to a benighted world, yet, in every place where he spoke, he was greeted with warmth, and after he had finished his lecture the applause came from both hearts and minds, for his hearers recognized that they had been listening to someone whose life had been spent in learning, searching, testing, and working in the service of the art for which he spoke with understanding, authority, and love.

The third book included in this volume is a collection of mis-
cellaneous writings ranging over thirty years. The long essay on
Beethoven's Choral Symphony occupied R. V. W. during the
autumn weeks of 1939. The Leith Hill Musical Festival was founded
in 1905 and he had conducted it for its thirty years of existence.
He had led the choirs through a long exploration of old and new
choral music and had planned to make the Choral Symphony the
main work for the Towns division in 1940. With this hope he had
been restudying the work. When war started it was obvious that
such an undertaking would be impossible, but he wrote down all
the things he would have told his singers. He had done this once
before, in 1937, when he gave the first Dorking performance of
the 'St. Matthew Passion', for he had then given a preliminary
lecture to the choirs, which had been illuminating to them and had
clarified his own thoughts: this was just such another essay, with
just such an audience in mind.

The other long paper is 'A Musical Autobiography', written for
Hubert Foss, who was both his friend and his publisher and to
whose own book, *Ralph Vaughan Williams*, it was a contribution.
The two papers on Bach are the essence of a lifetime's love, study,
and experience of performing his works. The essay and the note on
Gustav Holst are a record of the most important friendship in the
writer's life, and that on Stanford is a centenary broadcast made in
memory of a man who had been their teacher. 'Shrubsole' is a
statement of the unique value of musicians who may achieve only
one small, perfect work in their lives, and the theme of 'Nationalism
and Internationalism' restates many of the arguments in the Bryn
Mawr lectures. 'A Minim's Rest' is about poets as well as musicians
and starts from the crazy gang whose antics and devices are so
much a part of *The Merry Wives of Windsor* and of R. V. W.'s own
opera *Sir John in Love*.

Perhaps the heart of the matter, the composer's musical belief,
is most clearly stated in 'The Letter and the Spirit'. The argument
is that music must be heard. As he says, 'in our imperfect existence
what means have we of reaching what lies beyond the senses but
through those senses?'

In his essay *The Making of Music* R. V. W. quotes Mendelssohn's
saying 'the meaning of music is too precise for words'. These

collected writings on music all return to that truth, but all cast light on the approach to that meaning.

U. V. W.

January 1963.

Acknowledgements

The Mary Flexner Lectures on the Humanities were delivered by Ralph Vaughan Williams at Bryn Mawr College in October and November 1932, on a fund established by Bernard Flexner in honour of his sister. They were first published under the title *National Music* by the Oxford University Press, which also published *Some thoughts on Beethoven's Choral Symphony with writings on other musical subjects*.

'The Letter and the Spirit' and 'Gustav Holst' first appeared in *Music and Letters*; 'Gustav Holst—a note' and 'Composing for the Films' first appeared in *The R.C.M. Magazine*; 'A Minim's Rest' first appeared in *Essays Mainly on the Nineteenth Century presented to Sir Humphrey Milford* published by the Oxford University Press; 'Bach, the Great Bourgeois' (originally a broadcast talk) first appeared in *The Listener*; 'A Musical Autobiography' first appeared in *Ralph Vaughan Williams: a Study*, by Hubert Foss, published by Messrs. George G. Harrap & Co. Ltd.; 'Shrubsole' first appeared in the *Manchester Guardian*; and 'Charles Villiers Stanford' (also originally a broadcast talk) first appeared in *London Calling*. Grateful acknowledgement is made to the editors and publishers of these publications for permission to reprint these essays.

Thanks are also due to the following publishers for permission to print extracts from the works of Gustav Holst: J. Curwen & Sons, Ltd. (*The Planets* and *Savitri*); Stainer & Bell, Ltd. (*Hymn of Jesus* and 'Funeral Hymn'); and Novello & Co. Ltd. (*Ode to Death* and 'John Barleycorn').

The Making of Music was first published by Cornell University Press, to whom thanks are due for permission to reproduce it here. It contains the substance, though not necessarily the actual words, of a series of four lectures given at Cornell University in the autumn of 1954. The author has made some omissions and some additions; the epilogue is adapted from a lecture given at Yale University on 1 December 1954.

Contents

THE MAKING OF MUSIC

NATIONAL MUSIC

1

Should Music be National?

Whistler used to say that it was as ridiculous to talk about national art as national chemistry. In saying this he failed to see the difference between art and science.

Science is the pure pursuit of knowledge and thus knows no boundaries. Art, and especially the art of music, uses knowledge as a means to the evocation of personal experience in terms which will be intelligible to and command the sympathy of others. These others must clearly be primarily those who by race, tradition, and cultural experience are the nearest to him; in fact those of his own nation, or other kind of homogeneous community. In the sister arts of painting and poetry this factor of nationality is more obvious, due in poetry to the Tower of Babel and in painting to the fact that the painter naturally tends to build his visual imagination on what he normally sees around him. But unfortunately for the art of music some misguided thinker, probably first cousin to the man who invented the unfortunate phrase 'a good European', has described music as 'the universal language'. It is not even true that music has an universal vocabulary, but even if it were so it is the use of the vocabulary that counts and no one supposes that French and English are the same language because they happen to use twenty-five out of twenty-six of the letters of their alphabet in common. In the same way, in spite of the fact that they have a musical alphabet in common, nobody could mistake Wagner for Verdi or Debussy for Richard Strauss. And, similarly, in spite of wide divergencies of

personal style, there is a common factor in the music say of Schumann and Weber.

And this common factor is nationality. As Hubert Parry said in
his inaugural address to the Folk Song Society of England, 'True
Style comes not from the individual but from the products of
crowds of fellow-workers who sift and try and try again till they
have found the thing that suits their native taste. . . . Style is
ultimately national.'

I am speaking, for the moment, not of the appeal of a work
of art, but of its origin. Some music may appeal only in its immediate surroundings; some may be national in its influence and
some may transcend these bounds and be world-wide in its
acceptance. But we may be quite sure that the composer who
tries to be cosmopolitan from the outset will fail, not only with
the world at large, but with his own people as well. Was anyone
ever more local, or even parochial, than Shakespeare? Even
when he follows the fashion and gives his characters Italian names
they betray their origin at once by their language and their senti-
ments.

Possibly you may think this an unfair example, because a poet
has not the common vocabulary of the musician, so let me take
another example.

One of the three great composers of the world (personally I
believe the greatest) was John Sebastian Bach. Here, you may say,
is the universal musician if ever there was one; yet no one could be
more local, in his origin, his life work, and his fame for nearly a
hundred years after his death, than Bach. He was to outward
appearance no more than one of a fraternity of town organists and
'town pipers' whose business it was to provide the necessary music
for the great occasions in church and city. He never left his native
country, seldom even his own city of Leipzig. 'World Movements'
in art were then unheard of; moreover, it was the tradition of his
own country which inspired him. True, he studied eagerly all the
music of foreign composers that came his way in order to improve
his craft. But is not the work of Bach built up on two great foundations, the organ music of his Teutonic predecessors and the popular
hymn-tunes of his own people? Who has heard nowadays of the
cosmopolitan hero Marchand, except as being the man who ran

away from the Court of Dresden to avoid comparison with the local organist Bach?

In what I have up to now said I shall perhaps not have been clear unless I dispose at once of two fallacies. The first of these is that the artist invents for himself alone. No man lives or moves or could do so, even if he wanted to, for himself alone. The actual process of artistic invention, whether it be by voice, verse, or brush, pre-supposes an audience; someone to hear, read, or see. Of course the sincere artist cannot deliberately compose what he dislikes. But artistic inspiration is like Dryden's angel which must be brought down from heaven to earth. A work of art is like a theophany which takes different forms to different beholders. In other words, a com-poser wishes to make himself intelligible. This surely is the prime motive of the act of artistic invention and to be intelligible he must clothe his inspiration in such forms as the circumstances of time, place, and subject dictate.

This should come unself-consciously to the artist, but if he con-sciously tries to express himself in a way which is contrary to his surroundings, and therefore to his own nature, he is evidently being, though perhaps he does not know it, insincere. It is surely as bad to be self-consciously cosmopolitan as self-consciously national.

The other fallacy is that the genius springs from nowhere, defies all rules, acknowledges no musical ancestry and is beholden to no tradition. The first thing we have to realize is that the great men of music close periods; they do not inaugurate them. The pioneer work, the finding of new paths, is left to the smaller men. We can trace the musical genealogy of Beethoven, starting right back from Philipp Emanuel Bach, through Haydn and Mozart, with even such smaller fry as Cimarosa and Cherubini to lay the foundations of the edifice. Is not the mighty river of Wagner but a confluence of the smaller streams, Weber, Marschner, and Liszt?

I would define genius as the right man in the right place at the right time. We know, of course, too many instances of the time being ripe and the place being vacant and no man to fill it. But we shall never know of the numbers of 'mute and inglorious Miltons' who failed because the place and time were not ready for them. Was not Purcell a genius born before his time? Was not Sullivan a jewel in the wrong setting?

I read the other day in a notice by a responsible music critic that 'it only takes one man to write a symphony'. Surely this is an entire misconception. A great work of art can only be born under the right surroundings and in the right atmosphere. Bach himself, if I may again quote him as an example, was only able to produce his fugues, his Passions, his cantatas, because there had preceded him generations of smaller composers, specimens of the despised class of 'local musicians' who had no other ambition than to provide worthily and with dignity the music required of them: craftsmen perhaps rather than conscious artists. Thus there spread among the quiet and unambitious people of northern Germany a habit, so to speak, of music, the desire to make it part of their daily life, and it was into this atmosphere that John Sebastian Bach was born.

The ideal thing, of course, would be for the whole community to take to music as it takes to language from its youth up, naturally, without conscious thought or specialized training; so that, just as the necessity for expressing our material wants leads us when quite young to perfect our technique of speaking, so our spiritual wants should lead us to perfect our technique of emotional expression and above all that of music. But this is an age of specialization and delegation. We employ specialists to do more and more for us instead of doing it ourselves. We even get other people to play our games for us and look on shivering at a football match, instead of getting out of it for ourselves the healthy exercise and excitement which should surely be its only object.

Specialization may be all very well in purely material things. For example, we cannot make good cigars in England and it is quite right therefore that we should leave the production of that luxury to others and occupy ourselves in making something which our circumstances and climate permit of. The most rabid chauvinist has never suggested that Englishmen should be forced to smoke impossible cigars merely because they are made at home. We say quite rightly that those who want that luxury and can afford it must get it from abroad.

Now there are some people who apply this 'cigar' theory to the arts and especially to music; to music especially, because music is not one of the 'naturally protected' industries like the sister arts of painting and poetry. The 'cigar' theory of music is then this—I am speaking of course of my own country England, but I believe it exists equally virulently in yours: that music is not an industry which flourishes naturally in our climate; that, therefore, those who want it and can afford it must hire it from abroad. This idea has been prevalent among us for generations. It began in England, I think, in the early eighteenth century when the political power got into the hands of the entirely uncultured landed gentry and the practice of art was considered unworthy of a gentleman, from which it followed that you had to hire a 'damned foreigner' to do it for you if you wanted it, from which in its turn followed the corollary that the type of music which the foreigner brought with him was the only type worth having and that the very different type of music which was being made at home must necessarily be wrong. These ideas were fostered by the fact that we had a foreign court at St. James's who apparently did not share the English snobbery about home-made art and so brought the music made in their own homes to England with them. So, the official music, whether it took the form of Mr. Handel to compose an oratorio, or an oboe player in a regimental band, was imported from Germany. This snobbery is equally virulent to this day. The musician indeed is not despised, but it is equally felt that music cannot be something which is native to us and when imported from abroad it must of necessity be better.

Let me take an analogy from architecture. When a stranger arrives in New York he finds imitations of Florentine palaces, replicas of Gothic cathedrals, suggestions of Greek temples, buildings put up before America began to realize that she had an artistic consciousness of her own.

All these things the visitor dismisses without interest and turns to her railway stations, her offices and shops; buildings dictated by the necessity of the case, a truly national style of architecture evolved from national surroundings. Should it not be the same with music?

As long as a country is content to take its music passively there can be no really artistic vitality in the nation. I can only speak from the experience of my own country. In England we are too apt to think of music in terms of the cosmopolitan celebrities of the Queen's Hall and Covent Garden Opera. These are, so to speak, the crest of the wave, but behind that crest must be the driving force which makes the body of the wave. It is below the surface that we must look for the power which occasionally throws up a Schnabel, a Sibelius, or a Toscanini. What makes me hope for the musical future of any country is not the distinguished names which appear on the front page of the newspapers, but the music that is going on at home, in the schools, and in the local choral societies.

Can we expect garden flowers to grow in soil so barren that the wild flowers cannot exist there? Perhaps one day the supply of international artists will fail us and we shall turn in vain to our own country to supply their places. Will there be any source to supply it from? You remember the story of the *nouveau riche* who bought a plot of land and built a stately home on it, but he found that no amount of money could provide him straightaway with the spreading cedars and immemorial elms and velvet lawns which should be the accompaniment of such a home. Such things can only grow in a soil prepared by years of humble toil.

Hubert Parry in his book, *The Evolution of the Art of Music*, has shown how music like everything else in the world is subject to the laws of evolution, that there is no difference in kind but only in degree between Beethoven and the humblest singer of a folk-song. The principles of artistic beauty, of the relationships of design and expression, are neither trade secrets nor esoteric mysteries revealed to the few; indeed if these principles are to have any meaning to us they must be founded on what is natural to the human being. Perfection of form is equally possible in the most primitive music and in the most elaborate.

The principles which govern the composition of music are, we find, not arbitrary rules, nor as some people apparently think, barriers put up by mediocre practitioners to prevent the young genius from entering the academic grove; they are not the tricks of the trade or even the mysteries of the craft, they are founded on the very nature of human beings. Take, for example, the principle of repetition as a factor of design: either the cumulative effect of mere reiteration, such as we get in the Trio of the scherzo of Beethoven's Ninth Symphony, or in a cruder form in Ravel's Bolero; or the constant repetition of a ground bass as in Bach's organ Passacaglia or the finale of Brahms's Fourth Symphony. Travellers tell us that the primitive savage as soon as he gets as far as inventing some little rhythmical or melodic pattern will repeat it endlessly. In all these cases we have illustrations of the fundamental principle of emphasis by repetition.

After a time the savage will get tired of his little musical phrase and will invent another and often this new phrase will be at a new pitch so as to bring into play as many new notes as possible. Why? Because his throat muscles and his perceptive faculties are wearied by the constant repetition.

Is not this exactly the principle of the second subject of the classical sonata, which is in a key which brings into play as many new sounds as possible? Then we have the principle of symmetry also found in primitive music when the singer, having got tired in turn with his new phrase, harks back to the old one.

And so I could go on showing you how Beethoven is but a later stage in the development of those principles which actuated the primitive Teuton when he desired to make himself artistically intelligible.

The greatest artist belongs inevitably to his country as much as the humblest singer in a remote village—they and all those who come between them are links in the same chain, manifestations on their different levels of the same desire for artistic expression, and, moreover, the same nature of artistic expression.

I am quite prepared for the objection that nationalism limits the scope of art, that what we want is the best, from wherever it comes. My objectors will probably quote Tennyson and tell me that 'We needs must love the highest when we see it' and that we should educate the young to appreciate this mysterious 'highest' from the beginning. Or perhaps they will tell me with Rossini that they know only two kinds of music, good and bad. So perhaps we had better digress here for a few moments and try to find out what good music is, and whether there is such a thing as absolute good music; or even if there is such an absolute good, whether it must not take different forms for different hearers. Myself, I doubt if there is this absolute standard of goodness. I think it will vary with the occasion on which it is performed, with the period at which it was composed and with the nationality of those that listen to it. Let us take examples of each of these—firstly, with regard to the occasion. The Venusberg music from *Tannhäuser* is good music when it comes at the right dramatic moment in the opera, but it is bad music when it is played on an organ in church. I am sorry to have to tell you that this is not an imaginary experience. A waltz of Johann Strauss is good music in its proper place as an accompaniment to dancing and festivity, but it would be bad music if it were interpolated in the middle of the *St. Matthew Passion*. And may we not even say that Bach's B minor Mass would be bad music if it were played in a restaurant as an accompaniment to eating and drinking?

Secondly, does not the standard of goodness vary with time? What was good for the fifteenth century is not necessarily good for the twentieth. Surely each new generation requires something different to satisfy its different ideals. Of course there is some music that seems to defy the ravages of time and to speak a new message to each successive generation. But even the greatest music is not eternal. We can still appreciate Bach and Handel or even Palestrina, but Dufay and Dunstable have little more than an historical interest for us now. But they were great men in their day and perhaps the time will come when Bach, Handel, Beethoven, and Wagner will drop out and have no message left for us. Sometimes of course the clock goes round full circle and the twentieth century comprehends what had ceased to have any meaning for the nineteenth. This is the case with the modern revival of Bach after nearly one hundred and fifty years of neglect, or the modern appreciation of Elizabethan madrigals. There may be many composers who have something genuine to say to us for a short time and for that short time their music may surely be classed as good. We all know that when an idiom is new we cannot detect the difference between the really original mind and the mere imitator. But when the idiom passes into the realm of everyday commonplace then and then only we can tell the true from the false. For example, any student at a music school can now reproduce the tricks of Debussy's style, and therefore it is now, and only now, that we can discover whether Debussy had something genuine to say or whether when the secret of his style becomes common property the message of which that style was the vehicle will disappear.

Then there is the question of place. Is music that is good music for one country or one community necessarily good music for another? It is true that the great monuments of music, the Missa Papae Marcelli, or the *St. Matthew Passion*, or the Ninth Symphony, or *Die Meistersinger*, have a world wide appeal, but first they must appeal to the people, and in the circumstances where they were created. It is because Palestrina and Verdi are essentially Italian and because Bach, Beethoven, and Wagner are essentially German that their message transcends their frontiers. And even so, the *St. Matthew Passion*, much as it is loved and admired in other countries, must mean much more to the German, who recognizes in it the consummation of all that he learnt from childhood in the great traditional chorales which are his special inheritance. Beethoven has an universal meaning, but to the German, who finds in it that same spirit exemplified in its more homely form in those Volkslieder which he learnt in his childhood, he must also have a specialized meaning.

Every composer cannot expect to have a world-wide message, but he may reasonably expect to have a special message for his own people and many young composers make the mistake of imagining they can be universal without at first having been local. Is it not reasonable to suppose that those who share our life, our history, our customs, our climate, even our food, should have some secret to impart to us which the foreign composer, though he be perhaps more imaginative, more powerful, more technically equipped, is not able to give us? This is the secret of the national composer, the secret to which he only has the key, which no foreigner can share with him and which he alone is able to tell to his fellow countrymen. But is he prepared with his secret? Must he not limit himself to a certain extent so as to give his message its full force? For after all it is the millstream forcing its way through narrow channels which gathers strength to turn the water-wheel. As long as composers persist in serving up at second-hand the externals of the music of other nations, they must not be surprised if audiences prefer the real Brahms, the real Wagner, the real Debussy, or the real Stravinsky to their pale reflections.

What a composer has to do is to find out the real message he has to convey to the community and say it directly and without equivocation. I know there is a temptation each time a new star appears on the musical horizon to say, 'What a fine fellow this is, let us try and do something like this at home,' quite forgetting that the result will not sound at all the same when transplanted from its natural soil. It is all very well to catch at the prophet's robe, but the mantle of Elijah is apt, like all second-hand clothing, to prove the worst of misfits. How is the composer to find himself? How is he to stimulate his imagination in a way that will lead him to voicing himself and his fellows? I think that composers are much too fond of going to concerts—I am speaking now, of course of the technically equipped composer. At the concert we hear the finished product. What the artist should be concerned with is the raw material. Have we not all about us forms of musical expression which we can take and purify and raise to the level of great art? Have we not all around us occasions crying out for music? Do not all our great pageants of human beings require music for their full expression? We must cultivate a sense of musical citizenship. Why should not the musician be the servant of the state and build national monuments like the painter, the writer, or the architect?

Come muse, migrate from Greece and Ionia,
Cross out please those immensely overpaid accounts,
That matter of Troy and Achilles' wrath, and Æneas', Odysseus' wanderings,
Placard 'removed' and 'to let' on the rocks of your snowy Parnassus,
Repeat at Jerusalem, place the notice high on Jaffa's gate and on Mount
    Moriah,
The same on the walls of your German, French and Spanish castles, and
    Italian collections,
For know a better, fresher, busier sphere,
A wide, untried domain awaits, demands you.

Art for art's sake has never flourished among the English-speaking nations. We are often called inartistic because our art is unconscious. Our drama and poetry have evolved by accident while we thought we were doing something else, and so it will be with our music. The composer must not shut himself up and think about art; he must live with his fellows and make his art an expression of the whole life of the community. If we seek for art we shall not find it. There are very few great composers, but there can be many sincere composers. There is nothing in the world worse than sham good music. There is no form of insincerity more subtle than that which is coupled with great earnestness of purpose and determination to do only the best and the highest, the unconscious insincerity which leads us to build up great designs which we cannot fill and to simulate emotions which we can only experience vicariously. But, you may say, are we to learn nothing from the great masters? Where are our models to come from? Of course we can learn everything from the great masters and one of the great things we can learn from them is their sureness of purpose. When we are sure of our purpose we can safely follow the advice of St. Paul 'to prove all things and to hold to that which is good'. But it is dangerous to go about 'proving all things' until you have made up your mind what is good for you.

First, then, see your direction clear and then by all means go to Paris, or Berlin, or Peking if you like and study and learn everything that will help you to carry out that purpose.

We have in England today a certain number of composers who have achieved fame. In the older generation Elgar and Parry, among those of middle age Holst and Bax, and of the quite young Walton and Lambert. All these served their apprenticeship at home. There are several others who thought that their own country was not good enough for them and went off in the early stages to become little Germans or little Frenchmen. Their names I will not give to you because they are unknown even to their fellow countrymen.

I am told that when grape vines were first cultivated in California the vineyard masters used to try the experiment of importing plants from France or Italy and setting them in their own soil. The result was that the grapes acquired a peculiar individual flavour, so strong was the influence of the soil in which they were planted. I think I need hardly draw the moral of this, namely, that if the roots of your art are firmly planted in your own soil and that soil has anything individual to give you, you may still gain the whole world and not lose your own souls.

2

Some Tentative Ideas on the Origins of Music

In considering the national aspects of music we ought to think of what causes our inspiration and also to whom it is to be addressed, that is to say, how far should the origins of music be national, how far should the meaning of music be national?

And perhaps before we go on to this we ought to diverge a little bit and try and find out why it is we want music at all in our lives.

What is the origin of that impulse to self-expression by means of sound? We could possibly trace back painting, poetry, and architecture to an utilitarian basis. I am not saying that this is so, but the argument can be put forward. Now the great glory of music to my mind is that it is absolutely useless. The painter is bound by the same medium whether he is painting a great landscape or whether he is touching up the weather-stains on his front gate. Language is the medium both of *Paradise Lost* and of an auctioneer's catalogue. But music subserves no utilitarian purpose; it is the vehicle of emotional expression and nothing else.

Why then do we want music? Hubert Parry in his *Art of Music* writes, 'It is the intensity of the pleasure or interest the artist feels in what is actually present to his imagination that drives him to utterance. The instinct of utterance makes it a necessity to find terms which will be understood by other beings.'

Let us try to find out what is the exact process of the invention and making of music.

Music is only made when actual musical sounds are produced, and here I would emphasize very strongly that the black dots which we see printed on a piece of paper are not music; they are simply a rather clumsy device invented by composers; a series of conventional signs to show to those who are not within hearing distance how they may with the necessary means at their command reproduce the sounds imagined by the composer.

A sheet of printed music is like a map where you see a series of conventional signs, by which the skilled map reader will know that the road he is on will go north or south, that at one moment he will go up a steep hill and that at another he will cross a river by a bridge. That this town has a church, and that that village has an inn. Or to use another simile, heard music has the same relation to the printed notes as a railway journey has to a time table. But the printed notes are no more music than the map is the country which it represents or the time table the journey which it indicates.

We may imagine that in primitive times—and indeed it still happens when someone sits down at the pianoforte and improvises —the invention and production of sound may have been simultaneous, that there was no differentiation between the performer and the composer. But gradually specialization must have set in; those who invented music became separated from those who performed it, though of course till the invention of writing the man who invented a tune had to sing it or play it himself in order to communicate it to others. Those others, if they were incapable of inventing anything for themselves, but were desirous, as I believe everyone is, of artistic self-expression, would learn that tune and sing it and thus the differentiation between composer and performer came about.

What is the whole process, starting with the initial invention of music and leading on to the final stage when the sounds imagined by the composer are actually heard on those instruments or voices for which he designed them? What should be the object which the performer has in view when he translates these imaginings into actual sound? And what should be the object of the composer when he invents music?

We all, whether we are artists or not, experience moments when we want to get outside the limitations of ordinary life, when we see dimly a vision of something beyond. These moments affect us in different ways. Some people under their influence want to do a great or a kind or an heroic deed; some people want to go and kill something or fight somebody; some people go and play a game or just walk it off; but those whom we call artists find the desire to create beauty irresistible. For painters it takes the form of idealizing nature; for architects the beauty of solid form; for poets the magic of ordered words, and for composers the magic of ordered sound. Now it is not enough to feel these things; the artist wants to communicate them as well, to crystallize these vague imaginings into, as I have already said, ordered sound, clear and intelligible; and to do this he must make a synthesis between the thing to be expressed and the means of expression. Thus there has arisen the technical side of music. Musical instruments have been devised which will translate these ideas in the most sensitive manner possible; artists spend years discovering how to get the best results from these instruments and composers, of course, have to study how to translate their ideas into the terms of the means at their command. And first of all the composer has, as I have said, to devise a series of dots and dashes which will explain, it must be confessed, in a very inadequate manner, the pitch, the duration, the intensity, and to a certain extent the quality of the sounds he wishes the performer to produce. The composer starts with a vision and ends with a series of black dots. The performer's process is exactly the reverse; he starts with the black dots and from these has to work back to the composer's vision. First he must find out the sounds that these black dots represent and the quicker he can get over this process the sooner he will be able to get on to something more important. Therefore though a good sight reader is not necessarily a good musician, it is very useful for a musician to be a good sight reader. Then the performer has to learn how best to make these sounds. Here he is partly dependent, of course, on the instrument maker, but it is here that vocal and instrumental technique have their use. Then he must learn to view any series of these black dots both as a whole and in detail and to discover the relation of the parts to the whole, and it is under this heading that I would place such things as phrasing, sense of form, and climax—what we generically call musicianship. When he has mastered these he is ready to start and reproduce the composer's vision. Then, and then only, is he in a position to find out whether there is any vision to reproduce.

Thus we come round full circle: the origin of inspiration and its final fruition should be one and the same thing.

How are we to find out whether music as a whole, and especially the music of our own country, has a national basis? Or perhaps we may go further still and ask ourselves whether there is any sanction for the art of music at all, and if so, how we are to discover it. I suppose that most of you to whom I am speaking are studying music—some of you perhaps are teaching it and you find that at present your time is, quite rightly, largely occupied with the technical aspect of music, with the means rather than with the end. Do you not ask yourselves sometimes what is the end? Or perhaps I should put it better by saying, what is the beginning? You can hardly expect a gardener to be able to cultivate beautiful flowers in a soil which is so barren that no wild flowers will grow there. Must we not pre-suppose that there must be wild flowers of music before we occupy ourselves with our hydrangeas and Gloire de Dijon roses? Before the student undertakes the task of technical training he should satisfy himself that his art is something inborn in man. He should try and imagine whether the absolutely unsophisticated though naturally musical man—one who has no learning and no contact with learning, one who cannot read or write and thus repeat any-thing stereotyped by others, one who is untravelled and therefore self-dependent for his inspiration, one in fact whose artistic utterance will be entirely spontaneous and unself-conscious—whether such a one would be able to invent any form of music, and if so whether it would be at all like the music which we admire. 'Ought not I,' he may say, 'to expect it to illustrate in embryonic form those principles which I find in the music of the great masters? Unless I can imagine such a man surely this great art of music can be nothing but a house with no foundation, a sort of fool's paradise, a mirage which will disappear before the first touch of real life.'

In fact if we did not know from actual experience that there was such a thing as folk-song we should have to imagine it theoretically.

But we do find the answer to this inquiry in real fact. The theoretical folk-singer has been discovered to be an actuality. We really do find these unlettered, unsophisticated, and untravelled people who make music which is often beautiful in itself and has in it the germs of great art.

Some people express surprise and even polite disbelief in the idea that people who have never seen a pianoforte or had any harmony lessons and do not even know what a dominant or consecutive fifth is should be able to invent beautiful music: they either shut their ears and declare that it is not really beautiful but 'only sounds so', or they declare that these singers must have 'heard it somewhere'. Perhaps you know the story of the missionary who, hearing some savages chanting this rhythm ♩· ♪ ♫ 𝄽 , which after all is a very primitive one and very likely to be found among unsophisticated people, expressed his delight in discovering, as he thought, that Handel's 'Hallelujah Chorus' had penetrated to even these benighted regions. Or to give an example which came under my own notice. A distinguished English musician could not be persuaded to believe that a countryman who could not even read could possibly sing 'correctly' in the Dorian mode. He might as well have expressed surprise with M. Jourdain at being able to speak prose.

The truth is, of course, that these scientific expressions are not arbitrary rules, but are explanations of phenomena. The modal system, for example, is simply a tabulation by scientists of the various methods in which it is natural for people to sing. Again, nobody invented sonata form; it is merely a theoretical explanation of the mould into which people's musical thoughts have naturally flowed. Therefore far from expressing surprise at a folk-song being beautiful we ought to be surprised if it were not so, for otherwise we might doubt the authenticity of our whole canon of musical beauty.

Nevertheless the notion that folk-music is a degenerate version of what we call composed music dies hard, so perhaps I had better say a little more about it. If this were really so, if folk-song were only half-remembered relics of the composed music of past centuries, should we not be able to settle the matter by going to our museums and looking through the old printed music? We shall find there nothing remotely resembling the traditional song of our country except, of course, such things as the deliberate transcriptions of the popular melodies in the *Fitzwilliam Virginal Book*.

I cannot see why it should not be equally natural to presuppose an aptitude for singing in the natural man as an aptitude for speaking; indeed, singing of a primitive kind may be supposed to come before speaking, just as emotion is something more primitive than thought, and the indeterminate howls which travellers tell us savages make to accompany dances or ceremonies in which they are emotionally excited may be supposed to be the beginnings of music. However, the difference between real music and mere sound depends on the fact of definitely sustained notes with definite relations to each other. Some people hold that this definition of sounds can only have arisen after the invention of the pipe or some other primitive musical instrument; but I shall be able to give you personal evidence to the contrary. I have no doubt myself that song is the beginning of music and that purely instrumental music is a later development. Song, then, I believe, is nothing less than speech charged with emotion. The German words *sagen* and *singen* were in early times interchangeable and to this day a country singer will speak of 'telling' you a song, not of singing it. Indeed the folk-singer (of course I am speaking of England only, the only place of which I have personal knowledge), the English folk-singer, seems unable to dissociate words and tune: if he has forgotten the words of a song he is very seldom able to hum you the tune and if you in your turn were to sing the words he knew to a different tune he would be satisfied that you knew the song, and I believe the same is true of dance tunes. A country musician, so Cecil Sharp relates, took it for granted that when his hearers had got the tune of a dance they would be able to perform the dance as well.

The personal evidence I will give you is as follows. I was once listening to an open air preacher. He started his sermon in a speaking voice, but as he grew more excited the sounds gradually became defined, first one definite note, then two, and finally a little group of five notes.

The notes being *a*, *b*, *a*, *g*, *a*, with an occasional drop down to *e*.

It seemed that I had witnessed the change from speech to song in actual process. The increased emotional excitement had produced two results, definition and the desire for a decorative pattern. Perhaps I went too far in calling this song, perhaps I should call it

the raw material of song. I will now give you examples of actual
folk-songs built on this very group of three notes.

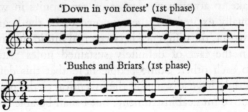

These are what we call the stock phrases of folk-song which
play an important part in folk-music just as the stock verbal phrase
plays an important part in ballad poetry. There is a good practical
reason for these stock phrases. Any of you who are writers, whether
you are writing a magazine article or a symphony, know that the
great difficulty is how to start, and the stock phrase solved this
difficulty with the ballad maker—so nine out of ten ballads start
with some common phrase such as 'As I walked out' or 'It is of a'
or 'Come all you' and so on. In the same way we find a common
opening to many folk-tunes, and this opening would naturally be a
variant of some musical formula which comes naturally to the
human voice. Now let us examine this little phrase again. Cannot
we suppose that our reciter in still greater moments of excitement
will feel inclined to add to and embellish his little group of notes?
Embellishment, we all know, is a natural consequence of heightened
emotion, and it is a good criterion of the more ornamental phrases
in a composer's work to make up our minds whether they are the
result of an emotional impulse or whether they are meaningless
ornament. Take, for example, the cadenza-like passages in the slow
movement of Brahms's Clarinet Quintet and compare them with
the flourishes, say, in a Vieuxtemps Concerto, or take the melismata
charged with feeling of which Bach was so fond and compare them
with the meaningless coloratura of his contemporary Italian opera
composers.

Increased emotional excitement leads to increase of ornament so
that our original phrase might eventually grow perhaps into this;

which is as a matter of fact an actual phrase out of a known folk-song. Here we have what we can call a complete musical phrase.

The business of the ballad singer is to fit his music to the pattern of a rhymed verse, usually a four-line stanza with some simple scheme of rhyme; so our melodic phrase has somehow to be developed to cover the whole ground. I assume for the sake of simplicity a single invention and will not discuss here the possibility of communal invention. If the singer is pleased with his initial little bit of melody he will feel inclined to repeat it. Repetition is one of the fundamentals of artistic intelligibility. Hubert Parry in his chapter on primitive music gives examples of savage music which consists of nothing else but a simple melodic phrase repeated over and over again. But supposing our ballad singer finds that the verse he has to recite is like the dream of Bottom the weaver in 8's and 6's. The music which he has adapted to the first line will not suit the second so something new will have to grow out of the old to fit the shortened number of syllables. This gives us a new funda-mental of musical structure, that of contrast. When he gets to the third line he finds 8 syllables again and to his great delight he finds he can use his first music that had pleased him so once more. Here we have a very primitive example of the formula *A.B.A.* which in an infinite variety of forms may be said to govern the whole of musical structure, whether we look for it in a simple ballad, in the Ninth Symphony, or in the Prelude to 'Tristan'. Let us analyse an actual example, 'Searching for Lambs', incidentally one of the most beautiful of the English folk-songs.

The words of the first stanza, which after all will largely determine the form of the music, are as follows:

> 'As I went out one May morning
>   One May morning betime
> I met a maid from home had strayed
>   Just as the sun did shine.'

The tune starts off with the elaborate form of our stock phrase (*A*). Then comes a short line; so a new phrase has to grow out of the old—a repetition in fact a third higher with a major third this time and an indeterminate ending, for we must not have any feeling of finality yet (*B*).

Now for the third line. You might expect a mere repetition of the first. But the third line of the words is not an exact metrical repetition of the first and moreover has a mid-rhyme. So some variety in the music is suggested. We start off with a repetition of line 2 which flows in a free sequence (suggesting by its parallelism the mid-rhyme (C)).

Now for the last line. Here we obviously need some allusion to the beginning to clench the whole. So the sequential phrase is merely carried on, and behold, we have our initial phrase once more complete, growing naturally out of the sequential phrase and, to complete all, 3 notes of coda added to make up the line (D).

What a wealth of unconscious art in so simple a tune! All the principles of great art are here exemplified: unity, variety, symmetry, development, continuity.

I will give you one more example of the growth of a tune from the same root idea. This time the third is major and the embellishing notes are consequently differently placed.

I need not analyse this tune in detail, but the same principles apply. The song is 'The Water is Wide'.

3

The Folk-song

We have now traced our course from the excited speech phrase to the complete song stanza. But we took no account of the element of rhythm.

The preacher of whom I told you, when he got excited established a definite relationship between the pitch of the notes he used but not between their duration, and it is this definite relationship between the duration of successive musical sounds which we call rhythm. Melody can exist apart from rhythm just as rhythm can exist apart from melody. But song can only be said to come into being when the two are in combination. Rhythm, I suppose, grows out of the dance, or out of the various bodily actions which we do in our daily life such as walking, or pulling on a rope. And even in speech we find that, unconsciously, if we want to be very emphatic or to impress something strongly on our memory we introduce a rhythmical pattern into what we are saying.

Now in primitive times before there were newspapers to tell us the news, history books to teach us the past, and novels to excite our imagination, all these things had to be done by the ballad singer who naturally had to do it all from memory. To this end he cast what he had to tell into a metrical form and thus the ballad stanza arose. As a further aid to memory and to add to the emotional value of what he had to say he added musical notes to his words, and it is from this that the ordinary folk-tune of four strains arose. Folk music, you must always remember, is an applied art. The idea of art for art's sake has happily no place in the primitive consciousness. I have already told you how the country singer is unable to dissociate the words and tune of a ballad. Song then was to him the obvious means of giving a pattern to his words. But this pattern is influenced by another form of applied music, that of the dance, the dance in which the alternation of strong and weak accents and precision of time are essential. Now let us take the dance-tune 'Goddesses' as an example of the rhythmical element applied to our initial formula. You will notice that the form is less subtle than in the song tunes. Regularity of pattern is essential to accompany the moving feet of the dancers.

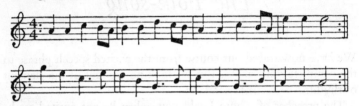

Next let me give you an example of a tune with very much the same melodic formula in which the rhythmical pattern is entirely governed by the words, a carol tune, 'The Holy Well'.

I have now tried to describe to you the folk-song, but before I go any further I had better give you some actual examples of what I mean by folk-song, and try and persuade you that I am telling you not of something clownish and boorish, not even something inchoate, not of the half-forgotten reminiscences of fashionable music mouthed by toothless old men and women, not of something archaic, not of mere 'museum pieces', but of an art which grows straight out of the needs of a people and for which a fitting and perfect form, albeit on a small scale, has been found by those people; an art which is indigenous and owes nothing to anything outside itself, and above all an art which to us today has something to say—a true art which has beauty and vitality now in the twentieth century. Let us take a few typical examples of English folk-song: 'The Cuckoo', 'My Bonny Boy', 'A Sailor From the Sea', or 'It's a Rose-bud in June'.

Can we not truly say of these as Gilbert Murray says of that great national literature of the Bible and Homer, 'They have behind them not the imagination of one great poet, but the accumulated emotion, one may almost say, of the many successive generations who have read and learned and themselves afresh re-created the old majesty and loveliness. . . . There is in them, as it were, the spiritual life-blood of a people.'

A folk-song is at its best a supreme work of art, but it does not say all that is to be said in music; it is limited in its scope and this for various reasons.

(1) It is purely intuitive, not calculated. (2) It is purely oral, therefore the eye does not help the ear and, prodigious though the folk-singer's memory is, owing to the very fact that it has not been atrophied by reading, it must be limited by the span of what both the singer and hearer can keep in their minds at one stretch. (3) It is applied music, applied either to the words of the ballad or the figure of the dance. (4) Folk-music, at all events European folk-music, and I believe it is true of all genuine folk-music, is purely melodic. These limitations are not without corresponding advantages. (a) The folk-singer, being unself-conscious and unsophisticated and bound by no prejudices or musical etiquette, is absolutely free in his rhythmical figures. If he has only five syllables to which to sing notes and those syllables are of equal stress he makes an unit or what in written music we should call a bar of five beats (to put it into the language of scientific music). If he is singing normally in a metre of 6/8 and he wants to dwell on one particular word he lengthens that particular phrase to a metre of nine beats. If he is accompanying a dance and the steps of the dance demand it he will lengthen out the notes to just the number of long steps, regardless of the feelings of the poor collector who is afterwards going to come and try and reduce his careless rapture to terms of bars, time signatures, crotchets, and quavers. We are apt to imagine that bars of five and seven, irregular bar-lengths and so on are the privilege of the modernist composer: he is probably only working back to the freedom enjoyed by his ancestor. (b) To pack all one has to say into a tune of some sixteen bars is a very different proposition from spreading oneself out into a symphony or grand opera, especially when these sixteen bars have to be repeated over and over again

B

for a ballad of some twenty verses. We have often experienced music which at first seemed attractive but of which we wearied after repetition. The essence of a good folk-tune is that it does not show its full quality till it has been repeated several times, and I think a great deal of the false estimates of folk-melodies which are current are due to the fact that they are read through once, or possibly hummed through without their words, or worse still strummed through once on the piano and not subjected to the only fair test, that of being sung through with their words.

And now as regards what I may call the vertical limitation of the folk-song; the fact that it is purely melodic. Modern music has so accustomed us to harmony that we find it difficult to realize that there can be such a thing as pure melody built up without any reference to harmony. It is true of course that we all whistle and hum tunes without harmony; nevertheless we are all the time unconsciously imagining an harmonic basis. Many of our most popular tunes would be meaningless unless in the back of our minds we supplied their harmonies.

Harmonic music, at all events during the eighteenth and nine-teenth centuries, presupposed the existence of two modes only, the major and the minor, with all their harmonic implications of the perfect cadence, the half close, the leading note and so on, so as to give points of repose, points of departure and the like. But in purely melodic music an entirely new set of considerations come into being. The major and minor modes hardly ever appear in true melodic music, but it must be referred to other systems, chiefly the Dorian mode, the Mixolydian mode and the Ionian mode, this last having of course the same intervals as the major mode, but otherwise quite distinct.

I do not propose to give you a disquisition on the modes; that would be quite outside the scope of these lectures, but I want to say just two things.

The epithet 'ecclesiastical' which has been applied to these modes has led to unfortunate misunderstandings. Because a folk-song can be referred to one of these 'ecclesiastical' modes it is often imagined that folk-song derives from church music. I believe that it is just the other way round, namely, that church music derives from folk-music. I shall have more to say about this in a subsequent chapter.

The only thing which the plainsong of the church and the folk-song of the people have now in common is that they can sometimes be referred to the same modal system because they are both purely melodic. It is surely hard to imagine that such a melody as 'The Cobbler' can be derived from, say, 'Jesu Dulcis Memoria' because they are both in the Dorian mode. You might as well say that the 'Preislied' derives from the finale of the Fifth Symphony because they are both in C major.

The other point I want to make is this. It is not correct to refer to the modes as 'old', or of pure modal harmony as 'archaic'. Real archaic harmony is never modal. When harmony grew out of the Organum, composers found that they could not work in the modes with their new-found harmonic scheme and they began to alter the modal melodies to give them the necessary intervals with which they could work. The harmony of Palestrina and his contemporaries is therefore not purely modal; this was reserved for the nineteenth century. As I have said, folk-song is pure melody without an harmonic substructure, but when modal melodies began to swim into the ken of composers, the first being probably the nationalists of nineteenth-century Russia, they began to suggest to them all sorts of harmonic implications. Up to that time harmony was always supposed to be considered as being built up from the bass. The Russian nationalists, perhaps owing to the fact that they were half amateur, evidently preferred to build their harmony from the melody downwards. We find this neo-modal harmony prevalent throughout Moussorgsky's 'Boris'. The lead was taken up by Debussy and the French contemporaries, some of the modern Italians and the modern English. It seems however to have passed by the Germans, possibly because their folk-songs have become tinged with harmonic considerations. Debussy's 'Sarabande' is a good example of pure modal harmony, as are the cadences in the minuet from Ravel's 'Sonatine'. I find it difficult to see what there is 'archaic' about these. If you look at real archaic harmony, going back even as far as Josquin and Dunstable, you will find nothing like it.

Some people are much worried about what they call the 'cult of archaism'. They are upset at all this 'borrowing' which is going on among composers and they are filled with indignation, but as far as I can make out on moral rather than on aesthetic grounds.

In an article called 'The Cult of Archaism' a recent writer says, 'In the writing of synthetic folk-music we have to deal with a form of equivocation which is probably quite as serious, being more insidious than the wholesale acquisition of folk-melody. It is reasoned apparently that though they may be musically unworthy to borrow on an extensive scale, the situation can be redeemed by writing artificial folk-melodies and presenting them as original themes. A student possessing the most elementary inventive ability can effect work of that kind without limit; it requires practically no skill and very little imagination.'

This seems to me to be nothing more or less than a protest by the 'trade', and the 'trade' as you know always adopt a high moral attitude when their profits are being interfered with. A brewer will be extremely annoyed if, when he has spent time, money, and skill on producing beer, he finds that someone has set up a free water tap just outside his house. So, when the members of the musical trade who have learnt how to construct melodies at great expense with all the latest devices and improvements find a composer writing a tune, not based on all these expensive models but built up on the natural music of his own people, they of course feel vexed: the fellow is not playing the game, in fact he is a blackleg. Which method results in the most beautiful music is not allowed to affect the issue. It is merely a trade question, a matter in going outside the regulations of the guild.

Contrast with this a recent writer on Moussorgsky: 'His invented themes recall those of popular art and it is to the phenomenon of "integration" that he owes his appealing originality.' Or as Mr. Kurt Schindler recently said about the same composer, 'It all depends on whether it is done with love.'

'Integration' and 'love'. These are the two key words. The composer must love the tunes of his own country and they must become an integral part of himself. There are, of course, hangers-on of the folk-song movement who want to be 'in the swim' and think they can do so by occasionally superimposing a modal cadence, or what they imagine to be a country dance rhythm, on to their cosmopolitan style compounded of every composer from Wagner to Stravinsky. These people, of course, have sinned against the light: whether they are also morally reprehensible does not seem to me to matter.

At the risk of wearying you I want to repeat that originality is not mere novelty. In the article I have already quoted Haydn is referred to as occasionally not taking the trouble to say something of his own. And is the same true of Beethoven when he used a theme from Mozart for his 'Eroica' Symphony? A composer at white heat of invention does indeed not 'trouble to say something of his own'; he knows instinctively what is the inevitable theme for his purpose. Music does not grow out of nothing, one idea leads to another and the test of each idea is, not whether it is 'original' but whether it is inevitable.

I should like to quote you the following lately written in the *London Mercury*: 'The best composers store up half-fledged ideas in the works of others and make use of them to build up perfect edifices which take on the character of their maker because they are ideas which appeal to that special mind.'

4

The Evolution of the Folk-song

The fact that folk-music is entirely oral and is independent of writing or print has important and far-reaching results. Scholars are too apt to mistrust memory and to pin their faith on what is written. They little realize how reading and writing have destroyed our memory. Cecil Sharp gives amazing examples from his own experience of the power of memory among those who cannot read or write. The scholars look upon all traditional versions of a poem or song as being necessarily 'corrupt'—as a matter of fact corruptions are much more likely to creep in in the written word than in the spoken. Any alteration in a written copy is likely to be due to carelessness or ignorance whereas when we do find variations in versions of traditional words and music these are as often as not deliberate improvements on the part of later reciters or singers.

There is no 'original' in traditional art, and there is no particular virtue in the earliest known version. Later versions are as likely as not developments and not corruptions.

There is a well-known saying of the folk-lorist Grimm that 'a folk-song composes itself'. Others replied to this with the common-sense view that in the words of our English critic I have already quoted with regard to the symphony, 'It only takes one man to make a folk-song.' Böhme, in the Introduction to his *Alt-deutsches Liederbuch*, says, 'First of all one man sings a song, then others sing it after him, changing what they do not like.' In these words we have the clue to the evolution of the folk-song. Let me quote you also from Allingham's *Ballad Book*. 'The ballads owe no little of their merit to the countless riddlings, siftings, shiftings, omissions and additions of innumerable reciters. The lucky changes hold, the stupid ones fall aside. Thus with some effective fable, story, or incident for its soul and taking form from a maker who knew his business, the ballad glides from generation to generation and fits itself more and more to the brain and ear of its proper audience.'

According to Gilbert Murray even a written book could be ascribed in primitive times to a communal authorship. Thus, the *Iliad* and the *Odyssey* are both the products of a long process of development.

It is interesting to note that almost up to the time of the invention of printing more trust was placed in the spoken than the written word. The Greek word Logos means a living thing, the spoken word, not the vague scratchings which in early times served for writing. Even in A.D. 135 it was possible for a historian to say, 'I did not think I could get so much profit from the contents of books as from the utterings of the living and abiding voice.'

Compare this with what we now realize of the strength and accuracy of oral tradition.

The book, as Professor Murray says, 'must needs grow as its people grew. As it became part of the people's tradition, a thing handed down from antiquity and half sacred, it had a great normal claim on each new generation of hearers. They are ready to accept it with admiration, with reverence, with enjoyment, provided only that it continued to make some sort of tolerable terms with their tastes. . . . The book became a thing of tradition and grew with the ages.'

Thus you see it is possible to ascribe communal authorship even to a book. To quote Professor Murray once again—'The *Iliad* and *Odyssey* represent not the independent invention of one man, but the ever-moving tradition of many generations of men.' If this be true of the book, how much more so of purely oral music and poetry.

Cecil Sharp, in his book on English folk-song, argues strongly in favour of the communal authorship of traditional music and poetry, but it must be noted that he does not claim a communal *origin*. He writes, 'The folk-song must have had a beginning and that beginning must have been the work of an individual. Common sense compels us to assume this much, otherwise we should have to predicate a communal utterance that was at once simultaneous and unanimous. Whether or not the individual in question can be called the author is another matter altogether. Probably not, because the continual habit of "changing what they do not like" must in course of time ultimately amount to the transference of the authorship from the individual to the community.'

However, though the case for communal origin cannot be proved yet I do not see how it can be disproved. No one, so far as I know, insists on the individual invention of the common words of our language and travellers tell us of musical phrases emanating from excited crowds of people spontaneously and simultaneously.

But I will grant for the sake of argument that the separate phrases of any folk-song you may like to name were invented by some individual. I will not go further than that because the 'skilled ballad-maker' of Halliwell could put musical phrases together to form a tune just as he could put lines of poetry together to form a ballad, and I have already shown you how certain stock phrases, some of which I have quoted, appear over and over again in folk-tunes, just as the stock phrases 'as I walked out', 'lily-white hand' and so on, appear over and over again in ballad poetry. But would it be right to call the ballad-maker who has strung these phrases together so skilfully into a tune the author of that tune? We will take it, however, for granted that a folk-singer has invented a whole tune just as Schubert invented a whole tune. When Schubert invented a tune he made it known to his fellow-men by writing it down; the primitive folk-singer could only make his invention known by singing it over to his hearers.

You will say, if that is all the difference between a composed song and a folk-song there is not much to choose between them. But it is on this apparently small difference that the whole question of individual as against communal authorship depends. If you hear two or three singers sing the same song—say by Schubert—they each will show slight differences in what we call 'interpretation' according to their various temperaments, but these differences can never become very wide because we are continually referring back to the printed copy. But supposing there was no printed copy, supposing three of you whom I will call A, B, and C learnt this Schubert song, not from the printed copy, but from the individual performances of the three singers I have imagined and whom I will call D, E, and F; that is to say, A learnt the song from D, B learnt it from E and C learnt it from F and then you three, A, B, and C, sang it to each other, adding of course your own individual pre-dilections—would there not be already a very wide margin of difference?

Let me give you a homely example. There used to be an army exercise called 'messages' in which the men were ranged in a row and an officer gave a verbal message to the first man who passed it on to the second, and so on to the end of the row; and the man at the end of the row had to report to the officer the message as he received it. Now you will understand that the message often came out at the end very different from what it went in at the beginning, and this in spite of the fact that each man was trying to be as accurate as possible.

Now this is what happens in the case of the folk-song, with this added factor which makes for divergence—the need for accuracy has disappeared. The second singer who receives the song from the first is at liberty, in the words of Böhme, to 'change what he does not like'.

This then is the evolution of the folk-song. One man invents a tune. (I repeat that I grant this much only for the sake of argument.) He sings it to his neighbours and his children. After he is dead the next generation carry it on. Perhaps by this time a new set of words have appeared in a different metre for which no tune is available. What more natural than to adapt some already existing tune to the new words? Now where will that tune be after three or four generations? There will indeed by that time not be one tune but many quite distinct tunes, nevertheless, but all traceable to the parent stem.

Now let us return a minute to our military 'messages'. It would often happen, of course, that the message in the course of trans-mission became hopelessly altered and indeed became nonsense when finally delivered. You may say, is not this the same with the folk-song? Are you not describing a process of corruption and disintegration rather than of growth and evolution? Let us remind ourselves once again that the folk-song only lives by oral trans-mission, that if it fails to be passed from mouth to mouth it ceases to exist. Now to go back once more to our soldiers. It might happen that by the time it reached the middle of the line the message had already become nonsense, but the soldier's duty, as you know, is not to reason why, but to pass on what he heard, whatever he might think of its quality. But a folk-singer is a free agent, there is no necessity for him to pass on what he does not care about. Let us suppose an example. John Smith sings a song to two other men, William Brown and Henry Jones. William Brown is a real artist and sees possibilities in the tune and adds little touches to it that give it an added beauty. Henry Jones is a stupid fellow and forgets the best part of the tune and has to make it up the best he can, or he leaves out just that bit that gave the tune its individuality. Now what will happen? William Brown's version will live from generation to generation while Henry Jones's will die with him. So you see that the evolution of the folk-song is a real process of natural selection and survival of the fittest.

Please forgive me if I return for a fourth time to our row of soldiers. Who is the author of the message in its final form as reported by the last soldier? Not he, obviously, because he was only repeating what he heard with possibly a few unconscious alterations. Neither is the officer who invented the original message, because we are supposing that its final form is only the same in outline and varies much in detail. Each of the soldiers had a hand in it, it is a product of their united minds; in fact it is a crude and rather ridiculous form of communal authorship. The folk-song in its evolution goes through exactly the same process, but as I have already shown, in the folk-song it is a case of growth and not of disintegration, of development, not of corruption.

This then is the much discussed and often ridiculed 'communal theory' of folk-song. This is what Grimm meant when he said, 'A folk-song composes itself.' To sum up, let me quote Cecil Sharp's definitions of art-music and folk-music. 'Art-music,' he writes, 'is the work of the individual, it is composed in, comparatively speaking, a short period of time and being committed to paper it is for ever fixed in one unalterable form. Folk-music is the product of a race and reflects feelings and tastes that are communal rather than personal; it is always in solution; its creation is never completed, while at every moment of its history it exists not in one form but in many.'

So you see the individual has his share in the creation of the folk-song and the race has its share. If I may venture to give my own definition of a folk-song I should call it 'an individual flowering on a common stem'. We folk-song collectors are often asked 'what is the origin' of a particular tune or 'how old' it is. There is no answer to either of these questions; there is no original version of any particular tune; any given tune has hundreds of origins. Nor can we say how old it is; in one sense any particular tune is as old as the beginnings of music, in another sense it is born afresh with the singer of today who sang it. Sometimes we are laughed at: the scoffer says, 'I expect that is not an old tune at all, the old man who sang it to you invented it himself.' Quite possibly to a certain extent he did. It is not the age but the nature of the tune which makes it a folk-song.

I should now like to give you some examples. First, of the same tune in various forms, or variants as we call them. The example I have chosen as the first is a tune which is very commonly sung in England, either to a doggerel ballad about the murder of 'Maria Martin' or sometimes to a carol 'Come All You Worthy Christians'. Before I do so I must give you a warning about the words of folk-songs. I do not intend to go into the large subject of ballad poetry, but shall only say just enough to explain the relationship of words and tunes. This ballad of 'Maria Martin, or the Murder in the Red Barn', is obviously a piece of broadsheet doggerel on the subject of a murder which was known to have taken place in the beginning of the nineteenth century. You might be led to think that as the words were comparatively modern and of doubtful folk-origin that the tune was equally suspect. We have seen that the folk-tune persists by oral tradition only; the same is true to a certain extent with the words of ballads, but in the case of the words the printing press began early to destroy this tradition, with the curious result that folk-music has preserved its vitality much longer than ballad poetry, which early began to be replaced by such broadsheets as 'Maria Martin'. When these broadsheets were sold at country fairs and elsewhere there was, of course, no music printed with them and the country singer would adapt to them his favourite tune with the result that the tune survived but that the words that went with it often disappeared before the ballad-monger's doggerel. And this is what has obviously happened in the case we are discussing.

Here are three variations of this tune; two with the minor third, one with the major, collected in various parts of England.

Æolian Mode

Dorian Mode

Mixolydian Mode

I will now show you the reverse side of the question, that is to say, two entirely distinct tunes, but which, I think I can show you, have the same outline and variations of the same phrases. The tunes are, (1) 'Bushes and Briars' (2) 'This is the Truth'.

And now I want to give you one or two examples of 'individual flowering on a common stem'. Here are two versions of the Morris dance-tune, 'Shepherd's Hey'. The first is the more usual version and the second is the same tune as played by Mr. Billy Wells, a well known folk-dance fiddler from Bampton in Oxfordshire. Notice that delightful little flourish in the second version of the

tune. Must we not suppose that Mr. Wells improvised this one day in a moment of especial artistic enthusiasm and that it has since become an integral part of the tune? Thus it is that folk-tunes evolve.

Here is another example—two versions of the tune 'Banks of Sweet Primroses', a plain and unornamented version, one from Sussex—the other, much more ornate, from Somerset.

You will notice that in the Somerset version the first and third phrase are the same—while in the Sussex variant it is only the third phrase which corresponds with the Somerset tune. We may suppose that this ornamented version so struck the imagination of singers that they sang it in both places instead of only in the third line.

(Sussex)

Thus it is that the folk-song evolves and becomes in reality the voice of the people.

Why am I sure that it is not a process of disintegration or 'corruption' as our scholarly friends are so fond of saying? For there are those who would have us believe that the folk-songs which have been sung during the last hundred years are corrupted, imperfect, half-remembered relics of some mysterious 'original'. But how with any semblance of accuracy can such tunes as 'Searching for Lambs' or 'My Bonny Boy' be described as corrupt, or imperfect, or disintegrated—are they not complete rounded, finished works of art? True, they may be different from other versions which have preceded them, but must they therefore be worse—cannot they be better? Is it not possible that the collector caught them at the climax of their evolution—if these are derelict relics, what were the originals?

I am far from saying that this is true of all folk-songs, there are dull and stupid folk-tunes just as there is dull and stupid music of all kinds, and it occasionally happens that a collector stumbles across a folk-tune just as it has got into the hands of an incompetent singer who has spoilt it; but we must remember this, that purely traditional music if it falls into bad hands tends to die a natural death while the written note, however bad it is, remains to cumber our national libraries.

One other point. The communal evolution of a folk-tune is in all points parallel to the evolution of a musical idea in the mind of an individual composer. We can sometimes, as in the case of Beethoven's notebooks, trace this evolution in all its stages in the composer's mind.

Is the final version then of the great tune in the Ninth Symphony a 'corruption' of the idea as it originally appears in Beethoven's sketch book? If the worshippers of 'originals' are to be logical this is what they will have to say.

It may be argued that since the folk-song has now ceased to evolve traditionally, it must be something dead, a mere archaism, interesting to the antiquarian, but with no living message for us in the twentieth century.

Our traditional melodies are, I am aware, no longer traditional. They have been noted down by experts and committed to printing, they have been discussed and analysed and harmonized and sung at concerts; they have in fact been stereotyped. They are no longer in a state of flux, they are no longer the exclusive property of the peasant, but have come into line with the composed music of which they are supposed to be the antithesis. From this you might suppose that their growth had stopped and that they are no longer something vital; that however beautiful they may be they belong to an age which is past and have nothing to say to the modern generation. The folk-song is I believe not dead, but the art of the folk-singer is. We cannot, and would not if we could, sing folk-songs in the same way and in the same circumstances in which they used to be sung. If the revival of folk-song meant merely an attempt to galvanize into life a dead past there would be little to be said for it. The folk-song has now taken its place side by side with the classical songs of Schubert, the drawing-room ballad and the music-hall song, and must be judged on its intrinsic merits.

When about twenty-five years ago Cecil Sharp collected and published his new discoveries in English folk-song he had in his mind the ordinary man, the 'divine average' of Whitman. And it is the ordinary man for whose musical salvation the folk-song will be responsible.

In the English-speaking countries where our artistic impulses are so apt to be inarticulate and even stifled, there are thousands of men and women naturally musically inclined whose only musical nourishment has been the banality of the ballad concert or the vulgarity of the music-hall. Neither of these really satisfied their artistic intuitions, but it never occurred to them to listen to what they called 'classical' music, or if they did it was with a prejudiced view determined beforehand that they would not understand it. To such people the folk-song came as a revelation. Here was music absolutely within their grasp, emotionally and structurally much more simple than their accustomed 'drawing room' music, and yet it satisfied their spiritual natures and left no unpleasant aftertaste behind it. Here indeed was music for the home such as we had not seen since the days of Thomas Morley when no supper party was complete without music when the cloth was cleared away.

Is not folk-song the bond of union where all our musical tastes can meet? We are too apt to divide our music into popular and classical, the highbrow and the lowbrow. One day perhaps we shall find an ideal music which will be neither popular nor classical, highbrow or lowbrow, but an art in which all can take part. You remember how the Florentine crowd carried Cimabue's great Madonna in procession to the cathedral? When will our art achieve such a triumph? Is this popularization of art merely a Whitmanesque fantasy? At present it is only a dream, but it is a realizable dream. We must see to it that our art has true vitality and in it the seeds of even greater vitality. And where can we look for a surer proof that our art is living than in that music which has for generations voiced the spiritual longings of our race?

5

The Evolution of the Folk-song

(*Continued*)

THE FOLK-SONG AND THE COMPOSER

In the last two chapters I described folk-songs. Now, I want to discuss the importance of all this to us, not as antiquarians or mere researchers but as musicians living in the twentieth century. Has it anything to say to us as creative artists? Well, I would suggest that to say the least of it, it acts as a touchstone. Artistic self-deception is the easiest thing in the world and we must be continually testing ourselves as to our sincerity, to make sure that our emotions are not all vicarious. Will not the folk-song supply this test? In the folk-song we find music which is unpremeditated and therefore of necessity sincere, music which has stood the test of time, music which must be representative of our race as no other music can.

This, then, or something like this is the foundation, it seems to me, on which all our art must rest, however far from it we spread and however high above it we build. As Hubert Parry says, 'All things that mark the folk-music of the race also betoken the quality of the race and as a faithful reflection of ourselves we must needs cherish it. Moreover it is worth remembering that the great composers . . . have concentrated upon their folk-music much attention, since style is ultimately national. True style comes not from the individual but from the products of crowds of fellow-workers who sift and try and try again till they have found the thing that suits their native taste and the purest product of such efforts is folk-song which . . . outlasts the greatest works of art and becomes a heritage to generations and in that heritage may lie the ultimate solution of characteristic national art.'

But what do we mean when we talk of building up a national art on the basis of folk-song? I, for one, assure you that I do not

imagine that one can make one's music national merely by introducing a few folk-tunes into it. Beethoven did not become a
Russian because he introduced two Russian folk-songs, out of
compliment to the Russian Ambassador, into his Rasumovsky
Quartets. Nor does Delius become an Englishman because he
happens to use an English folk-tune introduced to him by his
friend, Percy Grainger, as a *canto fermo* in one of his purely Nordic
inspirations. So I am far from suggesting that anyone can make his
music 'national' by adding a few touches of local colour. Nevertheless I do hold that any school of national music must be fashioned
on the basis of the raw material of its own national song; and this,
in spite of the fact that one could name many composers whose
music certainly reflects their own country, but who had confessedly
little or no knowledge of their own folk-music.

Such a composer was Tchaikovsky, but in his case the national
idiom was already, so to speak, in the air and he wrote his national
music as naturally as he spoke his own language. A stronger case
perhaps is our own English composer Edward Elgar. I have some
hesitation in discussing in public or venturing to appraise the music
of one whom we, in England, all revere as our leader, but the case
of Elgar is always quoted by those who oppose the theory of what
is known as the 'folk-song school of composers'. Elgar confessedly
knows and cares little about English folk-song. As you know, the
case in England is different from Russia. In the days when Elgar
formed his style, English folk-song was not 'in the air' but was
consciously revived and made popular only about thirty years ago.
Now what does this revival mean to the composer? It means that
several of us found here in its simplest form the musical idiom which
we unconsciously were cultivating in ourselves, it gave a point to
our imagination; far from fettering us, it freed us from foreign
influences which weighed on us, which we could not get rid of,
but which we felt were not pointing in the direction in which we
really wanted to go. The knowledge of our folk-songs did not so
much discover for us something new, but uncovered for us something which had been hidden by foreign matter. Now, in the music
of Elgar, in that part of it which seems to me most beautiful and
most characteristic, I see that same direction clearly pointed out.
When I hear the fifth variation of the 'Enigma' series I feel the same

sense of familiarity, the same sense of the something peculiarly belonging to me as an Englishman which I also felt when I first heard 'Bushes and Briars' or 'Lazarus'. In other works of Elgar I feel other influences not so germane to me and I cannot help believing that that is the reason why I love, say, the 'Be merciful' chorus from 'Gerontius' more, and the prelude to the same work less.[1]

Mr. Bernard Shaw, in what I think is one of his best plays, *The Dark Lady of the Sonnets*, imagines Shakespeare waiting on the terrace of Whitehall Palace for his lady and entering into conversation with the sentry he finds there. The sentry's conversation is racy and characteristic; he describes his sergeant as a 'fell' sergeant. When he is frightened he calls on 'angels and ministers of heaven' to defend him. Here, in truth, is the raw material of poetry and Shakespeare is soon busy with his notebook, preserving these pregnant sayings for future use. Mr. Shaw tells us in his preface to this play that he has been accused of impugning Shakespeare's 'originality' when he represents him as 'treasuring and using the jewels of unconsciously musical speech which common people utter and throw away every day'.

Or take the case of Burns—there can be no more original genius than Burns and yet it is well known that he founded much of his most beautiful poetry on traditional songs which his wife used to sing to him and which he gradually modified until the derivative material became his own. It all comes back to Emerson's well-known saying that the most original genius is the most indebted man. And if we all, whether geniuses or not, are in debt, why not be in debt among other things to that which is the fountain head from which all music must originally have sprung?

What is originality? Perhaps you know Gilbert Murray's aphorism that 'the genius may be a rebel against tradition, but at the same time he is a child of it'. Nobody has ever created or ever will create something out of nothing. We have a common stock of words and notes from which to select. The artist selects rather than creates. Originality is something much more subtle than being what advertisements call 'different'. A great artist can infuse a common thought with a special radiance. Schumann used to say that Beet-

[1] This was written in 1932.

hoven's chromatic scales sounded unlike anybody else's. Hundreds of people might have heard Mr. Shaw's sentry make his pithy remarks, but it required a Shakespeare to see their beauty, to realize their implications, to cut the diamond and give it its true setting.

I remember being told a story of how the artist Burne-Jones pointed out to a young friend that the blackened stone of the Oxford College buildings was beautiful. The young friend had, up to then, taken it for granted with everybody else that the colour was ugly. Now any fool can see that the Oxford Colleges are black, but it required an artist to see that this black colour was beautiful.

Probably one of the most original phrases in the world is the opening to the prelude of Wagner's 'Tristan', yet it is almost identical with one out of Mozart's C major Quartet. Its originality lies in the fact that with Wagner it had a definite emotional purpose, while with Mozart it was probably an harmonic experiment. We can be pretty sure that the Mozart phrase had not the same emotional effect on its contemporary hearers as the Prelude to 'Tristan' has on us, because the world was not then ready for such an emotional experience. When Mozart wanted to write amorous music, the mode of expression that suggested itself to him was 'La ci darem'. To take another example, it was not Debussy who was the inventor of the whole-tone scale; anyone can sit down to the piano and play that and probably composers have often experimented with it in private. I have it on the authority of Sir Hugh Allen that an English eighteenth-century composer, John Stanley, wrote a fugue on a subject in the whole-tone scale, but this of course was in the nature of an experiment; it was reserved for Debussy to see the significance of this method of expression and to explore its harmonic possibilities. And just as John Stanley before Debussy used the whole-tone scale without producing anything vital because it struck no corresponding sympathetic chord in his imagination, so the younger generation of composers since Debussy fail to make their whole-tone music vital because, to them, it is no longer a truth but only a truism. A composer is original, not because he tries to be so, but because he cannot help it. Monteverde and his contemporaries introduced an entirely new form of art, the opera, under the impression that they were reviving the declamation of the ancient

Greeks. Mozart's 'musical clock' Fantasia was a deliberate attempt to imitate the style of Handel, but Mozart sings to you in every note of it. I suppose there is nothing in the world more characteristic of its author than Coleridge's 'Ancient Mariner', but this was deliberately modelled on the ballads in Percy's 'Reliques'. A really original work remains original always. What is merely novel becomes stale when the novelty has worn off. The diminished seventh as a means of dramatic excitement is now considered an outworn device, but the 'Barabbas' from Bach's *St. Matthew Passion* remains as exciting and as unexpected for us today as it was when Bach wrote it two hundred years ago. When Brahms and Liszt were both new composers the music of Liszt was considered new and exciting, while that of Brahms was thought to be old-fashioned and obscurantist. Nowadays Brahms sounds as fresh as ever, while Liszt has become intolerably old-fashioned.

Do we not perhaps lay too much stress on originality and personality in music? The object of the composer is to produce a beautiful work of art and as long as the result is beautiful it seems to me it matters very little how that result is brought about. This idea of originality, especially in subject matter, is a very recent growth.

The great masters of music have never hesitated to build on folk-song material when they wished to. Certain musical critics cannot get out of their heads that it is a source of weakness in a composer to use what they call 'borrowed' material. I remember one writer saying unctuously that Bach never needed to borrow from folk-song. He could have known very little about Bach. I think he was an organist, which may account for it. As you probably know, about three-quarters of Bach's work is built up on the popular hymn-tunes which he loved so well, in fact, 'borrowed' material. Not all of these hymn-tunes are, of course, folk-songs in the technical sense of the word, though many of them are adaptations from traditional melodies.

But let us start a little further back.

Through all the ecclesiastical music of the fifteenth and early sixteenth centuries runs the mysterious figure of '*l'homme armé*', a secular tune which it became the fashion to introduce as a *canto fermo* into masses and motets.

Now why did these early choral composers introduce this and other secular airs into their Masses? As I daresay you know, the thing became a scandal and was prohibited because the congregations, when they heard the sound of the tunes they knew proceeding from the choir, would join in singing, not the words of the Mass but the words proper to the tune, which were often, I believe, not for edification.

I think these old composers felt that they must keep in touch with real life, that they believed, unconsciously, that music which is vital must preserve the popular element. If we look down the ages this is true of all great music. Could anything be more 'popular' than a fugue subject of the 'Cum Sancto' in Bach's B minor Mass, or the opening of the Finale of Beethoven's C minor? When hearers complained to Beethoven that his later quartets did not please, he did not reply that he was the high priest of an esoteric cult or that art was for the few, but he said, 'They will please one day.'

To return to '*l'homme armé*'. The practice was discontinued by papal edict in the sixteenth century, but I think we can trace the influence in the 'tuney' bits which Palestrina occasionally introduces into his motets and masses, when the metre of the words allows it, as at the 'Osanna'. A little later than Palestrina we find the Elizabethan Virginal composers doing much the same thing and we owe our knowledge of such tunes as 'Sellenger's Round', 'Carman's Whistle', 'John, Come Kiss Me Now' and dozens of others, in fact our whole knowledge of what was being sung in the streets of London in the reign of Elizabeth, to the fact that these Virginal composers introduced these songs into their compositions. Little they cared about 'originality'—perhaps they felt as we felt in modern England about twenty-five years ago, that these tunes must not remain unrecorded, that the fashionable English ladies who played on their virginals and were then, as now, apt to look with an exaggerated reverence on anything that came from overseas, would be all the better for a good honest English tune.

May I interpolate here our personal experiences in England in modern times?

In the early days of the 'Folk-song Movement' when we were all students, we felt there was something to be expressed by us Englishmen, that we had not got to the bottom of it; we saw signs of it in the works of our older composers; but we could not help feeling that foreign influences occasionally cramped them. Then Cecil Sharp brought to the notice of his countrymen the extraordinary wealth of beautiful English folk-songs, of which we had previously hardly had an inkling. Here was something entirely new to us and yet not new. We felt that this was what we expected our national melody to be, we knew somehow that when we first heard 'Dives and Lazarus' or 'Bushes and Briars' that this was just what we were looking for. Well, we were dazzled, we wanted to preach a new gospel, we wanted to rhapsodize on these tunes just as Liszt and Grieg had done on theirs: we did not suppose that by so doing we were inventing a national music ready-made—we simply were fascinated by the tunes and wanted other people to be fascinated too, and our mentors in the public press have lost no opportunity of telling us so. Some clever journalist has invented the phrase 'synthetic folk-song' and has told us 'that any student with moderate inventive ability can write synthetic folk-songs literally by the yard'. What is meant by the word 'literally' I fear I do not know. Personally, I think it is just as good for the student to write synthetic folk-song as synthetic Strauss, Debussy, or Elgar 'by the yard' if his music paper is large enough. All student work is synthetic; he absorbs what appeals to him and I cannot help thinking that what appeals to him most naturally will be the music of his immediate surrounding unless his mind is forcibly turned in another direction by his training, by his environment, or, more subtle than these, by that dreadful artistic snobbery which poisons the minds of young artists in England and, as far as I can judge, in America as well. It is by synthesis that the student learns. Early Beethoven is 'synthetic' Haydn. Early Wagner is 'synthetic' Weber and I believe that for a student to do a little 'synthetic' folk-song writing is a better way of arriving at self-knowledge than imitation of the latest importations from Russia or Spain which after all only cause him to write 'synthetic' Russian and Spanish folk-song, and that at second-hand.

Possibly we of the older generation were self-conscious and 'synthetic' in our devotion to folk-song. But it is the younger generation which matters: they are no longer self-conscious, they speak the language without thinking. Largely owing to the labours of Cecil Sharp our folk-tunes are now known to English people from their earliest youth. These tunes have become part of the national basis of musical language to every child in England. Cecil Sharp was never under the delusion that a national music could be 'made out' of folk-song; but he did believe the more these tunes became the property of the young, true composers would arise among them. His prophecy came true.

We have been told that the folk-song movement in England is dead. The arguments used prove that it is not dead but that it has just begun to live, that we are now taking folk-song for granted, whether we like it or not, as part of our natural surroundings; that its influence is no longer self-conscious but organic.

We are told that many of our younger composers are as yet untouched by the influence of folk-song, but those of us who can see rather deeper into things and with more imagination, know that they can no more help being influenced by their own folk-songs than they can help being nourished by their mothers' milk. Of course they are touched unconsciously and so the superficial journalist cannot see the influence; probably they do not recognize it themselves and would be most indignant if it was suggested to them; for them the folk-song is no longer synthetic, it is spontaneous.

I have had the privilege of looking at the early work of our younger English composers, written while they were still *in statu pupillari*, while they were still in the imitative stage, and it was largely what we have been taught to call 'synthetic folk-song'. Later on of course, as some of them took the trouble to explain to me, they put away childish things, saw the errors of their ways and so on. This is just what we should wish. They are in fact, once again to quote Gilbert Murray, 'rebels against tradition but at the same time children of it'.

I know in my own mind that if it had not been for the folk-song movement of twenty-five years ago this young and vital school represented by such names as Walton, Bliss, Lambert, and Patrick Hadley would not have come into being. They may deny their birthright; but having once drunk deep of the living water no amount of Negroid emetics or 'Baroque' purgatives will enable them to expel it from their system.

But this is a digression from historical order.

Do we find the folk-song influence in the classical period, Mozart, Beethoven, Schubert?

One would at first be inclined to say no. I hope I shall not be accused of inventing a paradox if I say that it is not noticeable because it is so very plain. If we look at a collection of German Volkslieder we are apt to be disappointed because the tunes look exactly like the simpler Mozart, Beethoven, and Schubert tunes. The truth of course is the other way out. The tunes of Mozart, Beethoven, and Schubert are so very much like Volkslieder.

We talk of the 'classical tradition' and the 'grand manner'. This really means the German manner because it so happened that the great classical period of music corresponded with the great line of German composers.

What we call the classical idiom is the Teutonic idiom and it is absolutely as narrowly national as that of Grieg or Moussorgsky. But there is one composer of the classical period whose case is different—Joseph Haydn. Haydn's themes, indeed the whole layout of his work, has really nothing in common, except purely superficially, with that of Mozart, though they have the same technical background and show some of the conventions of the polite music of the period. Sir Henry Hadow in his interesting essay on Haydn's nationality, called 'A Croatian Composer', proves definitely, I think, that he was not a Teuton, but a Slav of Croatian nationality. It is a curious comment on the strength of the German influence on all music that up till quite lately, we habitually spoke not only of Haydn, but even of the Hungarian Liszt and of the Polish Chopin, as 'German' composers.

That Haydn's musical ancestry is different from that of his German so-called compatriots is obvious in all his characteristic work. Of course before he attained maturity he followed the lead of his teachers and even in latter life, in the enormous amount of his output, there is a certain proportion of mere journeyman work, and it is noticeable that in these the national characteristics are not so apparent. It is when he is most himself that he owes most to the music of his own country. It has been suggested that Joseph Haydn owes nothing to a national bias because we do not find the same bent in the compositions of his brother Michael. But Michael of course was not a genius, but just an honest practitioner who never got beyond the commonplaces of the 'polite' music which he absorbed in Vienna, just as Joseph does not show his national characteristics except in his inspired moments.

Some explanation surely is required of all the irregular metres and characteristic phrases which distinguish Haydn's music. They derive from nothing in the music of Emanuel Bach or any other of his Teutonic forerunners. What is their ancestry? These themes and many others are found to be nearly identical with certain Croatian folk-tunes.

It goes without saying that Hadow has been accused of charging Haydn with plagiarism. This is what he writes on the subject:

'No accusation could be more unfounded or more unreasonable. He poached upon no man's preserve, he robbed no brother artist, he simply ennobled these peasant tunes with the thought and expression of which he was most nearly in accord . . . No doubt he was not only the child of his nation, he had his own personality, his own imaginative force, his own message to deliver in the ears of the world, but through all these the national element runs as the determining thread. . . . No doubt there are other factors; [besides nationality] the personal idiosyncrasy that separates a man from his fellows and again the general principles, fewer perhaps than is commonly supposed, that underlie all sense of rhythm and all appreciation of style. But to say this is only to say that the artist is himself and that he belongs to our common humanity. In everything, from the conception of a poem to the structure of a sentence the national element bears its part with the other two; it colours the personal temperament, it gives a stand-point from which principles of style are approached and wherever its influence is faint or inconsiderable the work of the artist will be found to suffer in proportion. . . . It is wholly false to infer that music is independent of nationality. The composer bears the mark of his race not less surely than the poet or the painter and there is no music with true blood in its veins and true passion in its heart that has not drawn inspiration from the breast of the mother country.'

The debt of the Russian nationalist school of composers to their own folk-song I need hardly dwell on, it meets us at every turn.

Chopin wrote national dances, the Mazurka and the Polonaise; Moussorgsky and Borodin frankly made use of folk-songs. Grieg and Dvořák avowedly and Smetana less frankly imitated them. In each case they have made the so-called 'borrowed' tunes their own.

In the eighteenth century an enterprising Scottish publisher commissioned Beethoven to harmonize some Scottish melodies. The result was curious and not satisfactory, but the strange thing is that the accompaniments added by the great master gave a decided German tinge to the tunes.

In the nineteenth century Brahms harmonized a collection of his own German Volkslieder—they sound exactly like Brahms, but here there is no misfit because the composer felt at home with his material. One of the tunes, 'Du mein einzig Licht', has been harmonized in another collection without sympathy or under-standing by Max Friedländer (though I admit he was also a German). A comparison between the two settings is instructive.

I will not give you any more detailed examples but I will try and tell you what I mean by the connexion between the composer and the folk-song of his country. Supreme art is not a solitary phenomenon, its great achievements are the crest of the wave; it is the crest which we delight to look on, but it is the driving force of the wave below that makes it possible. For every great composer there must be a background of dozens of smaller ones. Professor Dent has given us examples of a crowd of small practitioners in Vienna, who, so to speak, went to make up one Schubert.

There never has been and never will be a great artist who appeared as a 'sport'; a supreme composer can only come out of a musical nation and at the root of the musical quality of a nation lies the natural music whose simplest and clearest manifestation is the folk-song.

Historians of early English music are continually being puzzled and slightly annoyed by the occasional outcrop in medieval times of a magnificent piece of music like 'Sumer is icumen in' or the 'Agincourt Song' without apparent reason. There is no written record of a musical soil which could have produced such wonderful flowerings as when the wonderful Tudor school suddenly appeared, as they pathetically complain, 'from nowhere'. Of course, these things do not spring from nowhere, of course, the English were 'carolling' as Gerald the Welshman puts it, all through the Middle Ages, disregarded by the Frenchified court and the Italianized church, but coming to their full fruition in the age of Elizabeth. True, there is no written record of these happenings—therefore the historians are at a loss to account for their results; but there are more things in heaven and earth than are dreamt of in the book-man's philosophy.

The scholar's pathetic trust in the written word often leads him into difficulties. The only medieval music of which we have written record is that of the church and that of the Troubadours. Therefore, according to the scholars, this was the only medieval music worth notice. Popular music was made not according to rule but according to instinct—therefore it was negligible. This attitude of mind is well illustrated in Mr. Gerald Cooper's article on the Troubadours in the *Oxford History of Music*.

He writes that 'the music of the Troubadours in spite of certain points in contact with popular music was an aristocratic and intricate art with none of the haphazard characteristics of folk-music'. I take this to mean that the Troubadours were amateurish, i.e., 'aristocratic', that they wrote by rule, i.e., 'intricate', and not by instinct, i.e., 'haphazard'. The Troubadours, judging from results, had no instincts to guide them and therefore invented elaborate rules. But elaborate rules cannot produce live music: instinct is the sure guide. These rules reached their limit of absurdity in the music of the Meistersingers, the bourgeois descendants of the Troubadours.

Beckmesser thoroughly distrusted instinct and says to Walther, '*Oho! von Finken und Meisen lerntet ihr Meisterweisen? dasz wird dann wohl auch darnach sein.*' Again, Professor Dent writing also on the Troubadours says that 'from a social point of view the Troubadours are important because their art gradually led to the acceptance of music as an independent art, to its cultivation among the leisured classes, and so to a wider sphere of influence than could ever be permeated by an art of music which remains subservient to an ecclesiastical ritual'. But this is surely to put the cart before the horse. Music has always spread from below upwards, the spontaneous song of the people comes first. Quantz did not play the flute because Frederick the Great played it, but the other way out. Quantz learnt the flute presumably because it was indigenous to the country where he lived. The people have always sung and danced. Historians are too apt to take it for granted that, because there is no written record of this, it did not exist, or that at all events it is quite unimportant.

I cannot make out that Troubadour music flourished in England, at all events as an indigenous art. There is a simple explanation of this. The fashionable language was French and English was the despised speech of the peasants, so that fashionable England was probably in those days as it has so often been since, an importer of foreign goods. Perhaps it was just as well, for it allowed our native music to pursue its quiet way undisturbed so that 'Sumer is icumen in', almost certainly a popular melody, is still the despair and wonder of historians, and other popular tunes that have come down to us such as the 'Salutation Carol' and the 'Agincourt Song' are still vital, while the songs of the Troubadours are mere museum pieces. When the great School of Tudor music arose, it could go straight to the fountain head for its inspiration, fructified of course by the skill of the great Belgian contrapuntists, but inheriting its energy and vitality from the unwritten and unrecorded art of its own country-side.

6

The History of Nationalism in Music

In primitive times, when each small community was self-sufficing and every outsider an enemy, nationalism, or rather, parochialism was not so much an ideal as a necessity. But with the growth of mobility and its consequences of foreign trade, foreign wars, and the breaking down of natural boundaries by the purely artificial action of international treaties, people began to feel that their sheet anchor was dragging, that something that they loved and which peculiarly belonged to them was slipping away from them. It was not until they were threatened that they realized for the first time how much their customs, their language, their art meant to them.

Thus arose on the one hand the self-conscious cosmopolitans and on the other the self-conscious nationalists with their evil counterparts, the truculent chauvinist and the lovers of every country but their own. I am afraid it is true that nationalism first appears as hatred and fear of enemies, or at all events the fear of losing one's livelihood. English nationalism really came into being, strangely enough, as the result of the Norman Conquest. In the early Plantagenet days French, the language of the Conquerors, became the speech of the Court and of the educated classes and English was driven down to be the language of the peasants.

Then came the French wars and it became fashionable to regard French as an enemy language; the fashionable classes turned to the hitherto despised speech of the peasants in the same way, I suppose, as it becomes fashionable occasionally among our bright young things to talk cockney. By the year 1362 English again became the official language and it is interesting to note that it was then for the first time called the mother tongue. In 1385 certain schoolmasters had the courage to teach English and not French to their pupils in the grammar schools. 'Thus,' writes Professor Trevelyan, 'did these humble schoolmasters prepare the road for Chaucer and Wycliffe in their own century, for Shakespeare and Milton in time to come, for the English Reformation and Renaissance and the whole development of English life and letters as something other than a northern offshoot of French culture.'

In early days the music of the people was of necessity national. They had to make their own music because there was no one else to make it for them. The music of Courts and Princes had always been and probably always will be cosmopolitan. The Kings, Emperors, and Bishops attracted to their courts the best that they could get regardless of country. The skilled musician seems to have had no national conscience, but went where he could get most recognition and best pay. Thus, Dunstable, Dowland, and Lassus, to mention only a few, gained their fame and their livelihood at foreign courts.

It was this same indiscriminate Court patronage which first produced a wave of nationalism in music, at first no more than a 'keep out the foreigner' movement, a desire for protection by those who had to make their living by music. Thus we find Locke and Bannister and other English musicians complaining bitterly of the preference given to foreign musicians at the Court of Charles II; entirely, I fear, on the grounds that their bread and butter was being taken away from them. Nationalism as a spiritual force in art was yet to come.

The nationalism of John Sebastian Bach was on the other hand unself-conscious and consisted not in a fear of the foreigner, but of a deep love for the spiritual values of Teutonism, as exemplified in the Lutheran religion and the great choral melodies which were one of the outward and visible signs of that spirit. In Bach's case there was no question of fighting the foreigner, except perhaps in the one instance of his famous victory over Marchand at the Court of Frederick the Great, because there was no foreigner to fight. Music, in Bach's time and in Bach's community, was looked on not as an international art but as a local craft. The citizens of the small German towns where Bach practised his art would no more have thought of importing a foreign Cantor than of importing a foreign Town Clerk.

An interesting but short-lived 'keep out the foreigner' movement arose during Mozart's lifetime at the instigation, curiously enough, of the Emperor himself who established opera as a national institution, abolished the old Italian opera and ballet, and started what was called the 'National Singspiel', and it was for this that Mozart wrote 'Die Entführung'. The experiment did not last long. In 1783 the German company came to an end, but isolated performances of German operas continued to be given, among them of course *Die Zauberflöte*. So we must be thankful for this short-lived outburst of nationalism. The ultimate effects did not stop there because it prepared an audience to be enthusiastic later about *Der Freischütz*, and if we had not had *Der Freischütz* there would certainly have been no *Ring des Nibelungen*.

I am no historian and I speak under correction, or perhaps I am telling you the obvious, but the outburst of artistic nationalism in the early nineteenth century appears to me to have been the natural reaction to the artificial carving up of Europe to suit the needs of Emperors and politicians after 1815.

Chopin is generally considered the first of the nationalist composers and he certainly was strongly influenced by the patriotic aspirations of his oppressed country. We must, however, distinguish between the Parisian Chopin of the waltzes and nocturnes and the national Chopin of the mazurkas, polonaises, and Polish songs. But in reality he was no more national than Schumann or Beethoven or Mozart; his inspiration simply came from a new source. His period was the heyday of the romantic movement when everything had to be exotic. One's own time and one's own place were not enough and one sought an escape from reality in the glamour of remote times and remote places, the forests of Poland or the mountains of Scotland. So when Chopin appeared on the scene with his Polish rhythms and cadences he was hailed as the first nationalist, though he was only building on his own foundations just as Beethoven and Mozart had built on theirs.

The most striking example of a national renaissance comes from Czechoslovakia, or Bohemia, as it was then called, and it is a clear proof that a self-conscious movement among a few patriots can spread so as to be a living force in the country. The Czech national movement started little more than a hundred years ago with a coterie of Bohemian littérateurs; yet now Czech language, Czech culture, and Czech music is a natural and spontaneous expression of its people. This would not have been so if the roots had not always been there. The plant had shrivelled under the chill blasts of foreign suppression. Perhaps these March winds were required before the April showers could bring forth the flowers of spring. Those who bring about revivals are often scoffed at by the ignorant as foisting on the people something 'unnatural'—if it is 'real' we are sure it will come about 'naturally'. But does not life itself start for us in nine cases out of ten 'artificially'? Ask any doctor. And when life is nearly extinct can it not be revived by artificial breathing, artificial feeding, artificial blood pressure? If a healthy life ensues why quarrel with the means employed?

Smetana, the recognized pioneer of Czech musical nationalism, received his first impulse from 1848, the year of revolution, when he wrote his choruses for the revolutionary 'National Guards'. It is curious, however, that Smetana denied that he owed anything to folk-song and would indignantly protest that he never committed what he called 'forgery'. When we think of the polka out of his string quartet, of the dance movement in 'Ultava' or the opening chorus of *The Bartered Bride*, this seems difficult to swallow. The truth probably is that Smetana's debt to his own national music was of the best kind, unconscious. He did not indeed 'borrow', he carried on an age-long tradition, not of set purpose, but because he could no more avoid speaking his own musical language than he could help breathing his native air.

The national movement in Russia is too well-known for me to have to dwell long on it, but I will call your attention to two points. The Russian movement had small and humble beginnings as all great artistic movements do and I believe should do. And the Russian nationalist composers drew frankly and unashamedly on their own folk-songs. These are really two aspects of the same factor. The Russian movement started in the late eighteenth century with a revolt against the boredom of the heavy Italian operas which led people to look out for something lighter, some entertainment in which their own popular tunes might have a place.

This led to a series of 'people's' operas in which folk-tunes were introduced rather after the manner of the *Beggar's Opera*. Then came 1812 and the resultant outburst of Russian patriotism. Thus the way was prepared for Glinka who deliberately, as he said, wanted to write music which would make his own people 'feel at home', music which was sneered at by the Frenchified Russian aristocrats as 'coachman's music'. Mrs. Newmarch rightly says that whereas Glinka's predecessors had been content to play with local colour he 're-cast the primitive speech of the folk-song into a new and polished idiom'. From Glinka we pass on to the splendours of Moussorgsky, Borodin, and Rimsky-Korsakov surpassing their musical ancestor far in power of imagination, but like him, having their roots firmly planted in their native soil. It is a question how far the modern Russian school has not uprooted itself; possibly Stravinsky is too intent on shocking the bourgeois to have time to think about making his own people 'feel at home'. Cosmopolitanism has to a certain extent ousted nationalism. He seems deliberately to have torn up his roots and sold his birthright, cutting himself off from the refreshing well-spring of tradition. At one time he will toy with jazz, at another time with Bach and Beethoven seen through a distorted mirror. Or he will amuse himself by adding piquant 'wrong notes' to the complacent beauty of Pergolesi. This seems to be not the work of a serious composer, but rather that of the too clever craftsman, one might almost say, the feats of the precocious child. But in one branch of our art it is hardly possible for an artist to be untrue to himself, namely when he writes for the human voice, for then language takes command and the natural rise and fall of the words must suggest the melodic and rhythmic outline. And the human voice is the oldest musical instrument and through the ages it remains what it was, unchanged; the most primitive and at the same time the most modern, because it is the most intimate form of human expression. Instruments are continually being improved and altered, new inventions are continually increasing their capabilities both for good and evil. The pianoforte of today is not the instrument for which Beethoven wrote, the modern chromatic trumpet has nothing to do with the noble tonic and dominant instrument of the classics. Violinists can perform feats on their instruments undreamt of by our forefathers;

we can add mutes hard, soft, or medium to our brass instruments which change their features so that their own mothers would not know them. But through all this the human voice remains what it was with its unsurpassed powers and its definite limitations and in the face of these limitations the composer is forced to think of the essentials and not of the external trappings of music; thus he often finds his salvation. More important than all, the human voice is connected with our earliest associations and inevitably turns our thoughts back to our real selves, to that sincerity of purpose which it is so difficult to follow and so perilous to leave. And I believe this is especially the case in choral music where the limitations are most severe and the human element is the strongest. When Stravinsky writes for the chorus his mind must surely turn homeward to his native Russia with its choral songs and dances and the great liturgies of its church. And so I believe that it is in 'Les Noces' and the 'Sinfonie des Psaumes' that we find the real and the great Stravinsky which will remain fresh and alive when all the clevernesses of his instrumental works have become stale from familiarity.

7

Tradition

Closely connected with nationalism is the question of tradition. I have already quoted to you Gilbert Murray's great saying that a genius is the child of tradition and at the same time a rebel against that tradition. He develops this further by pointing out that in art tradition is essential. Art has to give a message from one man to another. As you can speak to a man only in a language which you both know, so you can appeal to his artistic side only by means of some common tradition. Consequently tradition cannot be disregarded. This is really the same thing as Emerson's epigram, 'The most original genius is the most indebted man.' Many of the most revolutionary artistic thinkers are in externals most obedient to traditional forms. In contrast to the iconoclasts of today there stand out one or two truly original figures, such as Sibelius, who have something to say that no one has said before, but who are nevertheless satisfied with the technical content which has been handed down to them by their ancestors.

Cecil Sharp wisely says, 'The creative musician cannot produce music out of nothing and if he were to make the attempt he would only put himself back into the position of the primitive savage. All that he can do and as a matter of fact does, is to make use of the material bequeathed to him by his predecessors, fashion it anew and in such manner that he can through it and by means of it express himself.'

It is true that tradition may harden into convention and I am entirely in sympathy with all artistic experimenters who break through mere convention. Let the young adventurer branch out into all known and unknown directions. Let the tree develop flowers and leaves undreamt of before, but if you pull it up by its roots it will die. Truly we cannot ignore the present and we must build for the future, but the present and future must stand firmly on the foundations of the past.

Walt Whitman says:

> 'Have the past struggles succeeded?
> Now understand me well. It is provided in the essence of things
> That in any fruition of success, no matter what,
> Shall come forth something to make a greater struggle necessary.'

But there may be bad traditions. Every generation, I suppose, thinks that the tradition of its immediate predecessors is bad, but the tradition is there and however much we want to we cannot help being the inheritors of those who have gone before us. We are inevitably the children of our fathers. We may curse our parents, but it is they that have made us, and not we ourselves. Effect proceeds from cause and always has done so; the sins of the fathers are visited on the children and it is up to us to see that the sins of one generation turn into the virtues of the next. Dr. Colles writes:

> 'Most of the best things in modern music come from composers who have kept close to their several native traditions and whose individual genius has enabled them to extend it in directions undreamt of by their predecessors.'

We cannot help building on the past. What is America building on? Have we possibly on both sides of the water a common tradition? Well, we have one thing in common and that is perhaps the strongest traditional force, namely, our common language—though even in that America and England in their divergent practical and emotional needs have to a certain extent drifted apart. And whether in fifty years' time we shall be mutually intelligible seems to me doubtful.

Now the musical style of a nation grows out of its language. To quote Dr. Colles again: 'A people's music grows in contact with the people's mother tongue, from the emergence of the vernacular in poetry and prose literature speech stamps its character with increasing decisiveness in the music of that people.'

The roots of our language and therefore of our musical culture are the same, but the tree that has grown from those roots is not the same. We cannot, if we wish to, jump back three hundred years and join up again where we parted. We have seen in the case of Bohemia and Russia how a tradition can be brought to fruition in a hundred years if the roots are well planted. America and England have had three hundred years of separate existence with different ideals and a separate culture. This must count for something. How are we each to find and preserve our own souls?

8

Some Conclusions

I will venture to say a little more about the future of music in America. I admit that I have not really got sufficient data to say much that is positive and you may think it very impertinent of me to attempt the task, but I feel that the future of music in America has something in common with that in England and that what is true of one may be true of the other. Here in America you have the finest orchestras in the world, you are determined to have nothing but the best, to engage the finest players, the finest conductors and to play the finest music. You have organized colleges and conservatories, you see to it that the study of musical appreciation and musical history are given a prominent place in your educational scheme; but I want you to ask yourselves whether because of these things, or might I say, in spite of these things, you are musical—or are going the way to become musical? Have you in the midst of all these activities the one thing needful? I am not going to answer the question because I do not know enough, but you may well ask me what do you mean by the 'one thing needful'? You may think, judging from previous lectures, that I think folk-song the one thing needful, and that conditions in America do not admit of folk-songs, because there is no peasant class to make and sing them.

Folk-song is not a cause of national music, it is a manifestation of it. The cultivation of folk-songs is only one aspect of the desire to found an art on the fundamental principles which are essential to its well-being. National music is not necessarily folk-song; on the other hand folk-song is, by nature, necessarily national. You may truly have got past that stage of development that makes folk-song possible. Nevertheless the spirit may be there all the same, the spirit of nationality. Or perhaps you may say that you have too many folk-songs. You have the folk-songs of the Negro, those of the Indian, those of the English settlers, and perhaps you will tell me that if I went to Oregon I should find the national music of the Swede, or that in New York I should be able to take my choice among the songs of every nation from Greece to China, and you might well ask me how a national music can grow out of that, since you cannot have a national art without a national language, a national tradition and so on.

But is it not perhaps the other way out? That some common art will be a bond of union and be one of the means out of which a national spirit will grow? Music *is* indeed in one sense the universal language, by which I do not mean that it is a cosmopolitan language but that it is, I believe, the only means of artistic expression which is natural to everybody. Music is above all things the art of the common man. The other arts have their practical counterparts; when we use our pen to order a ton of coal or our paintbrush to repair the damages made by our neighbour's motor car on our front gate, we are not necessarily expressing ourselves artistically; but the wildest howl of the savage, or the most careless whistling of the errand boy is nothing else than an attempt to reach into the infinite, which attempt we call art. And it seems to me that for this reason music is able to grow out of our ordinary life in a way that no other art can. We hear a great deal of the ugliness of modern life and we are making frantic attempts to preserve some visual beauty in the world. But we need no preservation societies, no national parks to preserve the amenities of music. The more sordid our surroundings, the more raucous the mechanical noises that assail our ears, the more I believe shall we turn to that art which comes entirely from within, as a means of self-expression. Music is above all others the art of the humble. We are laughed at in England for our bourgeoisie—personally I am proud to be described as a bourgeois. I remember a young exquisite saying to me that he didn't like Bach 'because he was so bourgeois'. I am not at all sure that it is not a true criticism and that that is why Bach appeals especially to me and my fellow bourgeois. I feel sure that it is not necessary for great composers to imitate Margaret Kennedy's Sanger and to banish themselves on to Austrian mountainsides. I believe that every community and every mental state should have its artistic equivalent.

I was told the other day that some of the English music which appeals to us at home was considered 'smug' by foreign critics. I was delighted to hear it because it suggested to me that our English composers had some secret which is at present for our ears only. That it is not also for others does not distress me. One day perhaps our 'native woodnotes wild' may cross the frontier hand in hand with Shakespeare, but they will not do so unless they are true to the land of their birth.

I expect the American composer has some secret to tell his own people if he will only trouble to find out what it is, if he will search for lights hidden under bushels or for nuggets of gold in heaps of dross. Why not look below the surface occasionally and find out what it is in the direct appeal of the popular tune which makes the audience go home whistling; to see if there is not some genuine artistic impulse hidden in unlikely corners? I don't suggest for a moment that a composer should ever write down to a supposed public; he must of course be true to himself in order not to be false to any man; the universal popular art is, alas, still a dream. But music is the youngest of the arts. We have perhaps not yet started to explore the promised land and before we can do so we may have to experience a change of heart.

I have been told that my talks turn into sermons. I hope that up to the present I have managed to keep off sermons, but now I fear that nature is becoming too strong for me and I propose to finish not by preaching you one sermon but three, each with its appropriate text.

My first text is 'Unless ye become as little children ye shall not enter the Kingdom of Heaven.' Education is said to be what a man has learnt and forgotten. I believe that in music we are still learning and do not yet know how to forget. Until our music becomes a really spontaneous expression, first of ourselves, next of our community, then and then only of the world, in fact until it is as unpremeditated as that of the folk-singer, it will not be vital. How should the childlike mind show itself in us? For one thing we must learn to walk before we can run. It is so easy now to be clever and to join in the race halfway without going the full course. But that is not the way to write true music. We cannot see perhaps why with all the wealth of the world at our disposal we cannot enter into the inheritance of a German or a Russian tradition straightaway without all these tiresome preliminaries. Any student can nowadays pick up all the tricks of the trade which go to make a Wagner or a Debussy or a Sibelius, but I assure you if we do this there will be something lacking in our music. We must in spirit though not in form start again from the beginning, even at the risk of appearing parochial, and do something, however small, which only we can do and our own people can appreciate.

Of course in recommending the childlike mind I am not speaking to the extremely young. I do not expect boys and girls under twenty-five to be childlike. Of course you have got to try your 'prentice hands on your symphonic poems, on your modernistic ballets or your atonal figures according to the period of musical history when the disease attacks you. But when you have got through your measles and tried your hand at everything and discovered how futile is the letter without the spirit, it is then that you will begin to examine yourselves and find out which is the straight way up the hill of difficulty.

After this necessary digression I can pick up the main thread again.

All artistic movements which have produced great men had small and humble beginnings. It was the humble *Singspiel* of Adam Hiller and other local German composers which led the way to Mozart's *Magic Flute*, and then on by way of Weber and Marschner to Richard Wagner. If Germany had not started with 'Der Dorf Barbier' she would never have finished up with *Die Meistersinger*.

Perhaps the history of the Russian school is more striking still. We are apt to think of the Russians in terms of the complexities of Stravinsky or the gorgeous colouring of Rimsky-Korsakov or the epic grandeur of Moussorgsky. But we must trace the history of Russian nationalism back to an almost unknown composer who wrote operas with the definite object of catching the humbler part of the Russian public by 'rendering native song in a national manner'. Close on his heels followed Glinka whose 'Life for the Czar' was a definite bid for popularity through patriotism. Glinka's avowed object in his music was to make his fellow countrymen 'feel at home'. Is it not a good criterion of the sincerity of our music whether it will succeed in making our own people 'feel at home'? The trouble of course is that we have so divorced art from life that people have got into the habit of thinking of music as necessarily something exotic. They do not want to be made to 'feel at home' and so the snobbery of the composer who wants to be sure that he is doing the latest thing and the snobbery of the hearer who wants to imagine that he is anything but his real self follow each other round in a vicious circle.

But you may say to me that our younger composers are doing just what you tell them to—they are raking out folk-songs from every conceivable quarter of the world and incorporating snatches of them into their compositions. Yes, but what are they doing with them when they have got them? It is of no use disguising them so that their fragrance is entirely lost or making them vehicles for mere cleverness as did the medieval composers with their *l'homme armé*. It is not enough for music to come from the people, it must also be for the people. The people must not be written down to, they must be written up to. The triviality which is so fashionable among the intelligentsia of our modern musical polity is the worst of precious affectations. But the ordinary man expects from a serious composer serious music and will not be at all frightened even at a little 'uplift'.

What the ordinary man will expect from the composer is not cleverness, or persiflage or an assumed vulgarity. He can get real vulgarity enough if he wants it in his daily life, but he will want something that will open to him the 'magic casements'.

Life is very exciting for the young composer nowadays; he is free of all rules, the means at his disposal for making new effects are almost unlimited; he is taking part in a breathless race to produce what is more and more unheard of. The temptations to beat all competitors in that race are great. Perhaps he is like the young novelist who is tempted to show off all that he knows about 'Life' and to cram his pages with night clubs and the amours of financial magnates about which he only knows at second-hand. This is all very alluring, but it is only first-hand experience which counts: simulated sentiment can only result in failure.

I receive from time to time a publication, issued from America, called *New Music*, consisting chiefly of compositions by young Americans. I do not pretend that I can make head or tail of what these young composers are saying, or what they are aiming at, but I am an old fogey and I realize that I am not justified in praising or blaming it. But I am justified in asking at whom it *is* addressed. Is it merely the music of a clique, or has it a genuine message to young America? All great music has the element of popular appeal, it must penetrate beyond the walls of the studio into the world out-side.

'They may prove well in the lecture rooms yet not prove at all under the spacious clouds and along the landscape and flowing currents.' Can these composers of the new music say, do they even want to say with Beethoven, 'It will please one day'?

The three watchwords of great music are sincerity, simpli-city, and serenity. Once more, and I believe for the last time, I will speak to you about folk-song. Let our composers and per-formers, when they can spare time from solving some new problem in atonality or exploiting the top register of the double-bassoon, refresh themselves occasionally with a draught of that pure water.

My next sermon is addressed not to the professional musician but to the amateur, and especially the listener, and my text is 'Be ye doers of the word, not hearers only.' A musical nation is not a nation which is content to listen. The best form of musical appreciation is to try and do it for yourself; to get really inside the meaning of music. If I were to visit a strange country and wanted to find out if it had a real musical life I should not go to the great cities with their expert orchestras, their opera houses and their much advertised celebrity concerts, but I should go to the small towns and villages and find out there whether enthusiastic quartet parties met once a week, whether there was a madrigal club, whether music was a normal form of recreation in their homes, whether the people met to sing together or play together under their local leader, whether they encouraged that leader to create music for the pageants and ceremonies of their town, whether they saw to it that the music in their churches was worthy of the liturgies performed there. Music is not only a form of enjoyment, it is also a spiritual exercise in which all have their part, from the leading hierophant down to the humblest worshipper.

Continuity is a necessary element of a living organism. In the hierarchy all have their place, the greatest expert and the lowliest amateur; they all share in building up the edifice. In the ideal commonwealth of music the leaders will be, not those who have come in from outside, but those who have started in the ranks with the Field Marshal's baton in their corporal's knapsack. And these leaders will have their duty—to speak to the people in the language which they understand.

The temptation to become a mere listener is nowadays very great. Gramophones and wireless have brought the world's riches to the doors of the humblest, but if we all become listeners there will soon be no one left to listen to. Modern invention is tending to make us content only with the cream of music, but where will the cream come from if there is no milk to skim it off?

This brings me to my third sermon and my third text, 'What shall it profit a man if he gain the whole world and lose his own soul?'

We are apt to look on art and on music especially as a commodity and a luxury commodity at that; but music is something more—it is a spiritual necessity. The art of music above all the other arts is the expression of the soul of a nation, and by a nation I mean not necessarily aggregations of people, artificially divided from each other by political frontiers or economic barriers. What I mean is any community of people who are spiritually bound together by language, environment, history, and common ideals and, above all, a continuity with the past.

The music of other nations is the expression of *their* soul—can it also be the expression of ours? If we possess our own soul surely and firmly, as indeed we do from the accident of language in our literature, then, indeed, we can afford to be broad-minded and to enlarge and enrich our own possessions by contact with all that is best in the world around us. But have we English-speaking people yet found our own soul in music? Gardeners tell us that it is dangerous to substitute artificial watering for natural rainfall because it tends to make the plants turn their roots up to meet the surface water instead of striking down to find the moisture deep in their native earth. Nations, like individuals, need periods of contact followed by periods of isolation. We must be careful that too much dependence on outside influences does not stifle rather than foster our native art. If we have no musical soul of our own, how can we appreciate the manifestations of the musical souls of others? In that case our love of music can be little more than a pose or at the best a superficial interest, not a deep-rooted intuition. If we have music in us it must show itself actively and creatively, not passively and receptively. An art which is not creative is no art.

I have told you how the national spirit in music has occasionally shown itself in a 'keep out the foreigner' movement. We have had it lately in England and doubtless it makes its appearance occasionally in America. It happens of course only in those countries and in those times when an influx of foreign influence tends to stifle native talent. The protest usually comes from professional musicians and is purely economic in its origin. They demand protection as members of other professions do so as to secure their means of livelihood. But there is this distinction in the case of the musical profession, that the case is often prejudged against them, and especially in English-speaking countries. That extraordinary mixture of self-depreciation and snobbery with which we view artistic questions makes us apt to take it for granted that the exotic art must be the best, and to refuse to believe the evidence of our eyes and ears. But it is not the economic side of the question that I want to discuss.

Music cannot be treated like cigars or wine, as a mere commodity. It has its spiritual value as well. It shares in preserving the identity of soul of the individual and of the nation. Some people will not believe this and tell us that music is a 'manufactured article' just like bacon and cheese, and they will have the music they like just as they will have the cheese they like regardless of where it comes from. And this view is not held only by the Lucullans of music, but by philanthropists and educationists as well, who tell us that we are not doing our duty by the young or the struggling masses by giving them anything except the best. They disregard the personal and national element in art and roundly declare we have no right to limit the outlook of those whose destinies are in our hands.

Does the same apply to us? I believe that in the long run it does apply; that, even at some immediate sacrifice of good we must develop our own culture to suit our own needs. Only in that way will art cease to be an excrescence on our life (an 'extra' as they used to call it in the school bills) and will become an indispensable element in our being. But I have to admit that those who hold with the spiritual value of the best art, regardless of its origin, have a strong case. Is not a compromise possible?

The Lucullan, of course, one who holds what I may call the 'commodity' theory of art, will say, 'When our composers and performers at home give us something better than I can get elsewhere I will willingly pay to hear it.' What are we to say to this? I have already suggested in an earlier lecture that there is no absolute good in art. We want to know for what end it is good. The Lucullan seems to take it for an axiom that, because the music he gets from elsewhere is different from the music he finds at home, it is necessarily better. It is of course better for those who made it, but is it necessarily better for us? Here I am afraid I am again compelled to point my finger at the creative artists and ask them whether they are content to let their music be something of itself, or whether they are trying to make it as much like that which comes from outside as possible? I find that young composers both in America and in England are inclined to say that they must go to Paris or Vienna in order to learn their technique. I am not going to argue this point for a moment, but will content myself with saying that technique is not a thing that can be added to a composer's outfit like the buttons on a suit of clothes. The technique must grow out of the desire for expression and ultimately is the discovery of the perfect balance between inspiration and realization. Gustav Holst once told me that a pupil once came to him and asked him to 'give him an idiom'. He might as well have asked him to give him a new set of bones. We are too apt to forget that the style is the man.

I now see that I can no longer avoid mentioning jazz. You will tell me you are tired of jazz and that it only represents a very small part of your psychology. I think you are wrong in despising jazz, but I do not go so far as to say as some thinkers do that it has in it the seeds of great further development. But it does show this:

that there is musical vitality in America which at any moment may manifest itself in some other form which has in it the elements of greatness. At all events jazz, whether you like it or not, is a purely indigenous art. No one but an American can write it or play it. Anyone who has listened to the helpless attempts of German or French bands to play jazz, or the pitiful efforts of some modern French or German composers to add a little sting to their failing inventiveness by adopting a few jazz rhythms, will realize this.

And the obverse is true. Certain attempts by American composers to make jazz 'polite' by dressing it out in the symphonic style of European tradition have also proved in my opinion to be failures.

I hope you do not think that I am preaching artistic chauvinism. That purely negative attitude of mind is, I trust, a thing of the past. If the civilized world is not to come to an end we must become more and more 'members one of another'. But as our body politic becomes more unified so do the duties of the individual members of that body become more, not less, defined and differentiated. Our best way of serving the common cause will be to be most ourselves. When the United States of the World becomes, as I hope it will, an established fact, those will serve that universal State best who bring into the common fund something that they and they only can bring. In 1926 Stresemann said, 'The man who serves humanity best is he who rooted in his own nation develops his spiritual and moral endowments to their highest capacity, so that growing beyond the limits of his own nation he is able to give something to the whole of humanity.'

It has been suggested that in order to save its own soul every nation should institute a kind of artistic 'five year plan' in accordance with which only indigenous music would be allowed for five years. In this way the people of each nation, being prevented from employing others to make music for them, would be obliged, if they wanted it, to make it for themselves. Then one of two things would happen. If there was no indigenous music to be had the art in that country would die out altogether, which in that case would be very right and proper because it would have been proved that music was not necessary to the lives of the people of that country and that it would sink to the level of a C3 nation in one of its most important means to a full life.

Or, on the other hand, being forced to make music for themselves, composers and performers would be encouraged to express themselves in terms which would voice the ideals of their fellow men. A new music would grow up which would be for that nation truly the best music and we should perhaps at last approach that consummation when art would be at the same time the treasure of the humble and the highest expression of the greatest minds.

If after the five years the foreign influence was again brought to bear, it would be acting on a strong and sturdy plant and would act wholesomely as an incentive and a corrective. It would no longer stifle, it would encourage. Personally I would like to see the experiment tried, but the objections are obvious. It could be said with some show of justice, 'Why condemn the present generation to a course of mediocre music in order that their descendants may find their souls?' This I think begs the question by taking it for granted that the music would be mediocre. I believe there would be some surprises in store for us. But there are other more subtle, but perhaps stronger objections. Would the nation rise to its opportunities? In those countries where the legend of foreign superiority is already strong the legend might gather strength rather than disappear when there were no means but traveller's tales of testing its authenticity. And would the composer seize the moment? He might be inclined to write what was expected of him by some clique, rather than what he genuinely felt and, when there was no real foreign music to dispute his sway, he might think it necessary to make a faithful imitation of it.

I offer no solution to the problem, but we must not imagine there is any short cut or easy road. The business of finding a nation's soul is a long and slow one at the best and a great many prophets must be slain in the course of it. Perhaps when we have slain enough prophets future generations will begin to build their tombs.

One more stray thought before I finish. I think there is no work of art which represents the spirit of a nation more surely than *Die Meistersinger* of Richard Wagner. Here is no playing with local colour, but the raising to its highest power all that is best in the national consciousness of his own country. This is universal art in truth, universal because it is so intensely national. At the end of that opera Hans Sachs does not preach about art having no boundaries or loving the highest when he sees it, but says what I may slightly paraphrase thus:

> 'Honour your own masters;
> Then even when Empires fall
> Our sacred nation's art will still remain.'

9

The Influence of Folk-song on the Music of the Church

This chapter is really rather outside my main subject which intends to deal with folk-song, only as one element of nationalism, but I have been specially asked to say a little about the influence of folk-song on the music of the church. 'Surely,' you may say, 'you have got the order wrong, you mean the influence of the church on the folk-song. Church music which has been committed to writing and reduced to rule and measure must be the firm rock and that which is merely spoken or sung as the shifting sand.'

Here is another instance of the unfortunate tendency among scholars to believe that the written words must be authoritative and oral tradition unreliable. The opposite is more often than not the case. Writing is a much more frequent cause of corruption than tradition. We can all read and write now and it is difficult for us to imagine the tenacity of memory which those possess who absolutely depend on it.

Cecil Sharp writes as follows: 'To those unacquainted with the mental qualities of the folk, the process of oral transmission would be accounted a very inaccurate one, the Schoolman for example, accustomed to handle and put his trust in manuscript and printed documents would look with the deepest suspicion upon evidence that rested upon evidence of unlettered persons. In this, however, he would be mistaken as all collectors of folk-products know well enough.'

You may be surprised at my suggesting that the elaborate, un-metrical, aloof plainsong of the church could have ever grown out of the joyful rhythmical song of the people. Nowadays we think of the church with its music and its ritual as something at the latter end of a long tradition, but each church had to begin somewhere and had to start with a popular appeal. In the eighteenth century John Wesley declared that he did not want the devil to have all the pretty tunes, and in the nineteenth century General Booth adapted all the popular melodies of the day to the service of what Huxley called corybantic Christianity. Is it not possible that the plainsong of the church originated in the same way? Frere in the *Oxford History of Music* admits the possibility.

There can be no doubt that popular music of some kind existed long before the Christian church organized the music of its ritual. The question is, how much did the church owe to popular song? At first it was naturally bitterly opposed to popular art which the churchmen labelled as 'infamous, nefarious, immodest and obscene', and Christians were forbidden to attend pagan ceremonies. But we must remember that the parish church probably stood in what would now be the public square which would be the great meeting place for the people. These pagan ceremonies with their accompanying music would be going on at the very church door making the struggle for existence between the two visible and audible to all. Now, as we know, the churchmen found it impossible to oust the pagan ceremonies. But they did the next best thing; they adapted them to their own use: if you can't defeat your enemy the only course is to take him to your bosom and hope to tame him by kindness. Thus the pagan ceremony of Yule became Christmas, the old Spring Festival became Easter, the worship of ancestors became the commemoration of saints, and so on. Surely it is impossible to believe that with these ceremonies some of the popular music connected with them did not creep in also.

We have direct evidence of the effect of folk-song on the plain-song or music of the church in the history of French song. The evidence comes from a most interesting account of Charlemagne's visit to Rome in 785. About two centuries before that date Pope Gregory had made an attempt to regularize the music of the church and had made a collection of what he considered to be pure and proper church music, in what is now known as the Gregorian chant, and this was the music in use at Rome at the time of Charlemagne's visit. But in other places local tradition was too strong and there were extant several local 'uses' besides the Roman or Gregorian, the chief being the Milanese or Ambrosian, the Spanish or Mozarabic, and most important for our present purpose the French or Gallican 'use', each with its peculiar music.

Now when Charlemagne went to Rome he took with him his French singers who performed the church services according to the Gallican use with their own melodies. Charlemagne was a great nationalist, convinced of the superiority of French art and was very sarcastic at the expense of the Roman singers. To his surprise the Romans in their turn despised the French singers and called them 'ignorant fools and *rustics*'. Note the word 'rustic'. The French music was to the Romans not harsh or unmelodious or too severe, but 'rustic'. In other words the Roman experts saw traces of that influence which is the bugbear to the academic mind—the folk-song.

As regards the poor French singers the story ends there. They were sent home by Charlemagne with their tails between their legs and two Roman teachers to show them the supposed pure style. But for us the romance unfolds itself like a detective story. According to Frere in the *Oxford History of Music* there appeared later in the Roman use 'a good many items which must have originated elsewhere than in the Roman rite and have come into the Roman collection from outside'. We may suppose that the Romans adapted something even from the despised Gallican use; it is not unknown for superior-minded people to make secret use of that which they affect to despise.

Of this again we have evidence. Among the melodies to which, in the Roman rite, the psalms are chanted is one very different in character from the rest, more 'tuney' if I can so describe it, more popular in character. Moreover it came to be known as the 'Foreign Tune', 'Tonus Peregrinus', and it is almost certain that this melody was taken by the Romans from the Gallican use. Now was this not one of the 'rustic' melodies, one of those adaptations from folk-song which the Romans in Charlemagne's time so strongly disapproved of? If such a folk-song exists where should we look for it? Should we not expect to find it connected with some primitive ceremony which might be among those which the French church had adapted for their own use? Tiersot gives us the proof we need in the 'Chant des Livrées', a song connected with the marriage ceremony, the melody of which suggests in its outline this very 'Tonus Peregrinus'.

Let me recapitulate the steps of the argument. First, here is a French folk-song. Secondly, it is connected with an ancient custom. Thirdly, French ecclesiastical music is accused of being rustic. Fourthly, it is likely, therefore, that this music should be based on folk-song, especially on ceremonial folk-song, and lastly, the family likeness between 'Le Chant des Livrées' and the 'Tonus Peregrinus'.

You may think that there seems to be very little connexion between the slow, solemn, long drawn out, unmetrical music of the church and the brisk, strongly accented songs of the French people, but we must remember that in plainsong as we have it now, we see the muse of the people, not as she was when she first stepped blithely out of the sunlight into the dim incense-laden atmosphere of the church, but as she is now after she has for years exchanged her parti-coloured *jupe* for the sad robe of the *religieuse*, her gay garland of flowers for the nun's coif and the quick country dance for the slow-moving processional. We shall then realize that the same features might be scarcely recognizable in such different circumstances.

Such transformations are not unknown in later times. Thomas Oliver reshaped the sprightly tune, 'Where's the mortal can resist me', so as to make the solemn melody 'Helmsley' for Wesley's Advent hymn, 'Lo, he comes'. And the English dance-tune, 'Sellenger's Round', lost its lilt in crossing the Channel and re-appears in Germany as a stately Chorale, 'Valet will Ich dir Geben', which we know so well in Bach's great setting from the *Passion According to St. John*.

Some of the French folk-songs were proof against the church influence even though they were used in the church services. The famous 'Prose de l'Ane' is a good example, though this was a definite invasion of the church from the secular world outside on a special occasion. Secular melodies naturally tended to keep their definite outline when they were set to metrical words. One of the most famous French ecclesiastical metrical melodies is the Easter Sequence 'O Filii et Filiae'. Now Easter suggests at once the Spring Festival. Is there any folk-song connected with that Festival to which this tune can be referred? Again Tiersot gives us the proof in two French May-day folk-songs which have a distinct likeness to the melody 'O Filii'. ('Trimouset' and 'Voici venir le joli mois'.)

These two songs are both called 'Chansons de Quête' and were sung, at all events till quite lately, by young men and women going out to get their 'étrennes' for the 1st of May. The very word 'Trimouset' is of obscure Celtic origin and points to some very primitive ceremony.

You will notice that it is in the beginnings and endings of the tunes that we find most likeness to the church melody. This is just what we should expect. The church was trying to attract people to its new religion. If you want to give people something new, start with what they are accustomed to, then having startled them with your new notions let them down gently at the end with the idea that what you had said is not so very new after all.

Having now established the possibility of folk-song affecting church music let us see how other churches were influenced.

Luther and his followers borrowed largely; partly from the melodies of the Roman church, but chiefly from secular tunes. It became the fashion to make what was known as a 'spiritual parody' of the words of a secular song and to sing these words to the same tune as the original. Böhme in his *Alt-deutsches Liederbuch* gives a list of over 250 of these word transpositions; thus 'Susanna will'st du mit' became 'Du Sündrin willst du mit'. 'Wach auf mein Herzens Schöne, zart allerliebste mein' became 'Wach auf mein Herz und Schöne, du christenliebe Schaar'.

The two most famous of these spiritual parodies have come down to us in the form of the well-known hymn-tunes, 'The Passion Choral' and 'Innsbruck'. The 'Passion Choral' was a secular love song 'Mein G'müth ist mir verwirret'. Böhme is of the opinion that this was not a folk-song, but was composed by Hans Leo Hasler in 1601. But to my mind Hasler's version has all the appearance of a folk-song and it is quite possible that Hasler only arranged it. Such things were quite usual in those days before the modern craze for personality set in. This tune had, by Bach's time, been adapted to Gerhardt's Passion hymn, 'O Haupt voll Blut und Wunden', or as Robert Bridges has it, 'O Sacred Head sore wounded'. Bach uses this tune over and over again, but you will have noticed he uses a simplified form of the melody. The original was a solo song. The version Bach uses was for massed, or as we should now say, for community singing; hence the simplifications. Thus a Choral can evolve like a folk-song, adapting itself to new uses and new circumstances, surviving in that version which is the fittest for its purpose.

The tune which we know as 'Innsbruck' is now, I believe, sung in Germany to the words 'Nun ruhen alle Wälder'; in the Bridges version 'The Duteous Day Now Closeth'. This tune is undoubtedly adapted from a secular folk-song, 'Innsbruck Ich muss dich lassen', one of the numerous class of 'farewell' songs popular in medieval Germany when the apprentice or workman might be leaving his native city for ever. We first know of it, with its secular words, in a version harmonized by Heinrich Izaac. The words were later paraphrased for church use as 'Ach Welt Ich muss dich lassen' and later still adapted to yet other words. In the later version of the tune we find the simplifying process again at work. For 'community' purposes the long melisma at the end of the tune which is such a common feature in German folk-song had to disappear and give place to a plain ending. This was the version that Bach knew, and he in his turn ornamented this plain cadence.

Both Bach and Mozart are reported to have said that they would have rather invented this tune than any of their own compositions.

If we turn to the Genevan Psalter of Calvin, we find the same story. When Clément Marot translated some of the psalms into French verse his versions caught the fancy of the young exquisites at the Court of François I and they sang them to well-known ballad-tunes. Each had his favourite, The Dauphin had his, Catharine de' Medici had hers and even Diane de Poitiers is said to have sung the 'De Profundis' to the melody of 'Baisez moi donc beau Sire'.

The Genevan Psalter as you doubtless know originated in these metrical versions of Marot. The origin of the tunes is unknown. We still find many of them attributed to Goudimel but all he did was to harmonize them. Another supposed author is Greiter, but he, it has been proved, was no more than a collector and adapter. We can find the solution I think in a sentence from Sir Richard Terry's pamphlet on the Strasburg Psalter of 1539. He writes, 'The bulk of the tunes in this Psalter have not been traced to any known source. [This] is not surprising if we remember that in the sixteenth century the sharp line of demarcation between sacred and secular music did not exist. . . . Just as the courtiers of François I sang Marot's psalms to any popular air that took their fancy, so the Huguenots adapted to their vernacular psalms and canticles tunes that were already familiar. . . . In the task of collecting tunes for the early metrical psalters all was fish that came to the compiler's net. . . . Just as the Lutheran Choral has preserved for us secular tunes of the moment which have long since died out at their original source, so has this book preserved for us a number of noble tunes which must have been popular in their day, but which now survive only as settings to Calvin's psalms.'

The Genevan Psalter contains many beautiful tunes; the best known to us probably are the following two; that which is known in England and America as 'The Old Hundredth' still, I am sorry to say, occasionally attributed to Goudimel, and a psalm-tune which is known to us as 'The Old 113th'. The 'Old Hundredth' comes from the Genevan Psalter of 1551 and was there set, not to the 100th but to the 134th psalm. This tune is undoubtedly derived from a folk-tune, or rather is likely to be a synthesis of more than one. The opening phrase occurs in other Lutheran Chorals and at least one other English psalm-tune. There are several secular folk-tunes in which phrases very like the 'Old Hundredth' occur. Douen, I think, quotes a French love-song in this connexion and Böhme has a Netherlandish Volkslied (*Altdeutsches Liederbuch* (103)) which is extraordinarily similar. This tune was printed in the *Souterliedekens* in 1540. As we saw in the case of 'Innsbruck' the melismatic cadences especially at the ends of the first and last lines have been simplified in the psalm-tune for the purposes of massed singing.

The 'Old 113th' appears as a psalm-tune in the Strasburg Psalter of 1539. We have no external proof that it is derived from a folk-song, but the internal evidence is very strong, the nature of the tune itself and the fact that several of its phrases appear in other tunes. The well-known Easter hymn, 'Lasst uns erfreuen', which we first know of in the Cologne Hymn Book of 1623 can hardly be anything else than an adaptation to different words of some source common to the two tunes.

Whether this tune was popular in origin or not, it has all the history of a folk-song, adapting itself to different words and different moods, showing slight variants in detail, and, finally, receiving illumination at the hands of J. S. Bach. In the Strasburg Psalter it was set to Psalm 36, 'My heart showeth me the wickedness of the ungodly', but later it was used to Psalm 68, 'Let God arise', or in the French metrical version, 'Que Dieu se montre seulement'.

In this guise it became known as the 'Battle-hymn of the Huguenots' and was to them what 'Ein' feste Burg' was to the Lutherans. The tune also became known in Germany, but changed its character from the martial to the penitential, being set to the words of Sebaldus Heyden's hymn, 'O Mensch bewein', and in this version forms a basis of the great chorus at the end of the first part of Bach's *St. Matthew Passion* and also of one of his most beautiful choral Preludes. The tune also came to England where it was set in rather a distorted form to fit a new metre to the 113th psalm. It is said to have been John Wesley's favourite tune.

It will be seen from these examples that even written music can, within limitations, evolve like the folk-song. Those who pin their faith on the written word call these changes deteriorations. There are some people who are always after the *earliest* version of a tune and call every later change 'corruption'. But the earliest version is by no means always the best; the voice of the people is often on the side of the angels and we can often trace a steady evolution until the tune reaches its climax illumined by the genius of a Bach. The best example I know is the 'Ein' feste Burg' which, if the earliest version is really what Martin Luther played on his flute to his friend Walther, is not much to be proud of. It is not until it has passed through generations of German congregations and has been glorified by Bach's harmony, that we realize its magnificence.

I sometimes wonder if we could trace this process of evolution through all music; if there is for composers a fixed stock of root ideas which each can make his own and use for his own purposes, good, bad, and indifferent. We could, for instance, perhaps imagine a melodic germ originating in the *Singspiele* of J. A. Hiller or one of his contemporaries, passing on through the early nineteenth-century ballad writers, lit up by the genius of Weber, finding its climax in Wagner, gradually deteriorating in the minds of Richard

Strauss and his followers, until it finally finds an unhonoured grave in the compositions of some twentieth-century conservatoire student.

In England and Scotland in Elizabethan times we find 'Ghostly parodies', as they were called, of such popular ballads as 'Go From My Window' and 'John, Come Kiss Me Now'. So we may suppose that the church in England was not averse to adapting secular music for her use. In the English psalters the names of composers of the tunes are not given, but only of those who harmonized them; but several of the tunes have local names, the 'Winchester' tune, the 'Windsor' tune, the 'Glastonbury' tune and so on. Why were these names given? May they not have been adaptations of folk-songs sung in those districts? This is, of course, merely a suggestion, but as far as I know, no other explanation has yet been given of these names.

I need not trace the secular influence any further; but in the nineteenth century it seems to have died out in the face of clerical disapproval. The tune 'Helmsley' was divorced from 'Lo, He comes' in the early editions of *Hymns Ancient and Modern*, and in one quite modern hymnal, the Editor tells us with conscious pride that there are no folk-songs in his collection. Perhaps we can find an explanation of this attitude from the following from Dyson's *Progress of Music*. Commenting on the modern relation of church and people he writes, 'Our churches are lovingly cared for, they are far cleaner and quieter and more decorous than our ancestors would have deemed possible, or even desirable. . . . We preserve with meticulous care everything of historic or local significance, everything that is, except the supreme historic fact, that the church was once the unchallenged centre and meeting place of the whole local community. . . . Our consecrated gardens may now be trim because the present world passes them by. . . . A church can be very peaceful when it is empty.'

SOME THOUGHTS ON

BEETHOVEN'S
CHORAL SYMPHONY
WITH WRITINGS ON OTHER MUSICAL SUBJECTS

1

Some thoughts on
Beethoven's Choral Symphony

This is not intended to be a learned disquisition nor an official guide
to this mighty composition. Nor is it an analysis; though I shall go
through the work as a whole showing its structure as it appears to me.

I have simply tried to set down, largely to clarify my own mind,
my personal 'reactions' (as our American cousins say) to what I
believe, together with the B minor Mass and the *St. Matthew
Passion*, to be the greatest of choral music.

In case this last sentence should appear to be an impertinent
truism, I ought to explain that the early nineteenth-century idiom
is naturally repugnant to me. My natural love is much more the
Gothic–Teutonic idiom of J. S. Bach and his predecessors—not
'Baroque', by the way, as it is fashionable nowadays to stigmatize
Bach's music. Bach has nothing to do with the mechanical orna-
ment of Baroque architecture, which is much more akin to
Beethoven, but should be compared to the natural exfoliation of a
Gothic cathedral. Thus it is, so to speak, in spite of myself, that I
have to acknowledge the supremacy of the Ninth Symphony.

When I admit that this Symphony is an unapproachable
masterpiece, I do not mean that I accept as perfect every note, every
phrase, every chord; perhaps even I do not consider it in every
detail a model work of art.

Tovey, in his masterly essay on this Symphony, pays lip service to imperfections in it, but when it comes to detail he fails to find any blemishes.[1]

For me there are certain passages in the Ninth Symphony which I find hard to swallow, but I do not include in this indigestible matter the choral finale, though even here there are certain things which stick in my gizzard.

I understand that the pious Beethovenite always makes an exception of this finale; but then I am not a pious Beethovenite. To me, the finale is potentially the greatest movement of the four.

Let me make my confessions and be done with it about some of the places which puzzle me.

For example—the 'Joy' tune in the finale is one of the greatest melodies of the world. Why does Beethoven always add as a refrain the following incredible 'tag'?

Again, is not the second subject of the third movement—especially with its counterpoint at its second appearance—though charming as a *morceau de salon*, quite out of keeping with the unearthly grandeur of the work as a whole?

Whence do difficulties such as these (I speak as a fool) arise? Is it not that Beethoven was for a moment conquered by the conventions? No composer can speak out of his period otherwise he

[1] All the references to Tovey's essays were written before his death in 1940.

will be either unintelligible or wilfully obscurantist. The great artist uses the conventions as his tools and bends them to his will, so that they are no longer conventions but a vital means of expression, but even the greatest artist is occasionally mastered by his machinery and allows convention to master him, not through fear of consequences, but from the fact that for the moment the engine has gone off the boil.

I remember that Sir Donald Tovey once in a broadcast lecture defended such passages by quoting as a parallel the famous, 'Pray you, undo this button' from *King Lear*, as an example of prosaic simplicity enhancing tragic emotion. I am obliged to quote Tovey from memory as there appears to be no written record of his lecture.

But the true parallel is not, to my mind, prosaic language but conventional verbiage spoiling noble simplicity. I would rather suggest as a parallel that unbelievable line in *Samson Agonistes*, which breaks the majesty of the final lament, 'unfortunate in nuptial choice'.

Perhaps it is Beethoven's method of ornamenting his melodies which puzzles me most. To start with, I cannot imagine why the melody of the slow movement, or of the 'Joy' tune, wants ornament at all. Is not this gilding the lily?

A great melody is for all time. When Beethoven, and often, Mozart, start ornamenting their melodies they seem at once to make them of their period and there they remain. Surely if a melody is to be ornamented at all the ornament should grow naturally out of the original thought, and not be mechanically added to it by a stereotyped process.

When Bach adds ornament to a melody I feel that this is the direct outcome of his overflowing emotion. When Haydn ornaments a melody it seems to me to be the natural childlike joy in a new plaything. But with Beethoven the ornament seems introduced by a conventional procedure. As soon as a melody has been stated simply it must be subjected to a process of appogiature, turns, and trills which are almost mechanical in the application. How otherwise can we account for the perversion of a beautiful melody in the slow movement of the 'Kreutzer' Sonata in the second variation? It is inconceivable to me how the composer who invented the wonderful tragic third variation could admit that other *variation de concert*[2] into his scheme.

The pundits will doubtless tell me that the second variation of the Sonata is a necessary foil to the third; but I have yet to learn that it is right to do evil that good may come.

Here are two examples from the Ninth Symphony:

Firstly, part of the melody of the slow movement in its simple and its varied forms:

To the possible objection that it is unfair to quote only a few bars of this passage I would reply that if I had quoted the whole my case would be stronger.

Secondly, part of the 'Joy' tune in the finale and the second variation for solo voices:

What do these variations do to enhance the beauty or give a deeper meaning to these two melodies? Are they not merely overlaid with trite and mechanical formulae, lending a commonness to them which intrinsically they do not possess?

With regard to this variation in the choral finale I discover from Tovey that I am not alone in my failure to see the point. Tovey duly censures us for this opinion, but I have to confess that after

---

[2] I am sometimes tempted to think that Bridgetower invented this variation himself.

reading his argument on the subject several times I still fail to understand it.

Compare for a moment with these ornamentations Bach's Variations on 'O Mensch bewein':

Here, so it seems to me, is an irrepressible exfoliation under the direct influence of deep emotion; not a plastered-on ornament according to a conventional formula.

I daresay I have laid too much stress on these minutiae which trouble me, but one is especially keenly alive to the faults of what is otherwise supreme. Also it is so much easier to explain one's criticisms than to voice one's wonderment. What are these moments after all but tiny darknesses which 'stain the bright radiance of eternity'?

In the presence of this work one, perhaps, only dares to point out one's disappointments and is left dumb in the presence of its greatnesses.

It will, by this time, be evident that I am not a loyal Beethovenite. For example, I love the 'Moonlight Sonata' and think it well named. This, I know, puts me out of court, for did not Beethoven himself prefer that dreary affair, the Sonata in F♯ major (Op. 78)?

Again, I think the 'Kreutzer' the greatest of the violin Sonatas, and I know that this is simply 'not done' in the best circles. Similarly, I believe the choral finale of the Ninth Symphony to be potentially the greatest of the four movements. This is in direct opposition, I

D

suppose, to the opinion of the pious Beethovenites (including Sir George Grove), who deplored the finale and considered it to be 'a pity', like the old ladies in Forster's *Room with a View*, who would only buy the head and shoulders of the photographs of Botticelli's *Venus* because they considered the complete figure 'a pity'.

It is admittedly harder to write good music which is joyful than that which is sad. It is comparatively easy to be mildly dismal with success. But to my mind, two composers and two only, and they but seldom, have been able to write music which is at the same time serious, profound, and cheerful—Bach in the 'Cum Sancto' of the B minor Mass and Beethoven in the finale of the Choral Symphony. Incidentally both these movements are in D major.

Readers will, of course, bring to my notice the *Meistersinger* Overture and 'Siegfried's Journey to the Rhine', but these are not cases in point. *Die Meistersinger* is admittedly comedy and the Rhine-Journey is a cheerful interlude to contrast with the gloom and tragedy of the rest of the opera.

I have said that the finale is potentially the greatest of the four movements. I use the word 'potentially' advisedly, because I am quite ready to admit that in this movement, Beethoven obviously does not achieve all that he intends. Too often, in performance, what should be a jubilant shout becomes a distressing wail. One could almost wish that Beethoven, while writing his voice parts, had had at his elbow a practical, uninspired, competent English choir-master. But 'almost' is not 'quite'. The English choir-master would probably have pointed out, with justice, that though D major is an ideal key for the 'Joy' tune when played by instruments, it is by no means so when sung by voices, owing to the awkward *tessitura*, which is either too high or too low. See, for example, the difficulties Beethoven encounters when his tenors have to dodge about from octave to octave when they try to sing the tune, and that therefore perforce, either the key or the tune must be altered—either course obviously unthinkable.

No, we must leave Beethoven with his magnificent failure (if failure it be) as something much more worth hearing than lesser men's successes.

As William Watson says of Shelley—he is greater than those others who have approached much nearer 'their meaner goal'.

I feel that the failure of many choirs to 'bring off' the chorus parts of this Symphony is due to a wrong method of approach. They, or their trainers, regard it as a very difficult vocal exercise and do not attack it boldly as a jubilant shout. The 'Ode to Joy' is a great song for 'all peoples, nations, and languages'. Never mind if the tone sounds rough and uncultivated; never mind if a few notes 'drop under the table', as Mozart said. Let the chorus sing their hearts out and their heads off and not trouble if they have sore throats for a week after.

But is this music so unsingable? Toscanini and Bruno Walter have proved to us that with an English choir, at any rate, a performance can be thrilling, brilliant, and musical, and there need be no (apparent) throat strain. Our English soprano soloists have also taught those dignified German ladies who were, till lately, considered the high priestesses of the Beethoven cult, that there is no necessity in those difficult high quavers of the Second Variation to make a noise like a dog being run over by a motor car.

Nevertheless, for a performance which I had hoped to prepare before the War, I made the experiment of modifying the voice parts in a few places—chiefly by adding alternative notes for second sopranos and tenors—so that those under the rank of Archangel could take part in it.

I know of four important essays on the Ninth Symphony, though there may be more which I have not read. By far the most interesting is that by Sir Donald Tovey, from which I must confess I have helped myself liberally, though I venture occasionally to disagree with him.

Then there is Richard Wagner's attempt to give the whole work a 'meaning', as was the fashion in that materialistic age, the age of 'romanticism'. That is, a 'meaning' which can be touched, tasted, and handled. The Ninth Symphony has, indeed, a meaning, but it is a meaning beyond the world of facts and words; it means itself and can be expressed in its own terms and no other.

There is also an excellent, but typically nineteenth-century essay by Sir George Grove. He is discreetly non-committal in his analysis of the choral finale, but writes at the end, 'If in the Finale a restless, boisterous spirit manifests itself, not in keeping with the English feeling of the solemnity, even the sanctity, of the subject, this is only a reflection and by no means an exaggerated reflection, of the bad taste which is manifested in parts of the lines adopted from Schiller's Ode and which Beethoven, no doubt, thought it was his duty to carry out in his music.'

And finally there is Weingartner's practical advice on the performance of the work, which should be read by every conductor.

A composer is most truly himself and at his greatest when he is least his superficial self, when he casts off all the trappings of his technique and period and enables his thought to stand out in all its nakedness. So, paradoxically, the first two and, with reservations, the last movement of this Symphony are the least 'Beethovenish', and therefore to my mind, the finest.

In the first two movements, at all events, Beethoven transcends even himself. The music is like no other music, either before or since. It seems sometimes to have come straight from the eternal source of truth without human intervention.

Standing on this ground Beethoven, I have to admit, is in a different sphere from my beloved Bach. Beethoven lived in a time of greater intellectual expansion than Bach, whose theology was purely anthropomorphic, and whose music does not look for the Supreme Being beyond the stars, but sees him humanly as the friend of souls, the Great King, the Bridegroom. Beethoven when he looks into eternity sees clearer and further than Bach; but Bach when he thinks of his very human deity has the richer and warmer consciousness. So on the human side Bach has Beethoven completely beaten. For example, when Beethoven touches the Crucifixion in the *Missa Solennis*, he achieves none of the profound mystery of human pity and divine suffering, or the absolute quiet of death of Bach's 'Crucifixus'. He has to be content with a conventionally sentimental, El-Greco-like setting. It was not in these terms that Beethoven could express himself.

For eternity we turn to Beethoven, for humanity to Bach.

Tovey describes the first movement as tragedy, the second—scherzo—as satiric drama. To my mind these movements transcend the human limitations of tragedy, satire, or drama and are direct visions of what lies beyond them.

In the slow movement, as it seems to me, we relapse on to the 'Beethovenish' Beethoven; the Beethoven whom the early nineteenth century called the 'sublime' Beethoven; the Beethoven who made strong men with whiskers brush away a silent tear. That is the reason, I suppose, why I care for this less than the other movements. I know it is all my fault. The opening subject, I feel sure, is beautiful, though not of the eternal quality of the other movements, but I *do* wish that Beethoven had not varied it. The second subject is entrancing in its sound, but always tastes to me a little of the Viennese drawing room, especially with the added counterpoint. But suddenly, even in this movement, we turn the page and come upon eternity again. The trumpets wake us out of our nineteenth-century slumber and a great organ-like passage intervenes. But it cannot last, the magic passes and we return to this kind of thing:

Why, O why, did Beethoven, after he had opened all heaven for us for the moment, return to earth thus!

No, there can be no doubt about it, I do not understand Beethoven—that is plain. It is not the 'obscure' parts which puzzle me but the plain-sailing ones. No, I do not understand Beethoven; and yet when I turn to the finale, I sometimes think that I understand him better than the inner circle.

We can divide those who object to the finale under two headings. First: The devout Beethovenites who think the finale 'noisy' and even 'in bad taste'; secondly: Those who are put off by the obvious, technical shortcomings in the texture.

I remember Gustav Holst saying to me (I quote from memory), 'I should not mind the end of the finale being noisy and vulgar. This is just feeble; it *tries* to be noisy and fails.'

I frankly admit the technical imperfections and in these few places am prepared to accept the will for the deed, when the will is plain in spite of the deed.

The pious hierophant would, I suppose, have preferred the smug solemnity of Mendelssohn's *Hymn of Praise*. If so he simply fails to realize what Beethoven was aiming at; he can be solemn enough in the 'Millionen' section.

The 'locus classicus' of these lily-livered critics is, I presume, the beginning of the final rampage.

There are to my mind plenty of banalities in the Ninth Symphony—banal chiefly because they seem to me out of place. But this passage is definitely not banal, because it is eminently in its right place. It might indeed be from an opera by Rossini; but here its absolute rightness sublimates it into a supreme piece of music—the Jubilation of a whole 'Fire-drunk' (*Feuer-trunken*) people.

When I was young I was told that Schiller originally wrote his Ode to 'Freedom' (*Freiheit*), not 'Joy' (*Freude*), and that Beethoven knew of this when he composed the music. I have never been able to find any confirmation of this legend, but we may profitably keep it at the back of our minds when we play or sing or read, or hear this great Symphony.

It is now time, I think, for a little formal analysis: not too formal I hope, but an attempt to show what are the principal musical themes and how they build up into an organic whole.

FIRST MOVEMENT—ALLEGRO MAESTOSO

The opening movement is, of course, in what is known as 'Sonata' form, but this is not in itself a justification of its structure. A musical form must be justified by its results.

I shall try to show, without any *a priori* reference to a stereotyped form, how this Symphony is built up.

In the first two movements this is easy, for though the movements are gigantic in stature, yet in actual length they are not outstanding and their pattern is clear-cut. Although the thought is profound the structure is simple and the themes are statuesque and straightforward.

If you read a text-book on composition you will probably be advised to start a symphony with a good square melodic subject which would from the first clearly define the principal key. Beethoven's first movement is, as we discover later, in D minor. However, he starts off with the chord of A—major or minor?—nobody knows. Where is it leading to?—nobody knows. On this chord there is a soft tremolando for the strings, above which the first violins, violas, and basses begin tentatively, picking out what may be the adumbration of a theme; the music grows louder and the theme more defined. Then the bassoon gives the game away by side-slipping on to D two bars early. Now the secret is out, D minor is the key, and like a bare mountain-side suddenly seen bleak and grey through a rift in the fog, the principal theme appears, a great unison arpeggio, gloomy in its stark nakedness, hereafter called the 'arpeggio theme'.

The complete subject is not a square-cut melody, as the text-books advise, but a series of short sharply defined phrases. As each of these is used separately in the development of the plot I will quote the theme in full as Example 1 and number the sub-sections a, b, c, d, e, f, and g.

Ex. 1.

With a rushing scale passage the music dies down and we start again, this time on the chord of D (again, major or minor?—there is no third in the chord). Again the bassoon helped by the horn side-slips two bars early, this time to B♭ in which key the 'arpeggio theme' bursts out once more.

Now B♭ is the key of the next group of themes which we are soon to hear. 'Never anticipate the key of your second subject,' say the text-books! Having landed in B♭ the composer brings us back to D minor by the repetition of a short phrase founded on

1(b), and when we are home again the fact is celebrated by this phrase:

Ex. 2.

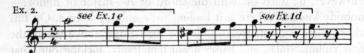

Tovey calls this a new phrase, but may it not be considered as a derivation from 1(e and d)? But the point is unimportant since the sense of unity is preserved and it is a mechanical view of musical structure which considers that this can only be done by unity of outline.

The phrase is repeated in canon and the bass changes to F, which is the Dominant of B♭, and an introductory phrase ushers in the new key and a row of new subjects placed, so to speak, end to end. It is the only really Beethoveny phrase in the movement, and is therefore not my favourite. Here is the introductory passage:

Ex. 3.

The mechanically-minded nineteenth-century romantics proclaimed this as a foreshadowing of the 'Joy' tune quoted in full later (Example 32), as if the mechanical fact that the outline is similar could give any spiritual affinity to the two themes. It is not thus that one phrase derives from another. Beethoven himself has shown us how to do this when later in this movement he makes

the logical continuation of

No two themes could be more different in spiritual content than Example 3 and Example 32.

We shall see later in this movement how Beethoven foreshadowed his 'Joy' tune.

Here is the row of new themes which the key of B♭ suggests to the composer: First a dialogue-melody between the various wind instruments accompanied by a mysterious semiquaver figure on the strings:

Ex. 4.

This continues for four bars and is followed by an ornamented repetition—a beautiful ornamentation—which contains a characteristic hovering between major and minor (G♮ and G♭) and leads to a similar thought further on.

A great organism like this movement is not merely a set of melodies neatly fitted into a pattern, it is a living growth, not a mechanical arrangement. One thought grows out of another, one idea develops out of a previous hint, so that, as in a tree, the topmost leaf and the deepest root are parts of one complete whole.

After a suggestion of 1(f), a phrase that is continually cropping up, like cement holding the structure together, there follows a mysterious scheme of descending scales played by the upper strings, with the lower strings continually climbing up the scale to meet them. In this there is a suggestion of 1(e).

Ex. 5.

This is repeated with the addition of a few bars. Then 1(f) becomes

Ex. 6.

which is repeated in the minor, so that the end of the second bar is G♭(=F♯). Thus we suddenly find it necessary to transpose the rest of the passage to the key of C♭(=B♮), where it stays for a few bars, softly sounding the first two bars of Example 6. Then the scale passages begin again, stressing the alternation between G♭ and G♮. Something is surely coming of this—and that something soon appears.

Ex. 7.

Note first the melody with its alternation of major and minor, which recurs again and again throughout the work. We remember that the opening of the Symphony was neutral in mode, that it decided first on the minor, then when the key changed to B♭, the major and minor alternations were already hinted at. Surely that is why at the outset the mode was left so vague. Then note the syncopated bass and finally the rhythm of Example 6 softly tapped out by the drum, a rhythm continually and ominously present, prefacing some denouement.

The excitement increases. The syncopated bass of Example 7 pounds on while the upper strings rush about in demi-semi-quavers. This phrase is played contrapuntally by the wind:

Ex. 8.

punctuated by the trumpets blazing out, (a) of Example 6, which finally takes possession and resolves itself into a great triumphal fanfare in B♭, hereafter called the 'fanfare theme'.

Ex. 9.

Here is momentary triumph, a great victorious unison growing inevitably from the mysterious distant unison of the opening, but the triumph is shortlived. The music dies down and easily slips back to where we started. On that primitive, sexless chord of A, the tremolando, the tentative fragments of subject begin again.

Are we going to go through that tension once more? No, there is a difference; listen to those sinister, soft barks on the trumpets and drums. We pass, not as before to D minor, but through D major to G minor, and here the music takes a new guise—in the technical language the 'development' has begun.

It may be asked, and was asked by the romanticists, why, when classical music passed the period of mere pattern-making and seemed to be telling of an adventure of the soul, was it necessary to stick to that A.B.A. pattern—statement, contrast, recapitulation. Why say it all over again when it has once already been said? Why not a continuous development, as in a story or an epic poem? Liszt and his fellow materialistic romanticists, who, as we are aware, thought that a 'meaning' must be tied on to every piece of music, tried the experiment, with the disastrous results which we know so well in their symphonic poems. Perhaps their failure is partly due to their intrinsic lack of musical invention and it was this very lack which led them away from symmetrical pattern into vague meanderings.

Music can indeed portray the very depths of the soul, but it does not do so on the lines of a story, but rather on those of a building. Symmetry is essential to music's vitality, and without it music can no more stand than a man without bones, or an arch without its two supporting pillars.

Further, the 'recapitulation' in a Beethoven symphony is not a mere saying of the same thing twice, but a restatement of the initial ideas now seen in a new light derived from all the phases the music has been through since it set out on its journey. And these new phases, these new lights on old faces are to be found in that part of the composition which leads back from the section of contrast to the section of restatement, or, to put it architecturally, the curve of the arch back to the supporting pillar, and this curve is known as the 'development' section.

Beethoven's development in the Ninth Symphony differs from his normal technique of development. In most of his works in the sonata form the music pursues a straight course, steering its way directly to the home port. But here there seems, as Grove points out, to be a curious hesitancy. Instead of using his thematic material as a means of leading directly home he seems rather to handle it and meditate on one aspect of it after another.

We shall discuss later the famous passage at the beginning of the finale where Beethoven passes his first three movements in review and dismisses them all. Is he not doing the same thing here?—considering each detail and interrupting his consideration each time by the now angry 'fanfare theme' (Example 9). First the bassoon discovers that the 'arpeggio theme' (1(a)) has a melodic value which we had not suspected, but this does not last long. Again the 'fanfare' theme interrupts, this time on a diminished seventh in G minor, and its place is taken by 1(b) which the oboe discovers also to have melodic qualities and which is answered in a short duet by the flutes. This leads to a seemingly insignificant, hesitating little cadence suggested by the end of Example 2. But we shall meet that little phrase again when its full tragic importance will be seen. Even so Anna Karenina met the little Moujik of her dream and he said the seemingly meaningless word at the tragic climax of her story.

Then Beethoven thinks it all out again: First, the 'arpeggio' phrase, this time given more emotional significance by the strings and by a new turn of phrase.

Ex. 10.

Is there some subtle connexion between this and Example 7? Again the fanfare theme interrupts and again the oboes with their version of 1(b); again the hesitating cadence.

Then Beethoven seems to make up his mind. Example 1(b and c) is no longer to be a softly singing phrase but to form part of a vigorous fugato starting in the bass:

Ex. 11.

Against this the second violins saw away at a counter subject in semiquavers and the upper instruments have another counter-subject of syncopated holding notes. At last we have got into our stride, the melodic leaps of the subject get wider and wider; the music soon quietens down again but the movement is maintained, though now declining on to the cantabile question-and-answer which we heard before. Finally, the semiquavers take possession and patter on the wood-wind while the basses rise in terms of Example 1 to meet them. This is one of those passages which look nothing on paper but are so astounding when heard. Then the semiquavers veer over to the strings and become the accompaniment to Example 4. Again 1(b) reappears with 1(c) in the bass elongated as in a distorting mirror. Finally the whole orchestra joins in a tornado of semiquavers and suddenly we are back in D major. No doubtful tonality now! The opening is given out with the full orchestra, first in D major (F♯ in the bass), and then changing to D minor (F♮ in the bass); over this, drums and basses tremolando, there enters with full force the opening of the Symphony once more, not now in a mysterious pianissimo nor in tentative suggestions, but cohering as a vast melody, expanding itself in imitative sequences while the drums keep up their inexorable roll.

Of all the great moments in this allegro this seems to me the greatest. Writers on Sibelius point out how he is apt to gather together the scattered fragments of his earlier themes into one great paragraph. This is just what Beethoven did here one hundred years previously.

Such fury cannot last for ever, and without much warning the music quietens down and becomes definitely in D major, and then there follow in succession all the themes from Example 3 to Example 9, varied by the subtle alternations of major and minor so characteristic of the whole movement. Especially should the elusive alteration of Example 6 be noted.

So we press on to the 'fanfare' phrase, not this time in triumphant major but in menacing minor. Are we going to finish here? No,

Beethoven's inexhaustible fertility has still more to say about his great themes which he embodies in a gigantic peroration or coda, very different from the terse little tail pieces of Haydn and Mozart.

The fanfare ends and we find that by some magic its end has become the beginning of a new theme, four bars long, made up by some chemical combination out of Example 1(a and b).

Ex. 12.

After twenty-eight bars this leads to Example 5, but the trumpets are continuously softly reminding us of the 'fanfare'; they grow in insistence and gradually submerge everything, mounting up step by step surely to some great climax.

Then a miracle happens. Suddenly the clouds lift and a mirage, like a vision of joy, appears for the moment, or, to put it in technical language, a sudden pianissimo supervenes and the themes 1(b) and 1(c) appear on the horn (see the fugato of the development section) in the major key for the first time, while the strings hold a pedal (A) in five octaves and the oboe gently accompanies with semi-quavers.

Here indeed is a foretaste of the 'Joy' tune, which the materially-minded Liszt school were not able to perceive. For those who have ears to hear the spiritual kinship is plain. But the light soon dies away. The theme is taken up by the strings in four octaves in the minor, first softly, then louder and louder, while the wind continues a little semiquaver figure. As the strings get louder the wind figure gets drowned, but as they die down again it is found that the wind is still persistently playing its part—a wonderfully poetical conception which is, I am sure, intentional. If it is a miscalculation, it is a lucky accident. These lucky accidents do happen—for instance, the unintentional omission of the bassoon bass in the finale, of which more later.

There is once more a reference to Example 5, which leads to a double statement of that seemingly insignificant hesitating cadence in the 'development' section. Now at last we understand its full, tragic force.

But Beethoven has one more surprise in store for us—the actual ending of the movement. The basses start softly muttering up and down in a chromatic scale, while the wind has an entirely new phrase, and in the last sixteen bars, too. What will the text-books say? But perhaps this theme derives in part from Example 1(a). In that case honour and the text-books are satisfied.

Ex. 13.

Over and over again the phrase repeats itself till it bursts with full power into the arpeggio phrase, and with this the movement abruptly ends.

SECOND MOVEMENT—MOLTO VIVACE

Beethoven's symphonic scherzos always retain the rhythmical dance nature which the later 'romantic' symphonists were to discard. Insistent, almost hypnotically constant rhythm is characteristic of both this scherzo itself and the 'trio' with which it alternates. In a scheme such as this a certain amount of formal regularity is essential to its vitality. We are not surprised, therefore, to find that each section is repeated, that there is an exact recapitulation of the first part of the scherzo after a contrasting section and that after the trio the scherzo is repeated in its entirety.

Rhythmical impulse being the basis of this movement, we naturally find that it is dominated by a rhythmical pattern (♩. ♪♩), which is essentially percussive in its nature, and that the drum soon finds this out and protrudes itself in this fashion in and out of season.

The opening bars, like the principal subject of the first movement, form the arpeggio of D minor, of which the D and A, tonic and fifth, are played by the strings, the F, third, by drum solo, a precursor of what is to follow, then the D, tonic, again by the whole orchestra minus the drums and the trombones. These latter instruments Beethoven reserves for later use. All this opening is in terms of ♩. ♪♩. Note also the silent bars. Unlike later composers, Mozart, Haydn, and Beethoven seldom used their trombones merely to add to the noise but to give a solemn, religious, or sinister colour to the music. After this exordium the movement starts in earnest in the shape of a five part fugue for the strings, of which this is the subject:

Ex. 14.

This theme naturally divides into two sections, the opening rhythmical figure a, and a pattern of crotchets three bars long b. It is started by the second violins and played by the strings with the wood-wind just punctuating the beginning of each bar.

The subject expands itself for forty-eight bars, chiefly in terms of the second half of the subject (Example 14(b)). For the first thirty-six bars the music maintains a mysterious pianissimo, but from that point it begins to grow in volume till at the forty-ninth bar the complete theme bursts out with the full force of the orchestra, except for the trombones, and the theme is extended by this figure:

Ex. 15.

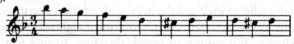

This is played twice in D minor, and then again one tone lower. We are evidently heading for C major. Surely we should have expected F major or A minor as the complementary key? But, no, the choice is C major.

Beethoven is sometimes accused by the bright young things as being too much of a tonic and dominant composer, and indeed, as, for example, in the C minor Symphony, his greatest strokes of musical effect seem to grow out of this very tendency. But here, as in other works of his third period, he seems to be breaking away from this tonal scheme. Was he on the brink of a fourth period? We shall never know.

On the dominant chord of C major Beethoven introduces a new theme:

Ex. 16.

This is the bare outline of the melody, what it sounds like, but in the score it does not look like this because it is divided up between the instruments. In Beethoven the melodic outline is ever present, but it does not always leap to the eye. We should remember Wagner's dictum: 'The business of a conductor is to find out where the melody lies.'

This leads to a definite new theme in C major, in technical language the 'second subject'.

Ex. 17.

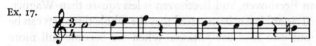

It is played by the wood-wind while the strings continue to pound away at (a) of Example 14. This passage is the best-known example of Beethoven's dynamic miscalculation. If the passage is played just as it stands it is almost impossible to hear the wood-wind melody against the hammering strings. Various conductors have suggested various remedies, which need not detain us here; none of them is quite satisfactory. When considering this and similar miscalculations we must remember that Beethoven never heard his work played. There is hardly a composer however keen his orchestral sense who does not wish to revise a few miscalculations after a first hearing. This was denied to Beethoven. Similarly, for a different reason, Schubert never heard his C major Symphony; if he had he would without doubt have corrected a parallel miscalculation at the end of his first movement. There are orchestral miscalculations even in Wagner, which any composer less conceited than he would certainly have corrected in performance.

But to return to our analysis: this 'second subject' leads to a series of two-bar sequences founded on the opening theme, Example 14, which in its turn leads to this—note the six-bar rhythm:

Ex. 18.

This may be a rhythmical alteration of Example 17. And finally to
a cadence figure, thus:

Ex. 19.

Before we go further I want to pause a moment on the theme in
six-bar rhythm, Example 18. There is a quaint idea prevalent that
Beethoven and other 'classical' composers are rhythmically 'square',
while the 'modern' composers are rhythmically 'free'. Nothing
could be further from the truth. As a matter of fact, Haydn is less
square than Beethoven, and Beethoven is less square than Wagner,
of whose 'Tristan' it has been stated that the whole three acts can be
parcelled out into four-bar phrases. When we become still more
modern as in Debussy, the squareness becomes even more apparent,
whole sections of his work consisting of two-bar sections each
played twice. While when we come to Stravinsky and Prokofiev,
one may almost say that every other two bars of their compositions
could be cut out without losing any music: some people might feel
inclined to add that the same is true of the pairs of bars which
remain! I can never understand why it is 'old-fashioned' to have
exact repetitions arranged in an architectural order, while it is
'modern' to arrange the repetitions in pairs. To my mind the one
is like an architect designing an arch, while the other is like an
orator who habitually repeats the last sentence while he is thinking
of what to say next.

After the cadence, a few bars of Example 14(a) lead back to a
repetition of all the first part from the beginning of the fugue.
These few bars of leading back, slight as they may seem, are in a
way the most important in the movement:

rhythmically: note the silent bars to complete the phrases.
   Beethoven was capable of keeping up the rhythmical impulse
   in silence as well as in sound.
harmonically: this middle cadence, as we know, is in C major. The
   opening to which we must get back is in D minor. There is no
   obvious relationship between the two keys.

Here is the harmonic scheme of Beethoven's return to D minor:

Ex. 20.

Now this is what is known as a 'modal' cadence—it seems either to hark back to Palestrina or forward to Moussorgsky. There is, so far as I know, nothing like it in the earlier Beethoven. What is this progression doing in the work of the 'apostle of the tonic and dominant'? The composer who in the Fifth Symphony had achieved his master strokes of power and originality by the use of these universal progressions of eighteenth-century harmony?

We find this same reaching out to new vistas and new horizons in others of Beethoven's later works, notably the 'Lydian Hymn', and parts of the Mass in D.

When we consider these passages we are led to a still further line of thought. The Ninth Symphony is generally regarded as the consummation of all that has gone before it, as the perfection, with the possible exception of the choral finale, of Beethoven's art. But is that the case? Is it not really an adventure into new territory, an imperfect and experimental work of art, stepping forward into an unknown region, but occasionally retreating on to familiar ground? Is not the symphony great, perhaps because of its very experiments, hesitations and imperfections, the sudden changes of style, the tentative nature of some of the choral writing? Is Beethoven in this symphony truly venturing

> toward the unknown region
> where neither ground is for the feet
> nor any path to follow?

Was Beethoven looking into a region where even he could not see clearly? Are not the great moments great for the very reason that the composer is seeing, as in a glass darkly, what no one has ever seen before or since?

After the repeat the curious quasi-modal passage extends itself till it lands us in the key of E minor. There is a strange pause on the third beat of the bar ♩. ♪♩ and the development of the fugue starts. The bassoon leads off, but in three-bar rhythm, cutting out the last bar of the subject; this leads to a wonderful passage, the drum, the 'enfant terrible' of this movement, always butting in where it is not wanted, now takes charge of the situation. The key has shifted to F major so that the drummer comes into his own and thunders out the first bar of the subject Example 14(a) alone, while the rest of the orchestra completes the three-bar phrase for him. Then with a sly wink and a magical diminuendo, the drum misses a bar and plays his figure on the *second* bar of the three while the orchestra continues its crochets.

The key changes, the drum has to yield to trumpets and horns, who kindly oblige with the notes the drummer cannot play having only two drums at his disposal. Then we find ourselves back in the principal key, D minor, and the oboe carries on the good work. Suddenly, and without warning, the rhythm changes back to four-bar phrases, a stretto starts in the bass, there is a momentary diversion to E♭, back to D minor, and a great crescendo on a dominant pedal leads back to the subject in its fortissimo form. All this, while the trumpets, horns, and the drummer, whenever he can fit it in, pound away consistently on the metrical figure ♩. ♪♩

From this tutti onwards the whole of the first part is recapitulated, with certain extensions and alterations to allow for changes of key and mode, minor or major, including the strange leading-back passage.

After a final crescendo, the time quickens and leads to this angry outburst, which is as a matter of fact a foreshortening of the opening phrase:

Ex. 21.

A blare on the trombone, its first appearance, announces a new section and a new theme: in technical language the 'Trio' of the scherzo. This melody is what Tovey calls 'as old as the art of music'.

Perhaps it is this primitive agelessness that gives the extraordinary newness to the music, that makes it something unlike anything before or since.

It consists of the notes of the scale of D up to A, and then back again, like the Duke of York and his ten thousand men. One is reminded of the schoolboy who said: 'I could have written all that Shakespeare stuff myself if I'd only thought of it.'

Absolute simplicity is beyond the reach of any but the greatest.

Here is the melody:

Ex. 22.

It is played by the wind only, with a moving bass on the bassoon, four times through without alteration. Then the strings with their rich warm colour have an answering phrase five bars long, repeated at once in varied form. Example 22 re-appears, this time on the horn, with soft light crotchets on the strings, a vision of distant blessedness. Did not Gluck use this same type of melody for his Elysian fields? The Elysian vision swells out louder and then dies away in soft, rich chords on the trombones; the blessed calm continues to the end except for one final cry of regret from the violins. And all of a sudden we are back in the battering turmoil of the scherzo.

Before leaving the trio there is one technical point to be noticed. According to the modern editions the tempo of this trio is ○ = 116: impossibly fast. Recent scholarship has, I think, proved that this is a misreading for ♩ = 116: absurdly slow. Wise conductors obey neither marking but take a middle course.

After the trio the scherzo is repeated note for note in its entirety, and we even overlap into the trio again, but the blessed vision breaks off abruptly, and with the savage outburst, Example 21, the movement suddenly stops.

I usually dislike Beethoven's jokes intensely. But this savage piece of humour is in an entirely different category from, say, the bassoon octaves in the finale of the Eighth Symphony.

So ends this amazing movement, so absolutely un-'Beethoveny', and yet the very quintessence of Beethoven.

THIRD MOVEMENT—ADAGIO MOLTO

Here we are back at real 'period' Beethoven, and therefore this is the movement which I like least. I know that it is all my own fault, and that the opening melody is beautiful and the first episode exquisite. I know that in my mind, but not in my heart. I cannot get out of my head the picture of Beethoven playing the pianoforte in a fashionable Viennese salon.

And yet there are that wonderful other-worldly third Variation, or interlude, the vision of unknown regions in the coda, and the unfathomable sigh of regret at the end. Truly, this symphony is an inexplicable mystery.

Technically this slow movement may be described as a set of variations separated by episodes.

I. There is an introduction, two bars long, played chiefly by the wood-wind and founded on two notes out of the main theme.

The theme itself is as follows:

Ex. 23.

The general scheme of this melody, as will be seen, is that it is played by the strings and that the end of each phrase is echoed by the wind. At the end of the last phrase an 'interrupted cadence' leads to the key of D.

II. Here is the melody of the episode, with a counter melody which only comes in at its second appearance:

Ex. 24.

Then by a masterly stroke of simplicity, we find ourselves back in
B♭.

III. First Variation, an ornamentation of the melody by the first
violins; the echoes by the wood-wind are not ornamented.

Ex. 25.

Again we have the 'interrupted cadence', but this time it leads to
G major.

IV. Episode repeated, but this time in G major and with a new
counter melody.

Ex. 26.

At the end an exactly parallel modulation to that of its first
appearance leads to E♭.

V. Second Variation: A free fantasia on the theme, Tovey prefers
to call it an interlude, the nomenclature does not matter. The point
is that it is one of those beautiful, far-off visions of happy things
which have already been noticed so frequently in this symphony.

The key is E♭. The clarinet starts off with the first two bars of
the theme, Example 23 (a and b), in its primitive form. It proceeds
to ornament the continuation of the theme in this beautiful manner
—worthy of Bach at his best. *O si sic omnia.*

Ex. 27.

Meanwhile, far below, the fourth horn booms out suggestions
of the opening bar of the theme. This is the famous passage which

Beethoven wrote especially for his friend the fourth horn-player, who possessed one of those new-fangled 'valve horns'. Then the key changes to C♭ and the horn takes up the ornamentation, Example 27, with magical effect.

Meanwhile, the strings accompany with soft plucked notes in triplets, which during the last three bars develop into an arpeggio figure accompanying a sort of cadenza on the horn. Alas, all too soon, the music fades into the light of common day. The key returns to B♭ and we reach the Third Variation. The wood-wind plays the theme in its simple form, but in compound 12/8 time, not simple 4/4 time, while the lower strings continue their pizzicato triplets and the first violins jump about in, to my mind, rather trivial arabesques. Sensible conductors keep these well in the background, as the merest accompaniment to the melody. Note, however, an entrancing swaying passage for the horn towards the end, which foreshadows the 'modern' treatment of the instrument.

Coda. The trumpets sound and wake us out of our complacency but only momentarily; another variation begins, a very beautiful variant of the opening phrase played by the first violins and echoed by the flute. I do wish, however, that Beethoven had not added that mechanical ornamentation in the second bar.

Ex. 28.

The theme is continued in the bass but is cut short by the menacing sound of the trumpets once again. Then follows this mysterious organ-like passage which it is worth while to quote at length—though this condensation can, of course, give no idea of the wonderful colour scheme.

What is the meaning of this stupendous passage? It stands apart, alone and unexplained, like Stonehenge on the Wiltshire Downs. Its isolation is in no way affected by the technical fact that it is built up on the opening bar of the theme.

Then once again the variant Example 28 returns, this time to lead to the second part of the theme.

Ex. 29.

Finally a new idea is hinted at, over the throbbing of the strings and the gentle tapping of the drums:

Ex. 30.

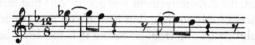

Is it possible that this is a reminiscence of the beautiful phrase (Example 7)

in the first movement?

At last, with a reference to Example 23, the movement quietly ends.

FOURTH MOVEMENT—FINALE

Now Hell breaks loose! Wagner thought it an inadequate Hell, and wanted to improve it: his emendations are chiefly concerned with the trumpet parts.

The opening chord of the finale is this grinding discord

But the trumpets and horns in Beethoven's day were incapable of
playing both the chord of D minor and the discordant B♭, which,
therefore, had to be left to the wood-wind, who, it must be confessed, perform the task rather feebly. Also Beethoven had a dis-
concerting habit, here and elsewhere in his tuttis, of putting notes
for the trumpets where their 'natural' scale fitted in to the harmony,
and leaving them out where they did not, which gives a scrappy
sound to the music. Wagner wished to use the possibilities of the
modern trumpet to fill in these gaps, but with doubtful success. It
seems that the only thing to do is to take Beethoven for better, for
worse, as we find him. At all events, the 'harsh din' is Hellish
enough to arouse a cry of remonstrance from the orchestral basses.
Again the din, and once more the protest from the basses. They
seem to be looking for some great tune which should solve all the
doubt and dismay of what has gone before. How about the first
movement? says the orchestra—again rejection and despair by the
basses. The scherzo is next suggested; angry dismissal by the basses.
Surely, then, the slow movement was good? 'Ah! that was lovely,'
the basses seem softly to sigh, 'but it won't do now. Quick! let us
find the solution of our troubles before it is too late—before joy
is lost for ever!'

Then the wood-wind answers: 'There used in the Golden Age
to be a tune which went somehow like this':

Ex. 31.

'That's it,' say the basses, 'we are saved; joy will once more be
ours', and with that they start softly, serenely, and seriously to hum
to themselves their 'immortal chant of old'—the 'Joy' tune as it
shall hereafter be called.

Then the violas take up the tune—still softly, but with full voice,
while the cellos join them in a loving unison: the first bassoon
improvises a heavenly descant, while the double basses far below
murmur a deep foundation.

It has been proved by musicologists that Beethoven intended the
second bassoon to play with the double basses here, as all good

Ex. 32.

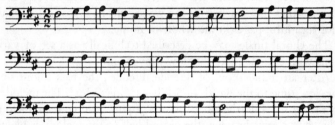

bassoons should when the double basses are left alone, *vide* Prout's *Orchestration Primer*, and that in printing the score it was accidentally omitted. The omission is one of those lucky accidents on which masterpieces often depend; the unobtrusive murmur of the double basses would be quite spoilt by a snorting bassoon.

Then the violins sing the tune, the bassoon helping from time to time, and the lower strings play sonorous counter-melodies, and lastly the trumpets take up the theme and make it into a solemn march.

After this last repetition Beethoven adds the refrain already discussed in these notes, which is, of course, suggested by the last phrase of the tune. This is extended, modulating in a perfectly orthodox fashion to the dominant A major, and we are led to expect a 'second subject' in regular symphonic form. But suddenly the composer appears to change his mind, a little wraith of a subject appears in an uncertain manner, both as to tonality and tempo, there is an angry outburst, and suddenly Hell breaks loose again with renewed force. This time it is rebuked, not by the orchestral basses, but by the human voice crying out to them to cease this din and to sing of joy.

What are we to make of all these hesitations, these apparent changes of purpose, which, as we have seen, are characteristic of the Symphony as a whole?

If we knew only the printed page and knew nothing of the historical facts, we might well guess that Beethoven originally designed a purely instrumental finale on 'sonata' lines, that he changed his mind and decided instead on a choral conclusion, but that he forgot when he sent the work to the printers to cut out the discarded version: if this were indeed so, we should have to count it as another lucky accident, for we should have lost some of the most beautiful pages in the whole of music.

The choral finale may be described technically as a set of variations with episodes, like the slow movement.

After an initial shout of 'Freude, Freude', the bass soloist sings the 'Joy' tune to the words of Schiller's 'Ode to Joy'. The melody is in the bass, while the oboe plays a joyful little counter-melody. The chorus joins in when the second half of the melody is played. Between each variation the refrain is repeated.

The first variation is not much more than a repetition of the theme with different texture, sung by the solo voices while the chorus joins in as before, but this time in four-part harmony. The second variation is an ornamentation of the theme in quavers, which has already been referred to in these notes. Like the first variation it is sung by the solo voices and taken up by the chorus. Again the refrain follows, this time covered by heavy minim chords for the voices, and the variation finishes with a shattering modulation to F major on the words 'vor Gott' ('before God'). I once played this passage to a pupil well versed in 'modern' harmony. I shall never forget her cry of surprise and delight at this modulation.

There is a pause: then what are we to expect? Well, Beethoven was a truly religious man, and was therefore not ashamed to place earthly jollity cheek by jowl with deep adoration.

Softly we hear the grunt of the bassoon and the thump of the big drum, gradually there emerges a jolly marching tune, a variant of the 'Joy' tune. This is, I believe, the music which deeply shocked the Victorian Beethovenites.

Ex. 33.

It is played chiefly by the wind band, very softly. The army of joy (freedom?) is advancing in the distance. Beethoven, great artist that he was, had no false shame in introducing this 'Turkish Patrol'

effect. Then, against the march tune, a man's voice is heard singing—probably a drunken soldier. (*Feuer*-trunken I assure you, Sir George Grove!) He is without doubt a Welshman, for he is obviously singing a 'Penillion' to the principal melody, though he probably has not obeyed all the rules of 'Penillion' singing. Gradually his companions join in, and the song culminates in a lusty shout.

Incidentally, it should be noted that Schiller's text here refers to the March of the Stars across the heavens. Beethoven evidently considered that the stars were jolly good fellows, fond of a rousing chorus, fond of a glass of beer and a kiss from the barmaid.

As the chorus finishes, the orchestra takes up the tale with a double fugue of daemoniac energy.

Here are the two subjects. One, it will be seen, is made up on the march tune; the other is a rhythmical variant of the 'Joy' tune.

Ex. 34.

Wagner, I believe, says that this figure 'means' the hero rushing into the fight. This unfortunate explanation has been the cause of much bad music by later composers, culminating in that outrageous piece of ineptitude, the 'battle' from *Ein Heldenleben*. It may be objected that I myself have also been giving a material meaning to Beethoven's music. This is far from my intention. I know full well that great music has no meaning in the material sense, and cannot be explained in terms of earthly facts. But, like all writers on music, I find it a convenient way, occasionally, of putting into words the scheme of the music.

The fugue continues with unabated exuberance for about a hundred bars. The quaver subject is unceasing, altering and extending itself as the occasion requires. The 'march' subject splits itself up into two phrases, a and b. Finally, b conquers and lands us on an F♯, the dominant of B, when the rhythm only is repeated; then comes a diminuendo on the horns.

The 'Joy' tune puts in a claim, sadly: 'Have you forgotten me?' 'No,' shouts the chorus, and plunges hurly-burly into the 'Joy' tune while the strings scamper around in excited quavers.

I know no parallel to this moment except perhaps the great 'Battle Piece', No. 5 of Bach's Cantata, 'Ein' feste Burg'.

The music ends abruptly: there is a silence. Then the trombones sound (for the first time since the scherzo) and the men's voices declare the brotherhood of man.

Ex. 35.

The full choir repeats the strain, then the orchestra, joined later by the chorus, with hushed voices gives the reason, that it is because man, lowly as he is, is made in God's image.

Ex. 36.

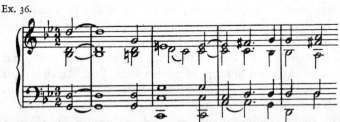

Note the wavering from minor to major – cf 1st Movement

Never has the mystery of the universe been so portrayed. Note the strange colour of the strings, without violins or double basses, enriched by the soft tones of low flutes, clarinets, and bassoons. Note also the strange quasi-modal melodic and harmonic scheme.

Then, at the words 'He lives beyond the stars', first a great shout and then an awe-struck whisper, we seem to see the whole star-studded universe and for a moment to penetrate into the mystery which lies beyond.

The great shout is on the chord of E♭. The whisper is on this harmony.

On this chord the strings shimmer, the wind throbs, the trombones and lower voices hold soft chords, while the women's voices murmur, or should do so, in their highest register. Alas, how seldom this supreme creation makes its effect in performance. I usually disbelieve those who declare that they prefer reading a score to hearing it. But in this case I dread this passage in performance, and even when it is well done, I breathe a sigh of relief when it is over. If ever I have the presumption and the good fortune to conduct this Symphony, I shall feel inclined to give this passage to a semi-chorus of picked voices, and to let the second sopranos sing the cruelly high alto part. It may be worth notice that Brahms thought this passage worth cribbing for his 'Requiem'.

Then joy breaks out again, joined with the assurance of the brotherhood of man in another wildly exciting double fugue, or rather, it would be wildly exciting when sung by a choir of super-men and women; of the two subjects, the upper is a rhythmical variant of the 'Joy' tune and the lower a version of the 'brotherhood of man' theme.

Ex. 37.

There is also a third subject or rather an ejaculation

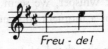

Freu - de!

which is thrown about from voice to voice.

The fugue rises to its highest point at the famous passage where the sopranos hold the high A for twelve bars, a terror to the average choralist. Then, at the very height of the excitement, a sudden hush; again we ponder in awe and wonderment on the deity and man's likeness to him.

This soft unison, these augmented intervals, the repeated notes: are they not well-worn devices for expressing mystery in eighteenth-century music? So is the diminished seventh of Bach's 'Barabbas' a

Ex. 38.

well-worn device; so are the chromatic scales in Beethoven's pastoral thunder-storm. But when a master hand guides these devices, they remain ever new and startling, and excite us more each time we hear them; while the far-fetched tricks of lesser composers seem stale even the first time.

This section ends with a great shout, 'brothers', and then the music softly and beautifully dies away as we once more contemplate the stars and the mysteries that lie behind them. Quite naturally, there succeeds to this a mood of childlike happiness. Beethoven did not put on his top hat when he went to church; indeed, if he had lived in modern times he would probably have joined the Salvation Army. At all events he could pass without any feeling of impropriety from awe-full wonderment to simple merriment, then back to the emotion of deeply-felt joy; and without a break to riotous junketing.

> I am of old and young,
>   of the foolish as much as the wise,
> Regardless of others, ever regardful of others,

> Maternal as well as paternal,
>   a child as well as a man,
> Stuffed with the stuff that is coarse
>   and stuffed with the stuff that is fine, . . .

The strings trip lightly on to the scene in terms of the 'Joy' tune. Then follow these two childlike tunes, the second of which is incidentally a canon in four parts.

Ex. 39.

Ex. 40.

Have these tunes a spiritual kinship with the 'Elysian' tune in the scherzo?

The chorus now takes it share, adding a great shout 'All men shall be brothers'—but suddenly the voices are hushed when they sing of the 'soft wings of Joy'. Then the music repeats itself in shortened form; again we have the great shout of brotherhood, and again the hush, but this time it takes the form of that famous vocal cadenza which Brahms was, again, not ashamed to crib in his 'Requiem'. Especially magical is the final cadence. The voices reach the chord of B major, with the sopranos holding the high B, then gently drop to F♯ while the alto sounds D♮, making the chord of B minor. Then the bass voice softly slides down to A and we are back in the home key: this progression has been foreshadowed earlier in the movement.

The orchestra takes up the idea with gusto: B, A, B, A, it repeats, over and over again, with ever-increasing speed, until at last we burst into the final unrestrained jubilation. No Sunday school about this, no angel choirs but real rowdy human beings:

> Pour out the wine without restraint or stay,
> Pour not by cups but by the belly full,
> Pour out to all that will.

The drums thump, the cymbals crash, the trumpets blare, the chorus sing this atrociously vulgar tune:

E

Ex. 41.

which nevertheless, or perhaps, therefore, is one of the great inspirations of the Symphony. But Beethoven has one more act of daring up his sleeve. The climax to all this rowdyism is a sudden chorale-like paean in praise of Joy, 'the daughter of Elysium'. Then once more the drums beat, the cymbals clash, the trumpets blare and in twenty quick bars the symphony is over.

(1939–40)

2

The Letter and the Spirit

Whereto serve ears if that there be no sound?
LORD VAUX

That the art of music is essentially one of sound is a proposition which would seem too obvious to need proof.

Yet it is the opinion of many people that the really musical man prefers not to hear music, but gets at his music silently by reading it to himself as he would a book.

Many years ago there appeared in *Punch* a picture illustrating the supposed growth in the near future of musical appreciation; the barrel organ was to be replaced by itinerant conductors turning over the leaves of scores and beating time. The picture represents two street-boys reading the score and watching the conductor, while the following conversation takes place: "Eavenly adagio ain't it, Bill?' 'Yes, but he takes the tempo too accelerato.'

Now Mr. Punch may be taken as always representing faithfully the average point of view. This then, is the average opinion, that when the street-boy becomes really musical he will no longer want to hear music but will be content to look at it. And this theory has the sanction of some of our acknowledged leaders of musical thought.

Sir Henry Hadow, in an address lately published with the imprimatur of the President of the Board of Education, says: '. . . It is a very low order of education which does not enable a person to read a page or write a letter without reading the words aloud. The same degree of education which enables us to read a page of Shakespeare to ourselves would enable us equally well to read a page of Beethoven.'

Again Dr. Arthur Somervell is reported to have said at an educational conference: 'When we go into a shop to buy a book we do not ask the salesman to read over a few passages to us, in order that we may see if we like it: we read for ourselves. Yet with music how many there are who ask that the piece shall be "tried over" for them before they buy. They ought instead to be able to read it for themselves without playing or singing.'

And to quote once again, the very distinguished amateur musician, Alexander Ewing, in a letter to Dr. Ethel Smyth wrote: 'A work of Bach's . . . exists for us on paper and in performance: two kinds of existence, differing in degree perhaps, but the one as real as the other.'

I venture to believe that the opinions quoted above are founded on a fallacy—namely, that to read silently a page of Beethoven is the exact counterpart of reading silently a page of Shakespeare.

Before going any further may we take it that the object of an art is to obtain a partial revelation of that which is beyond human senses and human faculties—of that, in fact, which is spiritual? And that the means we employ to induce this revelation are those very senses and faculties themselves?

The human, visible, audible and intelligible media which artists (of all kinds) use, are symbols not of other visible and audible things but of what lies beyond sense and knowledge.

The symbols of the painter are those which can be appreciated by the eye—colour, shapes, and the appearance of natural objects; the symbols of the poet are words and their meaning; and the symbols of the musical composer are those of the ear—musical sounds in their various combinations. To say that poetry when read aloud uses the symbol of sound is only to say that poetry then borrows to a slight extent from the sister art of music. But to realize how little part the ear plays in the poetic scheme one has only to imagine the spiritual effect of, say, Homer declaimed aloud to two listeners, one who did, and the other who did not, understand Greek. If the sound was a large factor in poetry the spiritual effect on both hearers would be nearly equal: as it is we know that the effect of declamation in an unknown language is almost negligible, and the reaction to the stimulus must be referred to music rather than to poetry. To a listener who understands the meaning of the words the actual sound of those words has a powerful emotional effect but only in connexion with the meaning and association of the words spoken. When a poem is read in silence the sound is absent, but the meaning of the words with all they symbolize is still there.

Where is the symbolic effect of a printed page of music? Can a page of musical notes and a page of poetry be compared in any way? It seems absurd to ask such a question; yet it is necessary, because there is a widespread notion (shared as we have seen by some of the most distinguished musical thinkers) that a printed page of music is the exact parallel of a painted picture or a printed poem.

The art of music differs from poetry and painting in this, that it involves two distinct processes—that of invention and that of presentation. It is just possible that in very primitive kinds of musical improvisation the acts of invention and presentation may be simultaneous. But it is difficult to say there are any cases in which the act of invention did not slightly precede the act of presentation; at all events in the ordinary case of a composer singing or playing his own composition he is simply acting in a dual capacity, first that of composer and then that of performer; the two processes are quite distinct.

In the other arts this is not so; the invention and presentation are one process. The painter paints his picture, and it is a complete work of art; all that is needed further is a pair of eyes and the heart and mind to realize what one sees. The poet writes his poem, and there it is for everyone who has learnt to read and who understands the meaning of words. But a musical composition when invented is only half finished, and until actual sound is produced that composition *does not exist*.

How then is the musical composer to make his invention live in actual sound? If it is a single line of melody or capable of being played on one instrument he may be able to complete the work himself. But how if his invention requires more than one voice or instrument? Then he must seek out others who are capable of making the sounds he desires and must instruct them when and where to make the sounds. For this purpose a clumsy and unprecise code of written signals has been evolved, which by convention indicate that certain sounds are to be made.

This code of signals or series of orders is known as a musical score, and has about as much to do with music as a time table has to do with a railway journey.

What the musical composer, in effect, says to his performers is: 'I desire to produce a certain spiritual result on certain people; I hope and believe that if you blow, and scrape, and hit in a particular manner this spiritual effect will result. For this purpose I have arranged with you a code of signals in virtue of which, whenever you see a certain dot or dash or circle, you will make a particular sound; if you follow these directions closely my invention will become music, but until you make the indicated sounds my music *does not exist.*'

So a musical score is merely an indication of potential music, and moreover it is a most clumsy and ill-devised indication. How clumsy it is may be seen from the importance of the 'individual renderings' of any piece of music. If a composer could indicate what he wanted with any precision there would be no room for this; as it is, two singers or players may follow faithfully the composer's intentions as given in the written notes and produce widely different results.

Under our present system of musical notation the composer can give only the most general indication of what he wishes. Perhaps future generations will devise something more precise; though whether this will be an advantage is doubtful.

The art of music, then, requires two minds (or one mind acting in two distinct ways) to produce the final result: the inventor and the presenter, or, in other words, the composer and the performer. If the composer is wise he will not try to make his score fool-proof, but will wait for that twin-mind which will translate his imaginings into sound, and consummate that marriage of true minds which alone can give his music life.

It is, of course, not to be denied that the power to realize to a certain extent by visual inspection what sounds will result from this code of signals (in other words to read a score) is an almost necessary part of a musician's equipment; but this power will not make him musical, any more than the knowledge of machinery which is necessary to a watchmaker enables him to tell the time. It is also true that the pleasure and exaltation of spirit of a certain kind is the result of this power; more especially is this true of the pleasure of memory evoked by reading the score of a well-known and often heard work.

A musical score is like a map. The expert map reader can tell fairly exactly what sort of country he is going to visit, whether it is hilly or flat, whether the hills are steep or gradual, whether it is wooded or bare, what the roads are likely to be; but can he experience from a map the spiritual exaltation when a wonderful view spreads before his eyes, or the joy of careering downhill on a bicycle or, above all, the sense of rest and comfort induced by the factual realization of those prophetic letters 'P.H.'?

So it is with music; the pleasure and profit of reading a score silently is at the best purely intellectual, at the worst it is nothing more than the satisfaction of having accomplished a difficult task successfully. It is not the pleasure of music. This can be achieved through the ear only.

In what does being 'musical' consist? It should be possible to be a first-rate musician and yet not be able to read a note of music, never to have heard of Bach or Beethoven, nor to know by sight the difference between an oboe and an organ; and conversely it is possible to know all these things and yet be no musician.

To be really musical one must be able to *hear*. The ear must be sensitive, the mind must be quick to grasp what the ear has heard and see its connexion with what has gone before, and to be prepared for what is to come, and above all the imagination must be vivid, to see the glimpses of the heart of things which the composer has crystallized into earthly sound.

To educate a child in music is to teach him to hear; then, and then only, is he a musician. I am far from saying that the power to read music, the knowledge of musical history, an intelligent interest in the technique of instruments will not be a great help to him when once he has learnt to love music, but they must never be allowed to take the place of music; we must first seek the Kingdom of God and all these things will be added unto us.

How does the composer invent? Does he hear the melodies and harmonies he makes with the mind's ear only? But what is it which he invents? Not the little black dots which he puts down on paper but the actual sounds those black dots represent. He wishes to be in spiritual communication with his hearers. To do that certain sounds are necessary; and until those sounds are heard the contact is not established. And does not the composer also need actual sound to produce in him that spiritual state which he hopes to induce in others? Does not the actual shock of sound help to fertilize his imagination and lead him on to still further musical invention? The text-books, of course, are horrified at the idea of 'composing at the piano' (as R. O. Morris writes, 'it is always considered as not quite playing the game') and hold it to be the sign of the incompetent amateur. The answer is that everyone must use the means which enable him to do the best. If the composer finds inspiration in the bass trombone or the accordion, by all means let him use them. There is fairly conclusive evidence that Beethoven, Wagner, and Elgar used the pianoforte in the course of composition and that Berlioz and Rheinberger did not. The inference is obvious.

In primitive times the intervention of the written note between the composer and the performer did not exist. The primitive composer either sang his simple melodies himself or else taught them orally to others; and there is, theoretically, no reason why a composer should not invent a symphony and teach it to an orchestra of performers without writing down a note, provided both he and they could cope with such a prodigious feat of mind and memory. The writing of notes is merely a convenience, necessary owing to the comparative feebleness of our memories and the want of concentration in our minds. To hold up this mere convenience as an ideal to be aimed at is surely to put the cart before the horse.

We have taken it for granted up to now that an expert musician can mentally hear the sound of any piece of music—that, though he cannot actually feel the emotion he can realize exactly what the effect on him of every harmony, melody, or rhythm which he sees written, would be if he heard it. But how far is this true?

Doubtless when the music is simple or of an accustomed type, the musician is on sure ground; but when anything in an unaccustomed idiom comes his way, is he not often out of his depth when trusting to the eye alone? Even in the case of comparatively simple music is it not possible to realize mentally the whole sound and yet miss the beauty? Any fairly equipped musician can look through a piece, say, of Purcell and realize exactly how all the notes would sound, but can he be sure whether he has realized its beauty?

Or to take a simpler example still—is it not a common experience with anyone to look through a single line of melody like a folk-song and be entirely deaf to its emotional appeal until he has heard it sung?

But a musician may answer: 'I can trust my powers of score-reading enough to judge a piece as beautiful if I can see beauty in it by a silent reading of the score.'

'Yes,' I should answer, 'but how if you cannot see beauty in it? Will you then trust your judgement? Will you not feel bound to hold it up to the test of the ear? If not, you have not given it a fair judgement.' Why is it that it is always the dull unimaginative music which gains the prize in a competition? Is it not because the adjudicators are content to look at the music and not to hear it— with the result that anything which looks right on paper is judged to be good, and everything that looks unfamiliar and awkward is rejected?

Are we then to be slaves of our bodies? Will not the mind be able eventually to free itself from all bodily trammels and get to the essence of things without physical intermediaries? It may indeed be argued that when we are actually hearing music the physical ear plays only a small part in our understanding of it. The physical ear can do no more than receive one moment of sound at a time, and our grasp of even the simplest tune depends on our power of remembering what has gone before and of co-ordinating it with what comes after. So that it seems that the mind and the memory play an even more important part than the ear in appreciating music. Why not go one step further and eliminate the physical ear altogether? Let us hear music with the mind's ear only.

Perhaps in future years this will happen—a new art will be evolved in which the mind of the composer will be in direct touch with his audience. But this art will not be music—it will be a new art; and with the new art a new set of means of communication will have to be devised. Our old system of dots and dashes which go to make up a music score, are, as we have seen, no more than a code of directions to the makers of musical sounds; if the sounds are not to be made, the code of directions will no longer be neces-sary, and our score-reader's occupation will be gone.

Certain types of musical thinkers seem to have inherited the medieval fear of beauty—they talk about 'mere beauty' and 'mere sound' as if they were something to be feared and avoided. But in our imperfect existence what means have we of reaching out to that which is beyond the senses but through those very senses? Would Ulysses have been obliged to be lashed to the mast if the sirens instead of singing to him had shown him a printed score? When the trumpet sounding the charge rouses the soldier to frenzy, does anyone suggest that it would have just the same effect if he took a surreptitious glance at *Military Sounds and Signals*? Would any amount of study of his own score have led Haydn to declare that his 'Let there be Light' came straight from Heaven?

Surely, while music is the art of sound, it is the ear which must be taught its language; when a new art supersedes it, a new language will necessarily follow in its train.

(1920)

3

Gustav Holst:
An Essay and a Note

In claiming for Gustav Holst that he is essentially a modern composer, I am from the outset laying myself open to misconstruction. The word 'modern' has been much abused, but I would point out that there is all the difference in the world between music which is modern and that which is 'in the modern idiom'. The 'modern idiom' consists of a handful of clichés of instrumentation coupled with a harmonic texture watered down from the writings of composers who flourished twenty-five years ago. With this kind of thing Holst's music has nothing to do; he does not serve up all the harmonic tricks of the last quarter of a century, he does not introduce a 'major ninth' regularly every eight bars, he is not afraid of long tunes (he has often the courage to let them stand alone, or with the merest suggestion of harmony),[1] he is not always making eight horns bellow out high D's, he owes much to Bach, to Purcell, to Byrd, and to Wilbye; and yet (or perhaps therefore) he is one of the few composers who can be called truly modern.

Modernity does not depend on certain tricks of diction but on the relationship between the mind that expresses and the means of expression. The modern mind needs a modern vocabulary, but the vocabulary will not make the modern mind. Some composers have the modern mind but have not found the idiom which suits it, many more have all the tricks of diction but not the informing mind. We are told that Richard Strauss is a 'modern of the moderns' but this is only superficially true; his mind is as early Victorian as that of his father-in-music Liszt—Strauss's music is nothing more

[1] E.g. 'This have I done for my true love', and the passage from *Savitri* cited later in this essay.

than Liszt plus one. Mentally he wallows in the German sentimentalism of the 'fifties. Delius, again, in spite of his bewitching
harmonic experiments (or is it because of them?), belongs mentally
to the 'eighties.

Mr. Bernard Shaw has written recently that Sir Edward Elgar
could if he chose 'turn out Debussy and Stravinsky music by the
thousand bars for fun in his spare time'. Doubtless he could; but
the result would probably be worthless because it would not be to
him a natural mode of diction, while Stravinsky's own music is
valuable in so far as his style is a real utterance. In the same way
Stravinsky could probably, if he chose, write a colourable imitation
of Elgar; but it would certainly miss the qualities which make the
Variations and the slow movement of the Second Symphony
beautiful music.

If Holst's music is modern it is not that he has acquired a few
tricks which today are hailed with wonder and tomorrow are as
flat as stale ginger-beer but that he has a mind which is the heir of
all the centuries and has found out the language in which to express
that mind. He shows his modernity equally whether he is straining
our harmonic sense to breaking point as in this example from the
Hymn of Jesus:

Or writing a simple broad melody like the middle section of 'Jupiter', No. 4 of *The Planets*.

Incidentally, it is a pity that this theme is hidden in the middle of 'Jupiter' which it does not seem altogether to fit. It ought to be the climax of some great movement which would take the place in the public affections of the sentimentalities of *Finlandia*. Or it might be used by the League of the Arts, set to appropriate words (not the rhyming homilies of the *Motherland Song Book*) and sung at points of vantage when next we have a peace celebration (which heaven forfend).

Indeed, Holst's work never sounds 'modern' in the narrow sense of the word (except now and then when he is exceptionally off his stroke) and the reason is that he knows what he wants to say and the way in which he means to say it. There is no attempt to tickle jaded nerves with 'new effects' and thus the very strangeness of much of his harmonic texture escapes the notice of the curio hunter, because it is absolutely germane to the whole conception. So it is with his masterly writing for the orchestra—it is so masterly that it escapes notice. Again the curio hunter is foiled. He hears no squeaks on the piccolo or grunts on the bass-tuba to make him sit

JUPITER

up and say 'modern orchestration' (though the strange devices are there all the same—for example the glissando for full organ in 'Uranus'). Holst knows his orchestra from the inside, having been an orchestral player; he does what he wants with it without conscious effort, and the result is that we think not of the orchestration, but of the music. When one is sitting in a Rolls Royce one may be travelling sixty miles an hour, but it does not feel like it.

The modernity of Holst is the result of the simple fact that he is a modern Englishman and that his music is in direct relation with real life; moreover he has not shrunk from life, but has lived it intensely. To 'live' is an expression which has had much harm done it by second-rate writers who seem to think that 'life' is limited to pretending you like absinthe and keeping a mistress in Montmartre. But Holst has pursued the calling of a hard-working, revered, and inspiring teacher, he has been a good citizen, a firm friend, a reliable helper in time of trouble. If to have 'lived' it is necessary to have eloped with a prima donna, to have played mean tricks on one's friends, to be dirty and drunken—if life means no more than that, then indeed the word has little meaning for a man like Holst. But if to live may be summed up in the words 'Whatsoever thy hand findeth to do, do it with thy might', then Holst has lived to the full; he has learnt his lesson in the hard school of necessity; he has not run away from the battle but has fought and won.

So many artists are conquered by life and its realities. Money-making, marriage, family cares, all the practical things of life are too much for them, and as artists they succumb and the creative impulse shrivels and dies. But to Holst the interests, responsibilities, and realities of life are not a hindrance but a stimulus—they are the very stuff out of which he has knit his art, the soil on which it flourishes. To a foolish friend who once said to him: 'I suppose you did not marry to help your composition', he answered: 'That is exactly what I did do.' Life and art are to Holst not enemies but the complements of each other; and as time goes on and his life gets busier and more varied, his artistic production becomes larger and finer, his style more mature, pronounced, and individual.

The Bohemian is not a natural growth in England. Our Café Royals, our Chelsea Arts Balls, our all-night clubs are shams: importations from Paris which have suffered a good deal on the voyage. It is not on such a basis as this that our English art will grow, and it may be well to add here that 'in spite of all temptations' which his name may suggest, Holst 'remains an Englishman'. On his mother's and grandmother's side he is pure English; on his father's side there is Swedish blood, but the Holst family came to England from Riga, where they had been long settled, more than a hundred years ago. There is a good deal of unclear thinking prevalent on the subject of race and nationality. Everyone is to a certain extent of mixed race. But race is only one factor in nationality; it is community of language, of customs, of laws, of religion as well as racial kinship, which binds men into a nation, and judged by these standards we should expect Holst's music to be the outcome of the English point of view.

We may sum up Holst's characteristics as exemplified in his life and reflected in his art as great force of character, indomitable energy, sense of thoroughness, and above all intense human sympathy.

Naturally frail in body and handicapped from the outset by a delicate childhood, he has done more work than many a strong and robust man. Although he is only just the wrong side of forty, his works include four operas, seven large works for orchestra and military band, two long scenas for solo voice and orchestra, three large compositions for chorus and orchestra and a huge quantity of shorter pieces of all kinds; besides which he has had to work hard at his profession of teacher, since his natural bent has led him to interesting rather than largely remunerative pupils. His energy and force of character show themselves in various ways; he has always been a great walker and in student days when money was scarce he would spend part of his holiday walking from London to his home in Gloucestershire. He is a wide reader and an original thinker on all subjects; when he was already approaching middle age, and though early ill-health and the necessity of entering his profession young cut short his classical education at *mensa, mensae*, he set to work to learn enough Sanskrit to be able (with a 'crib', of course, as all good scholars do) to make his own version of the Vedic Hymns on which so much of his music is based.

It was his feeling for thoroughness which led him when he left the College of Music to abandon the eminently respectable career of an organist for which he was destined and to get at music from the inside as a trombonist in an orchestra. Holst has sometimes thought that all the trashy music he had to endure in these early days has had a bad influence on his art. Personally I do not think so. To start with, the very worst that a trombonist has to put up with is as nothing compared to what a church organist has to endure; and secondly, Holst is above all an orchestral composer, and that sure touch which distinguishes his orchestral writing is due largely to the fact that he has been an orchestral player; he has learnt his art, both technically and in substance, not at second hand from text-books and models but from actual live experience. Holst has no use for half measures; all the little vanities, insincerities, and compromises which go to make up our daily life are entirely outside his ken; they leave him dumb and puzzled and at these moments he seems to retire from the world which we call 'real' into a mystical world of his own. To know all is to forgive all, and in early days, when Holst's knowledge of human weakness was less than it is now, his sincerity and thoroughness occasionally brought him into conflict with the half-hearted standards of the world; I remember a certain choral society which in his youthful enthusiasm he over-dosed with Bach's cantatas, with the result that he was asked to retire in favour of some other conductor and the society returned to its wallowing in the mire.

It was Holst's strong sense of human sympathy which brought him when a young man into contact with William Morris and the Kelmscott Club. The tawdriness of London, its unfriendliness, the sordidness both of its riches and poverty were overwhelming to an enthusiastic and sensitive youth; and to him the ideals of Morris, the insistence on beauty in every detail of human life and work, were a revelation. No wonder then that the poetic socialism of the Kelmscott Club became the natural medium of his aspirations; to Morris and his followers 'comradeship' was no pose but an absolute necessity of life. And though as years go on Holst has grown out of the weak points in Morris's teaching, yet his ideal of thoroughness, of beauty and above all of comradeship have remained and grown stronger. It is this almost mystical sense of unity which is the secret of Holst's power as a teacher. He writes himself of 'the wonderful feeling of unity with one's pupils when teaching, a feeling of contact with their minds other than the contact occasioned by speech'.[2] Like all great teachers Holst not only gives but expects to receive, and he will have no half measures: he is sympathetic to ignorance, over-exuberance, or even stupidity—but half-heartedness, insincerity, or laziness have no chance with him; for that reason he will never become a 'fashionable' teacher whose métier is to impart useless accomplishments to rich people who do not want to learn them. Everyone who comes to Holst must take music seriously—indeed they cannot help it—and it is his very insistence which has made the success of his musical directorship of Morley College. When he first began teaching there he found music treated as a side issue—a sort of decoy to attract students to the College. The authorities were rather alarmed when he openly rejoiced at the fact that the old type of music student began to fall off when he took over the directorship, and there was the inevitable anxious period when the old students left and the new ones had not begun

[2] 'The Mystic, the Philistine, and the Artist', a paper read before the 'Quest' Society.

to arrive. The directors looked glum and seriously thought of asking Holst to resign; but in the end he won through, the right students came flocking in—those who really wanted to learn—and now the authorities recognize the music classes at 'Morley' as one of their greatest assets.

One of the outstanding events of Holst's connexion with Morley College was the performance in concert form of Purcell's *Fairy Queen* (the first performance, I believe, since Purcell's time). The work of preparation was enormous, everyone worked like a slave (indeed one has to when Holst drives, he spares neither himself nor others), every part had to be copied in manuscript, sometimes transposed and re-arranged to suit the limited resources of the College. It is to this performance that we largely owe the magnificent stage production of this work at Cambridge last February, and the fact that the score is now printed in available form and has taken its place as one of our classics.

With all his idealism and mysticism Holst has never allowed himself to become a mere dreamer. He is a visionary but he never allows dreams to inhibit action. He has also a strong saving sense of humour—indeed he might, if he had chosen, have made a name for himself as a comedy actor. His letters, in their peculiar but beautifully clear handwriting, are a precious possession to his friends.

As in his life so in his art Holst does nothing by halves. He can be nobly diatonic with the greatest effect if he wants to as in the preceding passage from the 'Funeral Hymn'.

Or if he wants a harmonic clash he makes a complete one, he never lets one off lightly—as this example from 'Neptune' will show.

That he is not afraid of a tune we have already seen in the example on page 132. Perhaps, sometimes, his rhythms and melodies may appear a little too pungent for timid souls, as this example (from 'Jupiter'):

Or perhaps some hearers may find a sense of strain in some of his later music; probably the strain is with the hearer rather than with the composer. Recently Holst's work appeared at a concert side by side with a composition in which all the commonplaces of the last fifty years were neatly laid out in rows. A critic described this work as 'far more satisfactory' than Holst's. He was right; Holst's work is not always 'satisfactory'—it is not meant to be 'satisfactory'. Holst's later work sometimes makes one feel uncomfortable—and why not? We live in uncomfortable times just now: we live in dread of what the future may bring. And such a work as 'Neptune' (the mystic) seems to give us such a glance into the

*Repeat this bar till the sound is lost in the distance

future—it ends, so to speak, on a note of interrogation. Many composers have attempted this, sometimes bringing in the common chord at the end as an unwilling tribute to tradition, sometimes sophisticating it by the addition of one discordant note, sometimes letting the whole thin out into a single line of melody; but Holst in 'Neptune' actually causes the music to fade away to nothing.

It is of the essence of modern music, as of all modern thought, to drive straight to the root of the matter in hand without artifice or subterfuge; to let the matter rule the form, not the form the matter; to obtain our rules from practice, not our practice from rules. Holst, as we have seen, is a practical musician, he knows what he wants to say and uses the most direct way of saying it. If he desires that a melody shall sound remote from its harmonic context he does not hesitate to make it remote—he does not compromise by making it look as if it 'fitted'. Equally, if he so wishes, he uses successions of sevenths or triads without any attempt to disguise them into respectability. I cannot illustrate this better than by two quotions from *The Planets*, from 'Saturn' and 'Mars'.

A large and important part of Holst's musical work consists of setting of hymns and lyrics from the Rig Veda and other Sanskrit

poetry. The fact that the originals of these poems are oriental has led people to expect a sort of pseudo-orientalism in his music. Nothing could be further either from his intention or his achievement. Holst has written only one definite piece of orientalism, namely, the brilliant tour-de-force *Beni Mora*, a work which if it had been played in Paris instead of London would have given its composer a European reputation, and played in Italy would probably have caused a riot. (It will hardly be believed that neither this work nor *The Planets* has yet [1920] found a publisher.) But it is not the orientalism but the mysticism of the Vedic Hymns which attracted Holst, he needed some expression of the mystical point of view less materialized and less systematized than anything to be found in occidental liturgies. In the Rig Veda personification of the unknown is reduced to a minimum.

> He the primal one
> Begetter of the universe
> Begotten in mystery
>
> . . . .
>
> How shall we name him
> When we offer sacrifice?

These settings of Eastern texts culminate in the magnificent choral song *The Cloud Messenger*, but the spirit which dictates them is in all essentials the same which prompted his musical expression in the *Hymn of Jesus* and the *Ode to Death*.

The mystical frame of mind naturally begets a certain austerity in Holst's later music. Austerity is sometimes a cover for artistic impotence; the composer says 'I will not' when he means 'I cannot'. This negative austerity is not, of course, what I refer to here. Holst is never negative, his very faults are those of commission not of omission. His austerity leads not to dullness or emptiness, but to harmony which is acrid rather than luscious, melody sometimes angular but never indefinite or sugary, orchestration which is brilliant and virile but not cloying.

Among the purely musical influences which have affected Holst we may count a boyish devotion to Grieg which influenced his student work and occasionally crops up even in his later music, without in the least detracting from its individuality. Again it goes without saying that Holst, like every young musician who approached manhood in 1890, came strongly under the influence of Wagner; the chief relic of this influence is the three-act opera *Sita* in which much beautiful music lies hidden in a rather intractable medium.

That Holst knows and loves his Bach is evident from the following quotation from the comparatively early *Mystic Trumpeter*.

It was to a mind thus familiar, both as student and performer, with all the most modern devices of music that a new field of thought was opened in the lately re-discovered works of Purcell followed by the publication of the masses and motets of Byrd and Dr. Fellowes's great edition of the English madrigalists. These came as a revelation to Holst, as to many other musicians; he quickly imbibed their spirit without abating one jot of his individuality or in any way harking back to a sham archaism. We can see the spirit of his great ancestors in such works as the *Hymn of Jesus* or the opening of *Hecuba's Lament*.

Another very marked influence on Holst's musical thought must not be omitted here. The subject of English folk-song is a thorny one and has been much misunderstood. It would be out of place to discuss it at length now; but this much may be said, that, to those who have understanding, the folk-song is a liberating and not a fettering influence. The contact with new types of melody bound by purely melodic considerations, with rhythms not tied by the convention of bars and time signatures, the expressiveness of short and simple tunes—all this cannot fail to suggest to anyone who is naturally sympathetic new vistas of musical thought which may, indeed, have nothing to do superficially with the curves and cadences of folk-song, but are suggested by its spirit if not by its letter. Holst's first introduction to his traditional melodies was in a collection of songs from Hampshire which he harmonized at the request of the late Dr. Gardiner. Such arrangements as the following must have come as rather a shock to those accustomed to the unpretending harmonies of *English County Songs* or *Folk Songs from Somerset*, and it must be confessed that they are not too well suited to their immediate purpose.

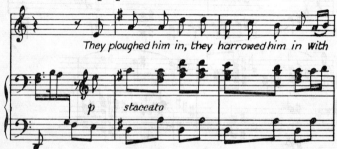

They ploughed him in, they harrowed him in with

clods   all   o-ver his   head;   and

But Holst was finding out what folk-song had to say to him and what he had to say to it, and in his latest essay in this form, the beautiful setting of the 'White Paternoster' tune, the melody and its treatment are absolutely at one.

Whatever the influence may have been it is obvious that Holst has freed himself from all conventions in the matter of rhythm and melody. If the nature of the musical idea or the accent of the words requires a rhythm of seven or five (rather than the accepted four, three, or six) he does not hesitate to employ such rhythms—indeed, rhythms of five or seven are characteristic of much of his later work. He often employs what we call for want of a better word 'modal' melodies (that is in other modes than the major and minor). Many people seem to consider that 'modal' melody and its corresponding harmony is a return to something archaic. We are told in the text-books that the harmony of Palestrina and his school is 'modal'. This, surely, is a fallacy. The two great sources of modal melody are the plainsong and the folk-song, and for this reason, that they are both purely melodic in their conception (the major and minor modes grew up from harmonic considerations). Now the music of the great choral period originates in attempts to harmonize these purely melodic plainsong tunes—but for some reason which no one has, so far as I know, investigated, these early harmonists found that the intervals of the melodic modes did not fit in with their harmonic scheme, and they accordingly altered the intervals to suit their purpose in accordance with the system known as 'musica ficta', until the various modes all merged into the major and minor of the great classical period, and (except for one or two experiments such as Beethoven's 'Lydian Hymn') up to quite modern times the major and minor modes were the basis of all music.

The harmonic possibilities of the purely melodic modes occurred, probably, first to the nationalist Russian composers; following on them we find Erik Satie using them in his earlier works; and from him, in turn, Debussy obtained suggestions for such things as his 'Sarabande' and the 'Fille aux cheveux de lin'.

Here is an example of a melody full of modal suggestions from Holst's *Savitri*.

Greet - ing to thee, my lov - ing Sa-vi-tri,

What wife in all the world is like to Sa - vi-tri?

It is sometimes argued that the particular idiom which a composer uses is a mere accident, that the fountain of inspiration flows or does not flow as the case may be, and that the particular vessel into which it flows is of no consequence. But idiom is part of the inspiration; it is not enough to have great emotions, the true way of materializing these emotions has also to be found. Many a composer who has had potentially much to say has failed because he did not discover the vocabulary from which he could choose the necessary means of expression. Of course, every true composer makes his own idiom. But bricks are not to be made without straw; and it cannot be doubted that the folk-song with its melodic curves, its free rhythm, its simplicity, and its sincerity has played its humble part in giving a tendency and direction to many composers to whom it was naturally sympathetic.

I am far from saying that there are no weak points in Holst's music—what piece of music has not its weak points? Did not Wagner fail at the very climax of his life work? When Brünnhilde throws herself on the flames as an act of supreme sacrifice some superhumanly beautiful melody was the only possible musical equivalent—but at that moment Wagner could invent nothing better than a tune which is hardly good enough for a third-rate German beer garden. Indeed, I can think of no piece of music (with the possible exception of the 'Sanctus' from Palestrina's *Missa Brevis*) which can be said to be absolutely without flaw.

Holst's weaknesses are the defects of his qualities—occasionally his magnificent technique masters him and the end gets lost in the means. Sometimes he spoils the noble simplicity of his work by an unnecessary piece of elaboration: at other times the very individuality of his thought which requires such a personal technique causes a flaw in his work; in his earlier music especially we do not always find complete unity of idea and expression; the *mot juste* fails him for the moment and he falls back on the common stock of musical device. But the very fact that these lapses are noticeable only goes to show how individual his music is. As time goes on these discrepancies get fewer and fewer and his style gets maturer, simpler and more individual, and this individuality shows through all his music; whether it is in the most extreme harmonic and rhythmical thought of *The Planets* or the absolute simplicity of the *Four Carols*, his signature is plain on every page.

There may be occasional moments in Holst's harmony which are not quite in the approved 'grand manner'. Sometimes we are pulled up in the middle of his most beautiful work by a melodic phrase which appears undistinguished (as for example a phrase in the *Hymn of Jesus* which has been adversely criticized). But these blemishes (if they are such) are the direct outcome of his vitality— he will never be content to say 'nothing in particular and say it very well'. If the harmony occasionally exhibits an error of style, it is because the intention at that moment became over-exuberant; if the melodic inspiration does not quite always hit the mark (as happens to all composers at times) it is because the composer is too honest and too whole-hearted to hide it under an indistinct muttering in the accepted style.

Holst's three last important works, *The Planets*, the *Hymn of Jesus*, and the *Ode to Death*, seem to sum up the whole of his aims; they exhibit in mature and perfect forms all that he has been striving for with more or less success in his earlier works. To one who has had the privilege of his friendship for the last twenty-five years, and has seen most of his compositions actually in the course of completion, it has been most interesting to watch the growth to maturity of a set, though perhaps unconscious, artistic purpose, to see experiments, at first perhaps not wholly successful, develop into finished methods of artistic expression, to see crudities gradually disappear and give place to maturity.

I cannot show this development better than by two quotations in which the same musical thought is evident, one from the early 'Mystic Trumpeter' and the other from 'Venus' (The Bringer of Peace).

The Planets consist of seven orchestral movements named after the seven planets with their various astrological characteristics.

MYSTIC TRUMPETER

VENUS

They are:

1. Mars (The Bringer of War).
2. Venus (The Bringer of Peace).
3. Mercury (The Winged Messenger).
4. Jupiter (The Bringer of Jollity).
5. Saturn (The Bringer of Old Age).
6. Uranus (The Magician).
7. Neptune (The Mystic).

They are in no sense programme music, the titles suggest the general character of the music and no more. The most individual and beautiful seem to me to be Venus (though the middle section is not quite so good as the rest), Saturn, Jupiter, and Neptune. Mercury is very brilliant and Uranus will probably be considered 'great fun', but to my mind they are not musically up to the level of the rest. Holst uses a very large orchestra in *The Planets*, not to make his score look impressive, but because he needs the extra tone colour and knows how to use it.

The text of the *Hymn of Jesus* is taken from the apocryphal *Acts of St. John* and is almost ideal for musical setting. It is probably part of some early ritual (perhaps a mystical dance, as the words suggest) and consists chiefly of a series of antiphonal phrases with an ever recurrent 'Amen'. Holst has used two choruses which sing antiphonally for the most part, joining forces occasionally for a great outburst on the words 'Glory to Thee'. There is also a semi-chorus which sings the recurring 'Amen'. Many musicians have set the 'Amen' to music—from the unknown composer of the 'Dresden'

Amen down to the too-well-known composer of the 'Sevenfold' Amen. In this hierarchy Holst's 'Amen' will surely take a high place by reason of its ethereal beauty.

The *Ode to Death* is a setting for chorus and orchestra of part of Whitman's 'President Lincoln's Funeral Hymn'. This has not yet [1920] been published or performed. Like the *Hymn of Jesus* it is a real work for chorus and orchestra—the orchestra is not occupied in doubling (and drowning) the chorus parts, but plays its independent part—the choral technique is characteristic of Holst at his best. (See following page.)

These three works represent Holst in his latest and maturest stage. What the future may have in store we cannot say—whether he will become simpler, or whether he will lead us into new paths where it will be difficult to follow; but of this we may be sure that there will be good reason behind whatever he does. He will not be simple merely through timidity, nor will he seek out strange

devices merely for the sake of eccentricity; he knows too well that whatever the future of music may be, it will always grow out of its great past.

(1920)

Some years ago I had the privilege of writing about Gustav Holst. I remember saying then that 'perhaps he will lead us into regions where it will be difficult to follow'. He may have now found in new regions that which his music ever seemed to be seeking.

All art is the imperfect human half-realization of that which is spiritually perfect. Holst's music seems especially to be a quest after that which in earthly life we can only partially fulfil.

This does not mean that his music was ever inchoate or groping. He had complete command of method. He was a visionary, but not an idle dreamer. He himself used to say that only second-rate artists were unbusinesslike.

At the same time his music has pre-eminently that quality which for want of a better word we call 'mystical', and this in spite of the fact that it was never vague or meandering: in all his works, whether in life or art, he was absolutely clear and definite. Indeed his music is usually robust and never shirks a definite tune when the occasion demands it. In spite of his masterful command of harmonic resource he never lets chordal complications interfere with clear outline and definite expression.

It is perhaps this very clarity which gives the 'mystical' quality to his music. It burns like a clear flame for ever hovering on the 'frontier to eyes invisible'. We all experience at times, most of us momentarily only, a vision beyond earthly sense. With Holst this vision seemed to be perpetually present, placing him outside the makeshifts and half-heartednesses and inconsistencies and compromises and insincerities that go to make up our daily life. Everything untrue or slovenly shrinks in his presence. In his life as in his art he seemed to be standing on the verge of ultimate truth.

For this reason his music has sometimes been described as inhuman and aloof. If this means that Holst never vied with the 'man with the muck-rake' we will willingly and thankfully endorse the criticism, but for those for whom humanity means something else than morbid abnormality Holst's music is triumphantly human. A

F

pure light always burnt in him, but he never lost sight of human possibilities; his writing is never unpractical, he demands much of his players and singers, from his singers especially, but he knew from long experience what even the most unpromising performers could achieve with enthusiasm, hard work, sure purpose, and good guidance.

It was these qualities—intense idealism of conception coupled with complete realism in practice, guided by his strong sense of humanity—which made Holst a great teacher as they made him a great composer.

I have myself known Holst as friend and teacher for more than thirty years. When I had a new work in the beginning stages my first idea would always be to show it to him. But sometimes I let a work go without his advice and counsel. I probably felt that there was some lapse in it from the highest endeavour and I felt ashamed to submit it to that truthful gaze. When this has been so I have always regretted it. I might have suffered in my self-pride from his judgement, but both my music and myself would have been the better for it.

The gift of inspiration is perhaps not so rare as we think. What is rare is the power of final realization in picture, poem, or music of that inspiration. This final realization is essential to a complete work of art. This power Holst possessed to the full. He never falters or gropes. He knows what he wants to say and says it without subterfuge or hesitation. He learnt his craft, not so much from books or in the study as from practical experience and from the nature of his material: not that he neglected book learning, and present-day students might note to their advantage that he spent several months previous to his entry at the College studying nothing but strict counterpoint. It was necessity as well as choice which brought Holst early face to face with the facts of music. Already in his student days he, like many others, had to be earning his living. He chose deliberately not to shut himself up in the organ loft or to give half-hearted pianoforte lessons to unwilling pupils, but to go out into the world armed with his trombone, playing, now in a symphony orchestra, now in a dance band, now in a Christmas pantomime in a suburban theatre. A reminiscence of these days still lives in my mind. At the end of our summer holidays some of us students met together to tell each other how we had spent our vacation. One of us had been at Bayreuth and gave, I am sure, a highly critical appraisement of the proceedings. Others, perhaps, had been to the Dolomites or to Brittany and were doubtless very poetical about it. In all this we listeners were mildly interested, but what remained in the memory of those who heard him was Holst's enthralling account of his experiences as a member of a seaside band, enthralling because of his great human sympathy, his unique humour, his strong sense of values.

In later years other activities, teaching and conducting, added to his experience which gave him that grip of the facts of music out of which he built up his wonderful technique. To many men this constant occupation with the practical side of art would have been a hindrance to inspiration, but to Holst it seemed to be an incentive. The fact that his creative work had often to be crowded into the few weeks of summer vacation gave him his great power of concentration and intensified his will to evoke at all costs those thoughts that lay in the depths of his being.

Holst had no use for half measures whether in life or art. What he wanted to say he said forcibly and directly. Like every other great composer he was not afraid of being obvious when the case demanded it—nor did he hesitate to be recondite on the right occasion. But whether he gives us the familiar chords and straightforward tunes of 'Jupiter' or leads us to the remotest confines of harmony as in 'Neptune' his meaning is never in doubt; he has something to tell us that only he can say.

I used sometimes to think that Holst occasionally pushed his love of definiteness too far. I remember once discussing 'Egdon Heath' with him. I suggested that the very clearness of the melodic outlines of that piece were at variance with its atmospheric nature; indeed that less robust melody would have been more successful in impressionistic suggestion. Holst, on that occasion, lived up to his own maxim 'Always ask for advice, but never take it.' I am glad that he did so for I now see that a less clear melody would have softened and thereby impaired the bleak grandeur of its outline.

Some timid-souled people, I believe, find his melody too strong and his rhythm too pungent for their effeminate taste. However this may be no one can ignore it. Whenever he puts pen to paper the signature 'Gustav Holst' is clear to read in every bar of the music.

(1934)

4

Nationalism and Internationalism

I believe that it was George Trevelyan who, in one of his early essays, wrote that the ideal would be for every nation to be different and all at peace; adding, prophetically, that what we are tending towards is to be all alike and all at war.

We all want peace, we all want international friendship, we all want to give up the hateful rivalries of nations; we must learn to plan the world internationally, we must unite or we shall perish. This is a very different thing from that emasculated standardization of life which will add cultural to political internationalism.

Is it possible to be a nationalist, and at the same time an internationalist? I believe that political internationalism and personal individualism are necessary complements: one cannot exist without the other. It is all very well for Wells and Curry to dismiss local patriotism with a sneer about Devonshire cream or Yorkshire pudding; but these things are small emanations of a deep-rooted instinct which we cannot eliminate if we would: and which we ought not to want to eliminate. I believe that the love of one's country, one's language, one's customs, one's religion, are essential to our spiritual health. We may laugh at these things but we love them none the less. Indeed it is one of our national characteristics and one which I should be sorry to see disappear, that we laugh at what we love. This is something that a foreigner can never fathom, but it is out of such characteristics, these hard knots in our timber, that we can help to build up a united Europe and a world federation.

In old days nationalism was not self-conscious because it was inevitable. When travel was slow and dangerous, when dissemination of news and knowledge was difficult, when it took longer to get from London to York than it now takes from London to New York, each country had to fend artistically, as well as economically, for itself. Now we have changed all that; we can get our music from Germany, our painting from France, our jokes from America, and our dancing from Russia. Has this brought us peace? Does not this colourless cosmopolitanism bring in its train wars, such as our isolated forefathers never dreamed of? I agree that this loyalty to one's country can only come to a full flowering when it is merged in a wider loyalty to the whole human race. But without that local loyalty there can be nothing for the wider issues to build on. I believe that all that is of value in our spiritual and cultural life springs from our own soil; but this life cannot develop and fructify except in an atmosphere of friendship and sympathy with other nations. Moreover, our national art must not be a backwater, but must take its part in the great stream that has flowed through the centuries. In that stream we must preserve our own current. We must not merely become an indistinguishable part of the general flow.

I believe, then, that political internationalism is not only compatible with cultural patriotism, but that one is an essential concomitant of the other. When the United States of Europe becomes a fact, each nation must have something to bring to the common stock of good. What we have to offer must derive essentially from our own life. It must not be a bad imitation of what other nations already do better. We should then be bad members of a world polity. I remember that soon after the First World War a distinguished British conductor toured Europe, playing British music to continental audiences. I asked him what sort of music he had played. He answered, 'I tried to give them something like what they were accustomed to.' Never was a greater mistake. What he ought to have given them was something that only we could do. They probably would not have liked it, but they would have recognized it as something which they could not and probably did not want to do themselves, but that if they did want it they would have to come to us for it.

At this point you will probably quote Tennyson at me, and tell me we needs must love the highest when we see it; or Rossini, who used to say, 'I know of only two kinds of music, bad and good.' Surely, you may say, we ought to want the best music wherever it comes from. If you go into a hot-house, pick a rare, exotic flower and put it in water in your room, it may perhaps, for a short time, seem better to you than the everyday rose which is growing in your garden outside the window. But in a short time the exotic will be a mere stalk, while the rose will live on, and even when it dies will be succeeded by others. Which then is the better of these two? The answer is that we want both. So it is with our art. We may say that the Covent Garden Opera of the pre-war years with its array of international celebrities was in one sense better than Sadlers Wells with its overworked and underpaid band of devotees. In the long run, which is going to make us more musical? Which is going to give the greatest impulse that is the foundation of all great art?

Do not think that I am decrying the foreign experts. We want the experts as the coping stone of our building, but even more do we want the humble practitioner as its foundation. Without the coping stone the edifice will not be complete; without the foundation it will collapse.

The problem of home-grown music has lately [1942] become acute owing to the friendly invasion of these shores by an army of distinguished German and Austrian musicians. The Germans and Austrians have a great musical tradition behind them. In some ways they are musically more developed than we, and therein lies the danger. The question is not who has the best music, but what is going to be best for us. Our visitors, with the great names of Bach, Beethoven, Mozart, and Brahms behind them, are apt to think that all music that counts must come from their countries. And not only the actual music itself, but the whole method and outlook of musical performance and appreciation. We must be careful that, faced with this overwhelming mass of 'men and material', we do not all become sham little Austrians or Germans. In that case either we shall make no music for ourselves at all, or such as we do make will be just a mechanical imitation of foreign models. In either case the music which we make will have no vitality of its own. It is again a case of the exotic flower in water. As long as our distinguished guests are with us we shall enjoy their art. But when they return to their own country, or when time inevitably puts an end to their activities, we shall find that we cannot successfully imitate their art, and that we have lost the power of initiating any for ourselves.

Perhaps the question of opera will illustrate these points the best. Serious opera has never flourished in this country; largely, I believe, because it was sung in a foreign language by foreign artists, or by English artists trying to be as foreign as possible, using that strange 'libretto language' which has no relation to any known tongue, and which they pronounce as a sort of bastard Italian. I remember the performance of a supposed English opera in the course of which the hero walked into the middle of the stage and called out, 'Whaa aas maa braad?'

England is the only country in the world, except perhaps the U.S.A., where opera is performed in a language foreign to that country. I remember when I went to Paris being puzzled by an advertisement at the opera of *Le Crépuscule des Dieux*. Opera, to English hearers, should be sung in English (not libretto English; it is this, and our sham Carusos who sing it, which would seem to justify the man who declared that if he knew every language in the world except one, he would choose to have his opera in that language). Or the lady who when offered a libretto said, 'We don't want to know what the opera is about, we've only come to hear the singing.' Opera in a foreign tongue will only appeal to the snobs who want to hear expensive foreign artists; or the prigs who cannot bear the sound of their own language. It will not touch the people, those who are eventually going to make opera in this country. Now this is where our Austrian and German friends come in: many of them have had great experience of conducting and producing opera, and we wish to enlist their help, but they will find that the question of opera in English carries a lot in its train; they cannot force their production, which is suitable for the German or the Italian language, as it stands, on to English artists singing the English language. The British attitude towards both tragedy and comedy is entirely different from the Teutonic or the Latin. I once had a painful experience watching a distinguished English singer trying conscientiously to be funny in the Teutonic manner. The hectic boisterousness which the German producer demanded was absolutely alien to the English nature whose comedy depends so much on understatement. What course are we to pursue? Are we to take the English standard of singing and mould it to opera, or are we to force the continental style down English throats? Or hold that singing, like champagne and caviar, is something that must be imported from abroad because the English climate will not support it?

Perhaps the way our distinguished visitors can help us is by becoming musically British citizens; by getting at the heart of our culture, to see the art of music as we see it, and then to stimulate it and add to it with their own unique experience and knowledge. If, however, they propose to establish a little 'Europe in England', quite cut off from the cultural life of this country and existing for itself alone, then indeed they will have the enthusiastic support of those snobs and prigs who think that foreign culture is the only one worth having, and do not recognize the intimate connexion between art and life. Indeed it is only lately that this connexion has been recognized by quite educated people in this country. A recent edition of the *Encyclopaedia Britannica* describes art as an ornamental fringe on the edge of life, a relaxation for those who can afford it. Nowadays I think we know better; we realize that art is not a luxury but a necessity. But do we even now realize the importance of active participation in art instead of passive submission?

Art can only thrive in an atmosphere of art. When we hear the fine flowering of Austrian or Italian music we are apt to imagine that these countries simply teem with Carusos and Kreislers. As a matter of fact you could probably hear more bad music in a day in Austria or Italy than in a week in England. But the point is that they do make music. They are not content to listen to lectures about it. What I want to see in England is everybody making music, however badly. Gustav Holst used to say that if a thing is worth doing at all it is worth doing badly. Out of all the bad music the good music will emerge.

English musical history is full of the tragedy of genius withering on barren soil—Dunstable, Purcell, Wesley, or Sullivan. Many young British composers have been ruined by abdicating their birthright in their most impressionable years. Before they knew what they wanted to achieve, before they had learned, so to speak, their own language, they went to Paris or Berlin or Vienna and came back having forgotten their own musical tongue and with only a superficial smattering of any other. My advice to young composers is—learn your own language first, find out your own traditions, discover what you want to do; then, go to Paris, Berlin, or anywhere else, rub musical shoulders with others, test your ideas against theirs, and so find out how far your art is 'built up four square'. You may say 'Is not this a very narrow point of view?' But is broad-mindedness after all such a blessing? Is it not too often a synonym for moral cowardice and inability to make up one's mind?

I do not want you to think that I do not welcome here all the great artists of the world. But I do so because I believe and hope that they will strengthen and stimulate our own art, and I do not want them to swamp it. In the same way I want us to perform all the great masterpieces of music; but we must perform them according to our own lights and our own artistic needs.

(1942)

5

Composing for the Films

Some years ago I happened to say to the composer, Arthur Benjamin, that I should like to have a shot at writing for the films. He seemed surprised and shocked that I should wish to attempt anything which required so much skill and gained so little artistic reward. However, he mentioned my curious wish to a well-known film conductor. The result was that, one Saturday evening, I had a telephone call asking me to write some film music. When I asked how long I could have to prepare it, the answer was, 'Till Wednesday.'

This is one of the bad sides of writing music for films—the time limit. Not indeed that it hurts anyone to try to write quickly, the feeling of urgency is often a stimulus; when the hand is lazy the mind often gets lazy as well, but the composer wants to have the opportunity, when all is approaching completion, to remember emotion in tranquillity, to sit down quietly and make sure that he has achieved the *mot juste* at every point. That is where the time limit inhibits the final perfection of inspiration.

On the other hand, film composing is a splendid discipline, and I recommend a course of it to all composition teachers whose pupils are apt to be dawdling in their ideas, or whose every bar is sacred and must not be cut or altered.

When the film composer comes down to brass tacks he finds himself confronted with a rigid time-sheet. The producer says, 'I want forty seconds of music here.' This means forty, not thirty-nine or forty-one. The picture rolls on relentlessly like Fate. If the music is too short it will stop dead just before the culminating kiss; if it is too long, it will still be registering intense emotion while the screen is already showing the comic man putting on his mother-in-law's breeches.

A film producer would make short work of Mahler's interminable codas or Dvořák's five endings to each movement.

I believe that film music is capable of becoming, and to a certain extent already is, a fine art, but it is applied art and a specialized art at that; it must fit the action and dialogue; often it becomes simply a background. Its form must depend on the form of the drama, so the composer must be prepared to write music which is capable of almost unlimited extension or compression; it must be able to fade-out and fade-in again without loss of continuity. A composer must be prepared to face losing his head or his tail or even his inside without demur, and must be prepared to make a workmanlike job of it; in fact, he must shape not only his ends, but his beginnings and his middles, in spite of the producer's rough hewings.

It may be questioned, is any art possible in these conditions? I say, emphatically, 'Yes, if we go the right way to work.' It is extraordinary how, under the pressure of necessity, a dozen or so bars in the middle of a movement are discovered to be redundant, how a fortissimo climax really ought to be a pianissimo fade-out.

There are two ways of writing film music. One is that in which every action, word, gesture or incident is punctuated in sound. This requires great skill and orchestral knowledge and a vivid specialized imagination, but often leads to a mere scrappy succession of sounds of no musical value in itself. On this the question raises: should film music have any value outside its particular function? By value I do not mean necessarily that it must sound equally well played as a concert piece, but I do believe that no artistic result can come from this complex entity, the film, unless each element, acting, photography, script, and music are each, in themselves and by themselves, intrinsically good.

The other method of writing film music, which personally I favour, partly because I am quite incapable of doing the first, is to ignore the details and to intensify the spirit of the whole situation by a continuous stream of music. This stream can be modified (often at rehearsal!) by points of colour superimposed on the flow. For example, your music is illustrating Columbus's voyage and you have a sombre tune symbolizing the weariness of the voyage, the depression of the crew and the doubts of Columbus. But the producer says, 'I want a little bit of sunshine music for that flash on the waves.' Now, don't say, 'O well, the music does not provide for that; I must take it home and write something quite new.' If you are wise, you will send the orchestra away for five minutes, which will delight them. Then you look at the score to find out what instruments are unemployed—say, the harp and two muted trumpets—you write in your sunlight at the appropriate second; you re-call the orchestra; you then play the altered version, while the producer marvels at your skill in composing what appears to him to be an entirely new piece of music in so short a time.

On the other hand, you must not be horrified if you find that a passage which you intended to portray the villain's mad revenge has been used by the musical director to illustrate the cats being driven out of the dairy. The truth is that within limits any music can be made to fit any situation. An ingenious and sympathetic musical director can skilfully manoeuvre a musical phrase so that it exactly synchronizes with a situation which was never in the composer's mind.

I am only a novice at this art of film music and some of my more practised colleagues assure me that when I have had all their experience my youthful exuberance will disappear, and I shall look upon film composing not as an art but as a business. At present I still feel a morning blush which has not yet paled into the light of common day. I still believe that the film contains potentialities for the combination of all the arts such as Wagner never dreamt of.

I would therefore urge those distinguished musicians who have entered into the world of the cinema—Bax, Bliss, Walton, Benjamin, and others—to realize their responsibility in helping to take the film out of the realm of hackwork and make it a subject worthy of a real composer.

If, however, the composer is to take his side of the bargain seriously the other partners in the transaction must come out to meet him. The arts must combine from the very inception of the idea. There is a story of a millionaire who built a house and showed it to a friend when it was near completion. The friend commented on the bare and barrack-like look of the building. 'But, you see,' said the millionaire, 'we haven't added the architecture yet.' This seems to be the idea of music held by too many film directors. When the photography is finished, when the dialogue and the barking dogs and the whistling trains and the screeching taxis have been pasted on to the sound-track (I expect this is an entirely un-scientific way of expressing it), then, thinks the director, 'let us have a little music to add a final frill'. So the music only comes in when all the photography is done and the actors dispersed to their homes or to their next job. Perhaps the composer has (unwisely from the practical point of view) already read the script and devised music for certain situations as he has imagined them before seeing the pictures, but what can he do about it? The photograph is already there, the timing is rigidly fixed and if the composer's musical ideas are too long or too short they must be cut or repeated, or worse still, hurried or slowed down, because, the photograph once taken, there can be no re-timing.

What is the remedy for all this? Surely the author, director, photographer, and composer should work together *from the beginning*. Film directors pay lip service to this idea; they tell you that they want the ideal combination of the arts, but when all is finished one finds that much of the music has been cut out or faded down to a vague murmur, or distorted so that its own father would not know it, and this without so much as 'by your leave' to the unhappy musician.

I repeat then, the various elements should work together from the start. I can imagine the author showing a rough draft to the composer; the composer would suggest places where, in his opinion, music was necessary, and the author would, of course, do the same to the composer. The composer could even sketch some of the music and if it was mutually approved of, the scenes could be timed so as to give the music free play. Let us suppose, for example, that the film contains a scene in which the hero is escaping from his enemies and arrives at a shepherd's hut in the mountains. The composer finds he wants a long theme to 'establish' the mountain scenery, but the director says, 'That will never do, it would hold up the action', and so they fight it out; perhaps the director wins and the composer has to alter or modify his music. Or the director is so pleased with the composer's tune that he risks the extra length. My point is that all this should be done *before* the photographs are taken. This would not prevent further modifications in the final stages.

An outsider would probably consider this procedure obvious, but so far as my limited experience goes, it has never occurred as a possibility to the author, or the director, and certainly not to the composer.

Again, when music is to accompany dialogue or action, surely the actors should hear the music before they start rehearsing; and at rehearsal, act to the music, both from the point of view of timing and of emotional reaction.

I need hardly say that the same give-and-take would be necessary here, that is, that the composer must be ready occasionally to modify his music to fit the action and dialogue.

It is objected that this is unpractical. One could not have a symphony orchestra day after day in the studio accompanying a long drawn-out rehearsal for each scene. The expense, it is said, would be impossible. When I hear of the hundreds of thousands of pounds which are spent on a film production, it seems to be rather queer to cavil at the few extra hundreds which this would involve, but let that pass. If an orchestra is impossible, how about the pianoforte? The trouble would be to eliminate the pianoforte sounds and substitute an orchestral equivalent which would absolutely synchronize. I am told that no method has yet been devised that can do this. I know nothing about the mechanics of the film-making, the skill of the whole thing fills me with awe, so I cannot believe that the engineers, if they really wished, could not devise a method—where there's a will there's a way. At present, where film music is concerned there is not the will. Yet another method would be to rehearse with the music played, I presume, on the pianoforte, and then, having registered the exact timing and the exact emotional reaction of the actors to the music, to act it all over again in exactly the same way without the music. I cannot help feeling that the result would be intolerably mechanical.

Of these three methods the pianoforte accompaniment (after-wards to be eliminated) seems to be the best solution of the problem. Does it really pass the wit of those marvellous engineers of the film to devise some method by which it can be achieved?

I believe that this and many other problems could be solved by those who have had much experience, if the composer insisted. As long as music is content to be the maid-of-all-work, until the musicians rise to their responsibilities, we shall achieve nothing.

Perhaps one day a great film will be built up on the basis of music. The music will be written first and the film devised to accompany it, or the film will be written to music already composed. Walt Disney has pointed the way in his *Fantasia*. But must it always be a cartoon film? Could not the same idea be applied to the photographic film? Can music only suggest the fantastic and grotesque creations of an artist's pencil? May it not also shed its light on real people?

Does what I have written sound like the uninstructed grouse of an ignorant tyro? I hope not, indeed. I venture to believe that my very inexperience may have enabled me to see the wood where the expert can only see the trees.

I have often talked over these difficulties with authors, directors, and conductors: they have been inclined in theory to agree with me. I acknowledge with gratitude that when I have worked with them they have, within their scheme, stretched every possible point to give my ignorantly composed music its chance, but they have not yet been able to break down the essentially wrong system by which the various arts are segregated and only reassembled at the last moment, instead of coming together from the beginning. It is only when this is achieved that the film will come into its own as one of the finest of the fine arts.

(1945)

6

A Minim's Rest

In *The Merry Wives*, Act I, Scene iii, occurs the following dialogue:

FALSTAFF: His filching was like an unskilful singer,—he kept not time.
NYM: The good humour is to steal at a minim's rest.

The word minim was apparently misheard by the reporters who took down the play, and they wrote 'minute's'. The eighteenth-century wiseacres, knowing nothing of music, except as an expensive noise, failed to understand the joke implied in the word minim and stuck to the nonsensical word, minute. This reading persisted right into the nineteenth century.

Why could Shakespeare make a joke about a minim's rest and be sure of his laugh, while the eighteenth century did not even know the musical term? Because, under Elizabeth, music was a living thing to old and young, rich and poor. At one end of the scale comes Morley's pupil who was ashamed because he could not take his part in a madrigal after supper, and at the other the 'groundlings' who did not misunderstand when Shakespeare called one of his most beautiful songs silly sooth, old and plain, sung by the spinsters and knitters in the sun. They knew that Shakespeare realized the beauty of their 'old plain' ballads; is he not always quoting them? What would Dr. Johnson have said if he were told that because he had no ear for music he was fit for stratagems and spoils? He refused to smile with the simple and feed with the poor—'Nay, my dear lady, let me smile with the wise, and feed with the rich.'

How came it about that in the eighteenth century music was driven underground except as an exotic luxury for the rich? Well, for one thing we had a German king who brought in his train one of the greatest of German composers, who finally planted his heavy heel on our island music-making. This German king was at the beck and call of a landed oligarchy which grew daily in power and wealth. The sons of these country gentry were sent on the 'grand tour' of Europe whence they returned laden with foreign pictures and sculpture and bringing home with them a voracious horde of French, German, and Italian musicians who did not try to understand our art, but planted their own standards in its place. They were at one and the same time worshipped as divine beings and despised as 'damned French fiddlers'—a wholesome state of things in which a national art might flourish!

Music came to be considered a foreign luxury to be enjoyed by the rich, together with their wine and their China tea, but to practise which professionally was entirely unworthy of John Bull. Thus the divergence between art and life grew ever wider. Art became isolated in cathedral closes, parish churches, and Nonconformist chapels. Perhaps this was not altogether a bad thing, for within these narrow confines there grew up the art of the eighteenth-century hymn, psalm, and chant tunes; something entirely *sui generis* and within its limits often very beautiful.

And what about the music of the people which had flourished exceedingly in Tudor times? We know that Squire Western still liked 'Bobbing Joan' while Sophia preferred Mr. Handel. In the end Handel won and the songs of the people were no longer sung in more prosperous circles. The peasantry, owing to the Enclosure Acts followed by the Industrial Revolution, became a depressed class indeed; the iron curtain descended on their activities—but were they dumb? Their music and their poetry were indeed ignored right into the nineteenth century by the manor house and the parsonage. In vain did the squire's daughter and the parson's wife try to interest their tenants and parishioners in the music of Mendelssohn and Spohr—no, they were 'entirely unmusical'. Poor ignorant ladies bountiful! They had only to listen outside the village alehouse or the labourer's cottage of an evening. There, age-old ballads such as Percy would have envied were sung to tunes of a classical distinction and beauty. Woe betide these interlopers if they were seen—the singer would at once shut up like an oyster and become once again 'entirely unmusical'.

George Trevelyan in his *History of England* has a wonderful passage in which he describes the submergence of the Anglo-Saxon tongue unwritten and unspoken except by the villein through three centuries till it emerged in Tudor times as the vehicle of the poetry of Shakespeare and Milton.

Is it possible that the same thing is happening with our music? Long it has lain underground. The old psalmody of the parish church was destroyed in the 'fifties and 'sixties by the Oxford Movement and *Hymns Ancient and Modern*. The church band was superseded by the wheezy harmonium and later by the American 'organ'. The folk-song ceased to be sung in its true environment after the Education Act, 1870. Why try to make your own music when it can be obtained much cheaper and nastier through the popular press?

But if the light of English music flickered, it never quite went out. Arthur Sullivan had the makings of a unique composer—but circumstances were too much for him. It seems fated that our musicians should be born out of due time. Purcell lived before the great period when his genius could have its full technical equipment. Wesley was tied hand and foot to the organ-stool. Sullivan also was bound by the convention of his time. He could, under happier circumstances, have written another *Figaro*—but 'light' music was obliged to be trivial; 'serious' music had to take on the smug solemnity of the mid-Victorian oratorio. Music which should be at once light and serious was unheard of.

Perhaps the darkest hour was before the dawn. The nineteenth century saw the birth and early development of Parry, Stanford, and Elgar. They were the pioneers who led the way to the great resurgence of music here in England. What was the life-giving power which led these men to hand on the torch of triumph? Time was when music by a British composer meant rows of empty seats. Now all is changed—why? Because all the composers of this renaissance from Parry to Britten, different and often antagonistic as their aims are, have this in common—that they realize that vital art must grow in its own soil and be nurtured by its own rain and sunshine.

But this alone would not be enough, It takes 1,000 bad composers to make one good one, it takes 1,000 mediocre violinists to make one virtuoso. Some people say that art is for the few—that may be true, but it is only from the many voices that one can pick out the few who know the password.

It was not so long ago that the *Encyclopaedia Britannica* could define Art as an ornament on the fringe of life, a luxury for those who could afford it, and to this day *The Times* classifies a performance of Bach's *Passion* in a church under the heading of 'entertainments'. But the mass of the people have by this time realized that music is not only an 'entertainment', nor a mere luxury, but a necessity of the spiritual if not of the physical life, an opening of those magic casements through which we can catch a glimpse of that country where ultimate reality will be found.

It seems that music, not only in its vague aspects but in its very details, was an essential part of the spiritual life of the sixteenth century. It was not for nothing that both Shakespeare and Milton were skilled musicians, or that George Herbert could write:

> Or since all music is but three parts vied
> And multiplied;
> O let thy blessed Spirit bear a part
> And make up our defects with his sweet art,

and make sure that he would be understood. How different from the mere dope of 'Music When Soft Voices Die' in the early nineteenth century.

The Elizabethans experienced a great revival of national consciousness which expressed itself in their poetry and music. Are we experiencing a similar revival? It is not mere accident that during the last War, when our national consciousness became very vivid, when everyone was keyed up to greater and greater effort, the need for music became greater and greater. The time will soon be due for the next supreme composer. He will arise in that community which is best fitted to receive him.

(1948)

7

Bach, the Great Bourgeois

When I was a small boy I was brought up almost entirely on Handel, and especially the Handel Festival. I once heard a Bach Gavotte at a village concert and asked whether it was right to put such a name on the same programme as the great masters, and my aunt told me that Bach was quite a good composer: but of course not so good as Handel (this being the accepted view in those days); and with the strange incuriosity of a child I left it at that and made no further inquiries until I went to school at ten years old.

There I was taken in hand by the music master, Mr. C. T. West, whose name I shall always hold in reverence. He soon realized that I did not much care for the 'Maiden's Prayer' or 'True Love' and one day—a momentous day for me—he brought me a Bach Album edited by Berthold Tours. Here indeed was a revelation; here was something undeniably belonging to no period or style, something for all time. This is where Bach differs from other composers. They, with the exception of a few outstanding Beethoven works, belong to their time, but Bach, though superficially he may speak the eighteenth-century language, belongs to no school or period.

There is a tendency nowadays to 'put Bach in his place'. He is labelled as 'Baroque' (whatever that may mean) and according to the latest orders from Germany he is to be performed as 'period music' in the precise periwig style. This is all part of a movement to 'play Bach as he wrote it'. To do this would be impossible even if we wanted to. Our violins are played on quite a different principle; our horns are soft and our trombones are loud. I should like to see Mr. Goossens confronted with one of those gross bagpipe instruments which in Bach's time stood for an oboe. The harpsichord, however it may sound in a small room—and to my mind it never has a pleasant sound—in a large concert room sounds just like the ticking of a sewing machine. We have no longer, thank Heaven, the Baroque style of organ, which we are told, with very insufficient evidence, was the kind of instrument Bach played upon. (By the way, I see there is a movement afoot to substitute this bubble-and-squeak type of instrument for the noble diapason and soft mixtures of our cathedral organs.)

We cannot perform Bach exactly as he was played in his time even if we wanted to, and the question is, do we want to? I say emphatically, No! Some music dies with its period, but what is really immortal endures from generation to generation. The interpretation and with it the means of interpretation differ with each generation. If the music is ephemeral it will disappear with any change of fashion. If the music is really alive it will live on through all the alterations of musical thought.

A young exquisite once said to me, 'I don't like Bach, he is so bourgeois', to which I probably answered that being bourgeois myself I considered Bach the greatest of all composers.

It is Bach's intense humanity which endears him to me and my fellow bourgeois. The proletarians (if there were any in this country) would be too much occupied with their wrongs, and the 'governing classes' (if indeed they existed outside the imagination of the *New Statesman*) would be too much occupied in preserving their rights to have time to be human. Those members of choral societies who sing Bach perhaps have not the exquisite literary taste of our high intelligentsia. The pietism of Bach's texts are not an offence to them even when they are translated into what the Rev. Dr. Troutbeck imagined was English. Well, the members of our choral societies are not literary experts and certain words which shock the esoteric sense of the literary aristocrats pass by them unnoticed. We English are not literary, we are not artistic, but we *are* musical.

But we must introduce Bach to our musical public not as a museum piece; we must do nothing to give the slightest hint of the scholar or the antiquarian. Does this involve, for example, the substitution of a pianoforte for a harpsichord; the doubling of the oboes with the clarinets in loud passages; the occasional substitution of strings for the harpsichord in the 'realization' of Bach's figured bass? Different circumstances require different treatment.

How did Bach hear his own cantatas and passions? He had a choir of sixteen voices, not very good according to his own account; a very ramshackle orchestra of about the same size and also a large organ. This is what he heard, and as Sir George Dyson justly says, it is doubtful if he ever heard a decent performance of one of his cantatas. What would he have said if he could have heard the Mass or Passion sung by three hundred voices from Leeds or Huddersfield? Would he not have been thrilled and uplifted? It might not be quite what he expected. He might have said:

'This is not what I ever hoped to hear, but it realizes and more than realizes what was in my mind. However with this enormous and splendid choir what is that wretched little orchestra of two oboes and two flutes doing. This, of course, must be altered.

'I see you have an instrument here called a clarinet. This would be very useful to increase the tone of your oboes, which to my mind is very thin, and to steady the occasional bubble of your trumpets. Again, where is your organ? It is essential to fill in the gaps of my orchestra. I see that you have an organ in your hall but you tell me it can't be used because it is the wrong pitch. Well, you are a funny people. How do you propose to do my "Confiteor" or the opening chorus of "Ein' Feste Burg" without an organ? Of course you must add something. No, I need not do it myself—any competent musician who understands my work can do that part of it. Some of your new instruments which I see in the orchestra could be brought in to help: your nimble horns which are soft, whereas mine were loud, and your trombones which are loud, whereas mine were soft: you have changed all that and in order to keep the spirit of my music you must, perforce, modify the letter.'

Purists may object that Bach never used trombones and trumpets in the same piece of music. This is true, and for this wonderful reasons have been given couched in the best jargon of aesthetic philosophy. The real reason was discovered by Professor Sanford Terry, namely, that the same performers played both instruments! Nowadays we have both trumpets and trombones at our disposal. May we not, in the absence of an organ, double our voice parts with trombones as Bach himself often did? Sir Hugh Allen was hardly an iconoclast, but he doubled the voices with trombones in the last pages of the B minor Mass. Doubtless Bach would have done the same if his players had not been already occupied mounting up to high D on their trumpets.

Can we not apply this principle to Bach's string parts as well? He had a very meagre band of strings and they were probably all double-handed—that is to say, they could play the violin or viola equally badly. Now in some of Bach's arias, notably the Agnus Dei of the B minor Mass, he wanted all the available strings for that wonderful opening melody. If you look at the score you will see that the first and second violins play in unison and that the violas are silent; this means, I have no doubt, that he made the violas change to violins for that number, leaving the inner parts to be filled in as best they could on the organ or harpsichord; and I feel equally certain that the continuo player filled in a flowing accompaniment and not those nasty detached twangs on the harpsichord which we hear nowadays. In our modern orchestras we have violins and violas galore, so there is no necessity for the violas to double the violins; therefore they sit idle, earning their guineas for nothing. To my mind, it would be justifiable to entrust the said flowing accompaniment to them. When I tried the experiment Sir Hugh Allen was slightly surprised but said, 'It sounded very beautiful.'

Closely connected with the problem of adaptation is the question of words. The purists in this matter can be divided into two classes— those who say that a performance must be in the original language; that Bach wrote for the German text and only the German text may be used, with the result of course that hardly any of the performers would be able to pronounce, or the audience understand, what is being sung (I am speaking of course not of an audience of specialists but of the great mass of people who are now crowding to sing and hear Bach). The other class are those who admit that performances must be in English, but that the words must be mauled about so that not a single note of Bach's recitative shall be altered. These people evidently have no feeling for the beauty of the Authorized Version and, rather than alter one note of Bach's music, they will countenance such horrors as 'One brief hour' as given in one of our English translations. In this case we are indeed confronted with a conflict of loyalties—loyalty to Bach's incomparable music and loyalty to the incomparable beauty of our English Authorized Version.

Of course when Bach has a definite melodic passage as in his arias and ariosos his notes must come first. But in the mere narrative where his object was to fit notes to the words so as to make correct declamation of the text, surely we may alter a note or two so as to preserve our superb English Biblical language, though of course, even here, when Bach has a magnificent expressive phrase for a particular word, we must, of course, place that word under the note which expresses it. Thus we are obliged to say, 'Go yonder and pray' instead of 'Go and pray yonder' so that the word 'pray' can be under Bach's wonderful musical illustration.

This point of view naturally does not occur to the distinguished foreign musicians who come here to conduct Bach. I remember once talking on the subject to a well-known and very talented foreign conductor. He was much horrified at the slight alterations in the recitative of the Bach–Elgar edition of the Passion. When I pointed out to him that they were made so as to preserve the text of the Authorized Version which we all loved in England he replied with scorn, 'I should like to know who authorized it', and when I objected that Troutbeck's literary style left much to be desired he only said that he believed he was a very religious man.

Did Bach always mean his orchestral directions to be carried out to the letter? For example, he scarcely ever specified what instrument is to play the continuo. I have heard the Agnus Dei from the B minor Mass accompanied by what Mr. Byard expressively calls 'plops' on the harpsichord and a full quota of double basses grunting out the bass. Again, when Bach writes an obbligato and marks it 'oboe col violini' does he really mean the doubling to go on all the time? May we not suppose that at the rehearsal he told the oboe to rest for a certain number of bars (indeed if the oboist tried to play the whole time as written he would probably burst); and occasionally told the violins to be silent and let the oboe be heard alone? I have tried this experiment with, I hope, success in the instrumental interludes of 'Jesu, Joy of Man's Desiring'.

Now we must tackle the problem of what is rather pompously called 'realization of the continuo'. In many of the arias and in the whole of the Evangelist's recitatives all that Bach provided was the bass and the necessary figures to indicate what harmonies should be played above the bass. (A figured bass by the way is something like the scheme which has been adopted for notation of the music for the ukelele in modern times.) The continuo part was given to the keyboard player whose duty it was to improvise a full accompaniment according to the indication in the figures.

It cannot be made too clear that what we find in the usual pianoforte scores of the Bach recitatives is not what Bach wrote. As I have already said, what Bach wrote for his recitatives was only the bass with the necessary figures to indicate the harmonies. In the usual vocal scores of the Passion this bass is 'realized' as a series of detached chords placed in the dullest part of the instrument and with hardly any variation of treatment which makes the cadences, particularly, almost intolerable. However, I hope and believe that these printed pianoforte parts are never played and, in justice to the arranger, I think they were never meant to be played. Perhaps really it would have been better in that case to print simply Bach's bass and figures and not give simple-minded people the idea that when they play these dreary chords they are playing Bach. How, then, are we to play Bach recitatives? We have some evidence that Bach and the pupils under his guidance did something interesting and elaborate by way of 'realization'. Will it be impertinent if we also try to do something interesting and elaborate, always of course keeping well within Bach's idiom? In this way, I believe we should truly interpret the word 'continuo' by a flowing melodic outline varying according to the nature of the narrative and the emotional content of the words.

'The letter killeth, but the Spirit giveth life.' If we adhere meticulously and mechanically to the letter of Bach we shall inevitably kill the spirit. Bach's hearers were eighteenth-century German Lutherans with minds very different from ours. They had, for example, a very personal reaction to theology; they saw no harm in singing 'Mein Jesu gute Nacht'. Our purists would have us sing 'My Jesus Now Good Night', but we quite rightly realize that in English this would be mere affectation. Again, these eighteenth-century German burghers liked full value for their money and they thought nothing of sitting in church listening to, or possibly sleeping through, three-and-a-half hours of music, plus a sermon. But we, with our quicker apprehension, are more easily exhausted and cannot really endure the emotion of this music for so long.

It is the fashion nowdays to perform Bach's Passion in its entirety with a 'Bach' luncheon party between the parts. I believe this to be a mistake. We must admit that Homer occasionally nods, and that some of the arias are not up to Bach's high standard. It is, I believe, wrong to include these for the sake of a mechanical completeness. It is not impossible that Bach never meant them all to be played on the same occasion, but that he made a different selection from year to year. I admit there is no evidence for this; but all the same it seems not impossible. Why should we perform Bach with all the disabilities under which he suffered any more than we perform Shakespeare in the Elizabethan pronunciation? If by modifying the letter we kill the spirit of Bach, then he had better remain dead and be put in the museum with the other mummies. Through all the changes and chances the beauty of his music abides because his music appeals to everyone—not only to the aesthete, the musicologist or the propagandist, but above all to Whitman's 'Divine Average'—that great middle class from whom nearly all that is worth while in religion, painting, poetry, and music has sprung.

Let me finish with one short story. The other day a messenger boy came to the door with a C.O.D. parcel. When I had paid the cash, signed along the dotted line and received his official 'thank you', he hesitated a moment and then added, 'When's the Passion?'

(1950)

8

A Musical Autobiography

My first teacher in musical theory was my aunt, Miss Wedgwood. When I was about six I wrote a pianoforte piece, four bars long, called, heaven knows why, 'The Robin's Nest'. It was shown to some musical visitors and my sister heard one of them say, 'Has he learnt any thoroughbass?' My sister and I pondered for long over what 'thoroughbass' could be. Of course, it never occurred to us to ask. However, soon after this my aunt took me through a book which I still have, called *The Child's Introduction to Thorough Bass in Conversations of a Fortnight between a Mother and her Daughter aged Ten years old: London, printed for Baldwin Cradock and Joy, 14, Paternoster Row*, 1819. Here is a specimen from conversation 8:

MARY: Mama, have I anything more to learn about the chord of the 7th?
MOTHER: Yes, you already know how a simple chord of the 7th is formed, but you are also to learn that there are 4 different kinds of 7th.

From this I went on to Stainer's *Harmony*, and when I was about eight I went in for a correspondence course organized by Edinburgh University, and, so far as I can remember, passed both the preliminary and advanced examinations. My handwriting was, at that time, considered too bad (I am told that some people still hold this extraordinary opinion) and I was allowed to dictate my exercises to my aunt.

Meanwhile, I had been taught the pianoforte, which I never could play, and the violin, which was my musical salvation. I remember as if it were yesterday, when I was about, I think, seven years old walking with my mother through the streets of Eastbourne and seeing in a music shop an advertisement of violin lessons. My mother said to me, 'Would you like to learn the violin?' and I, without thinking, said, 'Yes.' Accordingly, next day, a wizened old

German called Cramer appeared on the scene and gave me my first violin lesson.

I took my violin with me to a preparatory school at Rottingdean where I had lessons from a well-known Brighton teacher, Quirke. The climax of my career at Rottingdean was when I played Raff's 'Cavatina' at a school concert. Fifty years later, at one of the Three Choirs Festivals, I was suddenly moved to seize W. H. Reed's violin and play through Raff's 'Catavina' by heart, double stops and all, while Reed vamped an accompaniment, before a discerning and enthusiastic audience. But to continue my violin career to its bitter end: at Charterhouse I joined the school orchestra and played second violin, changing later to viola. I also played in Haydn string quartets with Colonel Lewin and his musical family in the holidays, and on Sundays at school I used to go to Mr. Girdlestone, one of the masters, where with several other boys we played through Concerti Grossi by the great Italian masters. I owe a great deal to these ensemble experiences.

I remember my first practical lesson in orchestration. The school band was playing the slow movement of Beethoven's First Symphony. The violas were quite close to the one horn in the orchestra and my first lesson in orchestral texture came from hearing the holding note on the horn which accompanies the reiterated figure of the violas. I believe I should have made quite a decent fiddler, but the authorities decided that if I was to take up music at all the violin was too 'doubtful' a career and I must seek safety on the organ stool, a trade for which I was entirely unsuited; indeed, I have the distinction of being the only pupil who entirely baffled Sir Walter Parratt, though I must add, for my own credit, that later on I passed the F.R.C.O. examination. Sir Hugh Allen always insisted that I must have bribed the examiners.

One great landmark in my musical education came, as I have mentioned earlier, while I was still at my preparatory school at Rottingdean. It was decided that I was to have some pianoforte lessons from the visiting teacher, Mr. C. T. West. First he gave me the ordinary music teacher's rubbish, 'Petite Valse' and so on; but he had the insight to perceive that I should like something better, and one day brought me a little book which I have always considered a great treasure—Novello's *Bach Album*. Bach had never been part of the home curriculum—Handel, Mozart, Haydn, and some early Beethoven was what we were fed on at home. My brother, sister, and I were encouraged to play pianoforte duets from funny old volumes containing choruses from 'The Messiah' and 'Israel' which I loved, and arias from *Don Giovanni* and *Figaro* which bored me, though I have to admit that we played the overture to *Figaro* at about minim = 50, my aunt complaining that it was the fashion to play it much too fast.

Later we added Schubert's marches and Haydn's symphonies to our repertoire. Since those early times I have never wavered in my admiration of Haydn. I remember one problem which disturbed me in my study of him. My aunt disapproved of waltzes and thought they were vulgar. Now, the second subject of Haydn's E♭ Symphony is undoubtedly a waltz. Haydn I knew was a great composer, a waltz I knew was something vulgar; surely a great composer could not write anything vulgar? The problem remained unsolved.

Of Bach I then knew nothing and I imagined vaguely that he was like Handel but not so good. This Bach album was a revelation, something quite different from anything I knew, and Bach still remains for me in a niche by himself.

One episode in my career at Charterhouse must be told. I had the temerity to approach Dr. Haig Brown, the headmaster (and headmasters were headmasters in those days, not the hail-fellow-well-met-young-feller-me-lads of modern times), to obtain the loan of the school hall to give a concert of compositions by myself and a school friend, H. Vivian Hamilton, who afterwards became well-known as a pianist. My chief contribution to the programme was a pianoforte trio in one movement. All I remember about it is that the principal theme is distinctly reminiscent of César Franck, a composer of whom I was not even aware in those days and whom I have since learned to dislike cordially. I must have got the theme from one of the French or Belgian imitators of Franck whose salon music was popular in those days. I remember that after the concert James Noon, the mathematical master, came up to me and said in that sepulchral voice which Carthusians of my day knew so well, 'Very good, Williams, you must go on.' I treasured this as one of the few words of encouragement I ever received in my life!

On leaving Charterhouse in 1890 I went direct to the R.C.M., but during the intervening summer holidays a very important thing happened to me. I went to Munich and heard my first Wagner opera. We found that *Die Walküre* was down for that evening. The opera, we were told, would start at 7, so at 6 o'clock we sat down to have a preliminary meal. Hardly had we started when the waiter rushed in—he had made a mistake, on a Wagner *Abend* the opera started at 6. The rest decided for dinner, but I, like the hero of a novel, 'left my food untasted' and rushed off to the Opera House. I arrived just in time to hear that wonderful passage for strings when Sieglinde offers Siegmund the cup. This was my first introduction to later Wagner, but I experienced no surprise, but rather that strange certainty that I had heard it all before. There was a feeling of recognition as of meeting an old friend which comes to us all in the face of great artistic experiences. I had the same experience when I first heard an English folk-song, when I first saw Michael Angelo's *Day and Night*, when I suddenly came upon Stonehenge, or had my first sight of New York City—the intuition that I had been there already.

That September I entered as a student at the R.C.M. and was determined, if possible, to study composition under Parry. I had first heard of Parry some years before, when I was still a schoolboy. I remember my cousin, Stephen Massingberd, coming into the room full of that new book *Studies of Great Composers*. 'This man, Parry,' he said, 'declares that a composer must write music as his musical conscience demands.' This was quite a new idea to me, the loyalty of the artist to his art. Soon after that I got to know some of his music, especially parts of 'Judith' and I remember, even as a boy, my brother saying to me that there was something, to his mind, peculiarly English about his music. So I was quite prepared to join with the other young students of the R.C.M. in worshipping at that shrine, and I think I can truly say that I have never been disloyal to it. Perhaps I can no longer, owing to the weakening digestion of old age, swallow Parry's music whole as I did then; but I still thrill to the magnificence of 'Job' and 'De Profundis', and I hereby solemnly declare, keeping steadily in view the works of Byrd, Purcell, and Elgar, that 'Blest Pair of Sirens' is my favourite piece of music written by an Englishman.

By a wise ruling of the College, which I fear no longer obtains, no one was allowed to study composition until he had passed Grade 5 in harmony. So for two terms I did my theoretical work with Dr. F. E. Gladstone. Under his guidance I worked through every exercise in *Macfarren's Harmony*, a discipline for which I have ever since been grateful.

After two terms I passed my Grade 5 harmony and was allowed to become a pupil of Parry. I will not try to describe what this experience meant to a boy. I was very elementary at the time. I blush with shame now when I think of the horrible little songs and anthems which I presented for his criticism. Parry's great watchword was 'characteristic'. He was always trying to discover the character revealed in even the weakest of his students' compositions. Before telling the following story I ought to explain that Parry, not content with the official lesson, used to keep his pupils' compositions to look at during the week. One day, through pure carelessness, I had written out a scale passage with one note repeated and then a gap—(i.e., CDEFGGBC instead of CDEFGABC). Parry said, 'I have been looking at this passage for a long time to discover whether it is just a mistake or whether you meant anything characteristic.'

I was painfully illiterate in those days, even more so than now. Parry could hardly believe that I knew so little music. One day he was talking to me about the wonderful climax in the development of the 'Appassionata' Sonata. Suddenly he realized that I did not know it, so he sat down at the pianoforte and played it through to me. There were showers of wrong notes, but in spite of that it was the finest performance that I have heard. So I was told to study more Beethoven, especially the posthumous quartets, 'as a religious exercise'. At that time I hated Beethoven. I was suffering from an overdose of Gounod, and I could not understand why the tune in the finale of the 'Eroica' Symphony was good music, while the 'Judex' from *Mors et Vita* was bad music. (I was only eighteen, please teacher.) To this day the Beethoven idiom repels me, but I hope I have at last learnt to see the greatness that lies behind the idiom that I dislike, and at the same time, to see an occasional weakness behind the Bach idiom which I love.

Parry was very generous in lending scores to his pupils. This was long before the days of miniature scores and gramophone records. I borrowed *Siegfried* and 'Tristan' and Brahms's *Requiem*, and for some time after, my so-called compositions consisted entirely of variations of a passage near the beginning of that work.

I remember one day when I came in for my lesson I found a fellow student, Richard Walthew, borrowing the score of the Prelude to *Parsifal*. Parry condemned it as the weakest of the Wagner preludes—'mere scene painting' was, I think, his description of it. He was always very insistent on the importance of form as opposed to colour. He had an almost moral abhorrence of mere luscious sound. It has been said that Parry's own orchestration was bad; the truth is, I think, that he occasionally went too far in his deliberate eschewal of mere orchestral effect. Years after this I was sitting next to Elgar at a rehearsal of Parry's 'Symphonic Variations' with its curious spiky sound. I said, 'I suppose many people would call this bad orchestration; I do not find it so.' Elgar turned on me almost fiercely: 'Of course it's not bad orchestration, the music could have been scored in no other way.'

Parry's criticism was constructive. He was not merely content to point out faults, but would prescribe the remedy. The last two bars of my early part song 'The Willow Song' were almost certainly composed by Parry.

Parry once said to me, 'Write choral music as befits an Englishman and a democrat.' We pupils of Parry have, if we have been wise, inherited from Parry the great English choral tradition which Tallis passed on to Byrd, Byrd to Gibbons, Gibbons to Purcell, Purcell to Battishill and Greene, and they in their turn through the Wesleys to Parry. He has passed on the torch to us and it is our duty to keep it alight.

I have already mentioned Richard Walthew.[1] We became great friends and though we hardly ever meet now I hope the friendship still subsists. This, however, is not a record of friendships but of musical influences, and I pick out Walthew's name among friends of that period because I learnt much from him. I used occasionally to go to his house at Highbury and play duets with him, or rather, he played and I stumbled behind him as best I could. In this way I learnt to know a lot of music including, I remember, Stanford's

[1] Richard Walthew died in 1952.

'Irish' Symphony. In those days, before the gramophone and the wireless and the miniature score, the pianoforte duet was the only way, unless you were an orchestral player, of getting to know orchestral music, and one really got to know it from the inside, not in the superficial way of lazily listening to a gramophone record. One day Walthew, who had a holy horror of anything high falutin in art, insisted on taking me to hear *Carmen*. By that time I had quite recovered from my Gounod fever and had become the complete prig. Bach, Beethoven (ex-officio), Brahms, and Wagner were the only composers worth considering, so I went to *Carmen* prepared to scoff, but Walthew won the day and I remained to pray. It must have been about the same time that I had another salutary disturbance of my musical prejudices: I heard Verdi's *Requiem* for the first time. At first I was properly shocked by the frank sentimentalism and sensationalism of the music. I remember being particularly horrified at the drop of a semitone on the word 'Dona'. Was not this the purest 'village organist'? But in a very few minutes the music possessed me. I realized that here was a composer who could do all the things which I with my youthful pedantry thought wrong, indeed, would be unbearable in a lesser man; music which was sentimental, theatrical, occasionally even cheap, and yet was an overpowering masterpiece. That day I learnt that there is nothing in itself that is 'common or unclean', indeed that there are no canons of art except that contained in the well-worn tag, 'To thine own self be true.'

In 1892 I went to Cambridge where I had lessons from Charles Wood in preparation for the Mus.Bac. degree. Charles Wood was the finest technical instructor I have ever known. I do not say necessarily the greatest teacher. I do not think he had the gift of inspiring enthusiasm or of leading to the higher planes of musical thought. Indeed, he was rather prone to laugh at artistic ideals and would lead one to suppose that composing music was a trick anyone might learn if he took the trouble. But for the craft of composition he was unrivalled, and he managed to teach me enough to pull me through my Mus.Bac. I also had organ lessons from Alan Gray. Our friendship survived his despair at my playing, and I became quite expert at managing the stops at his voluntaries and organ recitals.

G

In the year 1892 there also came to Cambridge, as organ scholar, an undergraduate rather older than the rest, H. P. Allen. I believe I had the honour of first introducing him to the music of Brahms. Allen at once took over the amateur University Musical Club, shook them out of their complacency and made them rehearse such things as the Schumann and Brahms pianoforte quintets and Schubert's string quintet. I got much musical instruction in listening to the rehearsal of these works which I came to know nearly by heart. Allen also gave me an opportunity of hearing, for the first time, a semi-public performance of a composition of my own, a quartet for men's voices. At the first performance the second tenor got a bar out and remained so nearly to the end. Allen organized an encore and it was done all over again, this time correctly. The audience disliked it the second time even more than the first. This may seem a small episode but it was my first experience of an essential and salutary, though unpleasant form of composition lesson, a performance in public, something quite different from a private rehearsal.

Allen did me the same service, though on a larger scale, in 1910, when after my Sea Symphony had had a very doubtful reception at the Leeds Festival he at once arranged for performances at Oxford and in London, though he confessed to me afterwards that he was rather frightened about it.

While I was at Cambridge I conducted a small choral society, which met on Sundays to sing Schubert's Masses. If a composer cannot play in an orchestra or sing in a choir the next best thing he can do in self-education is to try his hand at conducting and really find out what the performers are up against. The only way to learn to conduct is to 'try it on the dog'. This is much better than any amount of class teaching, about which I have grave doubts. According to Wagner, the duty of the conductor is to give the proper tempo to the orchestra. Elgar said, 'When I conduct I let the orchestra play.' A good orchestra will play well if the conductor will let them, and they play no better because he makes funny faces at them. (It is different with a chorus, they fail to come in altogether if they don't get the right grimace.) The two best conducting lessons I ever had were from my old friend Isidore Schwiller, the violinist, who taught me how to start an orchestra on an upbeat, and from

Mr. Henderson, the famous timpanist of the L.S.O. of old days, who said to me, 'You give us a good square 4 in the bar and we'll do the rest.' To which I may add Stanford's witty saying, 'A conductor need never be nervous, he can't make any wrong notes.'

After Cambridge I went back to the R.C.M. Parry was by this time Director, so I went for lessons to Stanford. Stanford was a great teacher, but I believe I was unteachable. I made the great mistake of trying to fight my teacher. The way to get the best out of instruction is to put oneself entirely in the hands of one's instructor, and try to find out all about his method regardless of one's own personality, keeping of course a secret 'eppur si muove' up one's sleeve. Young students are much too obsessed with the idea of expressing their personalities. In the merest harmony exercises they insist on keeping all their clumsy progressions because that is what they 'felt', forgetting that the art cannot mature unless the craft matures alongside with it.

The details of my work annoyed Stanford so much that we seldom arrived at the broader issues and the lesson usually started with a conversation on these lines: 'Damnably ugly, my boy, why do you write such things?' 'Because I like them.' 'But you can't like them, they're not music.' 'I shouldn't write them if I didn't like them.' So the argument went on and there was no time left for any constructive criticism.

Stanford never displayed great enthusiasm for my work. But his deeds were better than his words, and later on he introduced my work to the Leeds Festival, thus giving me my first opportunity of a performance under these imposing conditions.

When all is said and done, what one really gets out of lessons with a great man cannot be computed in terms of what he said to you or what you did for him, but in terms of the intangible contact with his mind and character. With Stanford I always felt I was in the presence of a lovable, powerful, and enthralling mind.

This helped me more than any amount of technical instruction.

The benefit that one obtains from an academy or college is not so much from one's official teachers as from one's fellow students. I was lucky in my companions in those days. Other students at the College were Dunhill, Ireland, Howard Jones, Fritz Hart, and

Gustav Holst. We used to meet in a little teashop in Kensington and discuss every subject under the sun from the lowest note of the double bassoon to the philosophy of *Jude the Obscure*. I learnt more from these conversations than from any amount of formal teaching, but I felt at a certain disadvantage with these companions: they were all so competent and I felt such an amateur. I have struggled all my life to conquer amateurish technique and now that perhaps I have mastered it, it seems too late to make any use of it. Curiously, however, as regards orchestral texture, when I hear my early works, written when my knowledge was still all out of books and I had to sit for an hour wondering what to do with the 2nd clarinet in a loud tutti, my orchestration seems fuller and richer than nowadays when my writing is backed by practical experience. And here I should like to mention the names of two men who have helped me in my orchestral work. Cecil Forsyth before he went to America 'vetted' many of my scores, giving out from his incomparable store of knowledge obtained 'straight from the horse's nosebag'. Gordon Jacob is the other name. He was at one time nominally my pupil, though there was nothing I could teach him which he did not know better than I, at all events in the matter of technique. Since then I have often asked his advice on points of orchestration, as indeed I would gladly do in any branch of the composer's art.

In 1895 I was appointed to my first and last organ post, at St. Barnabas, South Lambeth. As I have already said, I never could play the organ, but this appointment gave me an insight into good and bad church music which stood me in good stead later on. I also had to train the choir and give organ recitals and accompany the services, which gave me some knowledge of music from the performer's point of view. I also founded a choral society and an orchestral society, both of them pretty bad, but we managed once to do a Bach Cantata and I obtained some of that practical knowledge of music which is so essential to a composer's make-up. Composers who think that they will achieve their aim by ranging apart and living the life beautiful make the great mistake of their lives. Wagner could never have written 'Tristan' and *Meistersinger* if he had not had those years of gruelling experience at Dresden. Brahms ought certainly to have accepted that kapellmeistership in that small German town whose name I forget. Intimate acquaintance with the executive side of music in orchestra, chorus, and opera made even Mahler into a very tolerable imitation of a composer.

In 1897 I decided to have a few months' study and experience abroad. Stanford wanted me to go to Italy and hear opera at the Scala. He thought I was too Teuton already. He did not want me to take definite lessons with anyone. But I disregarded his advice and went to Berlin. My reason for this choice, I believe, was the extraordinary one that Berlin was the only town at that time where they performed the *Ring* without cuts! I had an introduction to Herzogenberg, who looked at my work and said it reminded him of Mascagni, and advised me to study with Max Bruch. It is difficult to say what it is one learns from a teacher. I only know that I worked hard and enthusiastically and that Max Bruch encouraged me, and I had never had much encouragement before. With my own pupils now I always try to remember the value of encouragement. Sometimes a callow youth appears who may be a fool or may be a genius, and I would rather be guilty of encouraging a fool than of discouraging a genius. A fool, after all, may find his own salvation in artistic self-expression even though it means nothing to anyone else, and as to the genius, perhaps one may by analogy quote Lord Chesterfield, 'If it's fine take an umbrella; if it's raining, please yourself.'

When I was under Stanford I used to vex him much with my flattened sevenths. He tried to prove to me that the flat leading note was pure theory and that all folk-songs descended on to the tonic, but I felt in my bones that he was wrong, though it was only later, when I heard traditional singers, that I was able to prove my point to my own satisfaction. Max Bruch was equally worried by this idiosyncracy of mine: he said, 'Sie haben eine Leidenschaft für die kleine Septime.' He also warned me against writing 'Augen-musik' as opposed to 'Ohren-musik'. This warning was wasted on me as I habitually and unashamedly use the pianoforte when composing. (I suppose this would be considered part of my amateurishness.) I heard all the music I could when I was in Berlin, especially operas. Among them were Lortzing's *Undine* and Meyerbeer's *Robert le Diable*. I also remember beautiful performances of Bach Cantatas at the Sing-Akademie. The Joachim and Halir quartets were at their zenith and there was a memorable performance at the Hoch-Schule of the Brahms Double Concerto played as a pianoforte trio by Joachim, Hausman, and Barth.

When I came back to London I soon left my organist post and settled down to try and learn how to compose, not by studying but by doing. However, I still felt the need of instruction, and in about the year 1900 I took my courage in both hands and wrote to Elgar asking him to give me lessons, especially in orchestration. I received a polite reply from Lady Elgar saying that Sir Edward was too busy to give me lessons but suggesting that I should become a pupil of Professor Bantock. I did not adopt his suggestion which was perhaps a mistake, as what Bantock did not know about the orchestra is not worth knowing. But though Elgar would not teach me personally he could not help teaching me through his music. I spent several hours at the British Museum studying the full scores of the Variations and *Gerontius*. The results are obvious in the opening pages of the finale of my Sea Symphony and I have discovered lately that I owe a good deal in this work to an early work of Holst's *The Mystic Trumpeter*. Holst used also to say that he cribbed from me, though I never perceived it. I do not think that composers ever know when they are being cribbed from. Cribbing is, to my mind, a legitimate and praiseworthy practice, but one ought to know where one has cribbed. I expect that Schubert knew that he cribbed 'Death and the Maiden' from Beethoven's Seventh Symphony, but I doubt whether Wagner realized that he had cribbed the 'Nibelungen' theme from Schubert's D minor quartet and the 'Rhine' theme from Mendelssohn's *Melusine*.

Deliberate cribbing is all right and the funny thing is that what is most deliberately cribbed sounds the most original, but the more subtle, unconscious cribbing is, I admit, dangerous. I was quite unconscious that I had cribbed from *La Mer* in the introduction to my London Symphony until Constant Lambert horrified me by calling my attention to it.

A strange episode occurred about this time which, though it had no direct bearing on my musical education, must be related here. I burst in on the privacy of Delius, who happened to be in London at the time, and insisted on playing through the whole of my Sea Symphony to him. Poor fellow! How he must have hated it. But he was very courteous and contented himself with saying, 'Vraiment il n'est pas mesquin.'

In 1900 I first met Cecil Sharp. He had not then shaken musical England with *Folk Songs from Somerset*. Indeed I did not imbibe folk-song from Sharp, and when I first started collecting, in 1903, and began boring my friends with my finds I left Sharp out of the list because I thought he would not be interested.

I must have made my first contact with English folk-songs when I was a boy in the 'eighties, through Stainer and Bramley's *Christmas Carols New and Old*. I remember clearly my reaction to the tune of the 'Cherry Tree Carol' which was more than simple admiration for a fine tune, though I did not then naturally realize the implications involved in that sense of intimacy. This sense came upon me more strongly in 1893 when I first discovered 'Dives and Lazarus' in *English County Songs*. Here, as before with Wagner, I had that sense of recognition—'here's something which I have known all my life—only I didn't know it!'

There has been a lot of cheap wit expended on 'folk-song' composers. The matter seems to boil down to two accusations: First that it is 'cheating' to make use of folk-song material. This is really nothing more than the old complaint of the vested interests who are annoyed when anyone drinks a glass of pure water which he can get free, rather than a glass of beer which will bring profit to the company. This appears to involve a moral rather than an artistic question; from the point of view of musical experience it seems to me that so long as good music is made it matters very little how it is made or who makes it. If a composer can, by tapping the sources hidden in folk-song, make beautiful music, he will be disloyal to his art if he does not make full use of such an avenue of beauty.

The second accusation is made by people who affect to scorn what is 'folky' because it does not come within the ken of their airless smuggeries, because it does not require any highly-paid teachers to inculcate it, or the purchase of text-books with a corresponding royalty to the author. It is really a case of the vested interest once again.

Why should music be 'original'? The object of art is to stretch out to the ultimate realities through the medium of beauty. The duty of the composer is to find the *mot juste*. It does not matter if this word has been said a thousand times before as long as it is the right thing to say at that moment. If it is *not* the right thing to say, however unheard of it may be, it is of no artistic value. Music which is unoriginal is so, not simply because it has been said before, but because the composer has not taken the trouble to make sure that this was the right thing to say at the right moment.

I have never had any conscience about cribbing.

I cribbed Satan's dance in *Job* deliberately from the Scherzo of Beethoven's last quartet; the opening of my F minor Symphony deliberately from the finale of the Ninth Symphony, and the last two bars of the Scherzo to my Sea Symphony from the Mass in D. (I expect Beethoven knew that he was cribbing the last movement of the 'Appassionata' Sonata from one of Cramer's pianoforte studies.) It is said that once when Wagner was rehearsing *Meistersinger* he stopped in the middle of that rather commonplace theme in the third act and said, 'Gentlemen, does not that come out of the *Merry Wives*?'

My intercourse with Cecil Sharp crystallized and confirmed what I already vaguely felt about folk-song and its relationship to the composer's art. With Sharp it was a case of 'Under which King, Bezonian? Speak, or die.' You had to be either pro folk-song or anti folk-song and I came down heavily on the folk-song side.

In 1904 I undertook to edit the music of a hymn-book. This meant two years with no 'original' work except a few hymn-tunes. I wondered then if I were 'wasting my time'. The years were passing and I was adding nothing to the sum of musical invention. But I know now that two years of close association with some of the best (as well as some of the worst) tunes in the world was a better musical education than any amount of sonatas and fugues.

As I have already said, I have always found it difficult to study. I have learnt almost entirely what I have learnt by trying it on the dog. Gustav Holst once said to me years ago, 'We ought to be writing now what will enable us to write well later on.' This is a precept I find very difficult to observe. Young composers are apt to think that what they have written is what the world has been waiting for come at last. This is an intelligible and healthy state of mind, but they are also apt to think that it is 'now or never' and that this is the last as well as the greatest work they are going to write; and it is this attitude of mind which prevents so many students from learning to compose.

In 1908 I came to the conclusion that I was lumpy and stodgy; had come to a dead-end and that a little French polish would be of use to me. So I went to Paris armed with an introduction to Maurice Ravel. He was much puzzled at our first interview. When I had shown him some of my work he said that, for my first lesson, I had better 'écrire un petit menuet dans le style de Mozart'. I saw at once that it was time to act promptly, so I said in my best French: 'Look here, I have given up my time, my work, my friends, and my career to come here and learn from you, and I am *not* going to write a "petit menuet dans le style de Mozart".' After that we became great friends and I learnt much from him. For example, that the heavy contrapuntal Teutonic manner was not necessary; 'complexe, mais pas compliqué', was his motto. He showed me how to orchestrate in points of colour rather than in lines. It was an invigorating experience to find all artistic problems looked at from what was to me an entirely new angle.

Brahms and Tchaikovsky he lumped together as 'tout les deux un peu lourdes'—Elgar was 'tout à fait Mendelssohn'; his own music was 'tout à fait simple, rien que Mozart'. He was against development for its own sake—one should only develop for the sake of arriving at something better. He used to say there was an implied melodic outline in all vital music and instanced the opening of the C minor Symphony as an example of a tune which was not stated but was implicit. He was horrified that I had no pianoforte in the little hotel where I worked. 'Sans le piano on ne peut pas inventer des nouvelles harmonies.'

I practised chiefly orchestration with him. I used to score some of his own pianoforte music and bits of Rimsky and Borodin, to whom he introduced me for the first time. After three months I came home with a bad attack of French fever and wrote a string quartet which caused a friend to say that I must have been having tea with Debussy, and a song cycle with several atmospheric effects, but I did *not* succumb to the temptation of writing a piece about a cemetery, and Ravel paid me the compliment of telling me that I was the only pupil who 'n'écrit pas de ma musique'. The fact is that I could not have written Ravel's music even if I had wanted to. I am quite incapable, even with the pianoforte, of inventing his 'nouvelles harmonies'. I sometimes wish that I could think of the strange chords of my old friend, Arnold Bax. I hope I am not like the fox without the tail, but I feel content to provide good plain cooking and hope that the proof of the pudding will be in the eating.

My French fever soon subsided but left my musical metabolism, on the whole, healthier.

Another potent musical influence was S. P. Waddington.[2] His is one of the best informed minds on all subjects that I have ever met, one of those people in the presence of whom it is impossible to be mean or petty. He never would give me formal lessons, but he often looked at my work and pronounced sound judgements on it. He was the finest sight-reader I ever met and as I could not play at all myself his playing was often the first occasion I really heard my work. His power of deciphering a manuscript score was almost uncanny. If the manuscript was too illegible he would guess and invariably guessed right. With this power of sight-reading went that of immediately spotting weak moments and redundant bars. He was a severe critic—'You try to run before you can walk,' he once said to me; this was perfectly true; I had not sufficient patience or application to study. I have learnt by trial and error, I have drawers full of these errors; attempts to run with a fatal stumble almost every other bar. But one bit of study I did undertake. One summer I retired for a month to a Yorkshire farmhouse with several classical scores and the themes of my own 'compositions'. These themes I proceeded to treat and develop according to my classical models, choosing of course themes which more or less corresponded in structure. I found this a wonderful discipline and I have passed it on to my pupils. (I believe Charles Wood used much the same method.) The difficulty is that if the pupils invent ad hoc themes they are so colourless that they are incapable of development and they steadily refuse to make use of themes that they have already composed as being too sacrosanct for such base purposes. The model I most frequently use is the slow movement of Beethoven's Sonata, Op. 2 No. 2. It has so many points of subtle

[2] Waddington died in 1953.

structure and development which only a close bar-by-bar analysis reveals.

It was in the early years of this century that I first met George Butterworth. I think it was I who introduced him to folk-song. This was his salvation; his music up to then had showed great promise, but was much overshadowed by Brahms and Schumann. To him, as to me, the folk-song was not an inhibiting but a liberating influence; it certainly helped Butterworth to realize himself and to cast off the fetters of Teutonism.

If I helped Butterworth, much more did he help me. We were talking together one day when he said in his gruff, abrupt manner: 'You know, you ought to write a symphony.' I answered, if I remember aright, that I never had written a symphony and never intended to. This was not strictly true, for I had in earlier years sketched three movements of one symphony and the first movement of another, all now happily lost. I suppose that Butterworth's words stung me and, anyhow, I looked out some sketches I had made for what I believe was going to have been a symphonic poem (!) about London and decided to throw it into symphonic form. Butterworth assiduously saw me through my trouble and when the original full score was lost, helped to make a new one from the band parts.

The greatest influence on my music is one about which I feel I can write least. I remember my first meeting with Gustav Holst in 1895 very vividly. He quoted something from Sheridan's *The Critic*. How soon we started our 'Field Days' I cannot remember, but it must have been soon. On these occasions we would devote a whole day or at least an afternoon to examining each other's compositions. As I say, these orgies must have started early and they continued to the end, that is to say, for nearly forty years. I think he showed all he wrote to me and I nearly all I wrote to him. I say 'nearly all' advisedly, because sometimes I could not face the absolute integrity of his vision and I hid some of my worst crimes from him. I regret now that I did not face even his disapproval. Without him and Waddington to criticize me I sometimes feel lost: they both had the power and the will to give all they had.

Holst would spend hours bringing his mastery, his keen vision, and his feeling for clear texture to bear on my work especially in those clumsy places where I was continually getting into holes and could not find the way out. He would not rest till he had found a solution for the problem which not only satisfied him, but one which my obstinacy would accept. This was all the more wonderful because Holst, I know, found it difficult to appreciate the amateurish attitude of mind; his absolute sureness of purpose inclined him to be unsympathetic to the vacillations of human nature. This is why, for example, I never showed him my comic opera, because he never would have been able to understand how I could at the same time consider it trivial and yet want to write it.

I should like to place on record all that he did for me when I wrote *Job*. I should be alarmed to say how many 'Field Days' we spent over it. Then he came to all the orchestral rehearsals, including a special journey to Norwich, and finally, he insisted on the Camargo Society performing it. Thus I owe the life of *Job* to Holst, just as I owe the life of the Sea Symphony to Stanford and Allen.

I remember after the first orchestral rehearsal of *Job* his almost going on his knees to beg me to cut out some of the percussion with which my inferiority complex had led me to overload the score. Overscoring has always been one of my vices, and it arises, I am convinced, from the fact that I am not always sure enough of myself and have not the courage of my convictions and that I must hide my nakedness with an apron of orchestration. Holst's orchestra could be naked and unashamed.

(1950)

9

Charles Villiers Stanford

It is an honour and a pleasure to be given the opportunity to write about my teacher, Charles Villiers Stanford, the centenary of whose birth we celebrate this year. Stanford was a great composer, a great teacher, a skilled conductor, and as befits a true Irishman, a lovable, quarrelsome, and generous man.

He has written some of the most beautiful music that has come from these islands. He realized that all art which is worth while must spring from its own soil. He made an exhaustive study of his own Irish folk music; some of his arrangements, notably those known to British hearers as 'The Arbutus Tree' and 'Father O'Flynn', are household words. Stanford dedicated his arrangements to Brahms, and presumably sent him a copy. Now the last movement of Brahms's pianoforte quintet contains a phrase out of one of these Irish melodies. . . . I am not sure enough of my dates to say whether the egg or the hen came first, but the coincidence is striking.

Of course in Stanford's enormous output there is bound to be a certain amount of dull music; but, after all, so there is in Beethoven and Bach. At times his very facility led him astray. He could, at will, use the technique of any composer and often use it better than the original, as in 'The Middle Watch', where he beats Delius at his own game. Sometimes he could not resist adding a clever touch which marred the purity of his inspiration, as in the sophisticated repetition of the words 'lead the line' at the end of the otherwise beautiful song 'Sailing at Dawn'. The bright young things of the younger generation do not seem to know much about Stanford, and not having had the advantage of his teaching are inclined to ignore what he did and what he taught. But I believe that he will return again. With the next generation the inevitable reaction will set in and Stanford will come into his own. His smaller works are still known and loved by our choral societies, and I cannot but believe that such splendid music as the *Stabat Mater*, *Requiem*, and *Songs of the Fleet* will not strike home as soon as opportunity is given to hear them. It is up to our concert societies, in this centenary year, to give us these works as well as the 'Irish' Symphony and Rhapsodies and the many fine songs. In any continental country the centenary of a composer of Stanford's calibre would have been celebrated in every opera house in the country. Covent Garden and Sadlers Wells cannot even give us an opportunity of hearing such splendid works with all the certainty of popularity as *Much Ado* and *Shamus O'Brien*. Instead of which they choose to shake the dead bones of *Norma* and *Sanson et Dalilah*.

Many of Stanford's songs were written for that fine but very individual singer, Plunket Greene. It is difficult, therefore, to capture their quality, but the printed line remains for any singer who will take the trouble to read the old spirit into the notes.

The belittling of Stanford's work was encouraged by one who ought to have known better. The late Bernard Shaw, in the first number of *Music and Letters*, used Elgar as a stick to beat what he called 'the Academic clique', forgetting—or pretending to forget—that it was the acknowledged head of this 'clique', Hubert Parry, who was instrumental in obtaining the first performance of Elgar's Variations. Shaw was rather proud of having called Stanford a 'gentleman amateur' since he repeated the expression more than once. Apparently the word 'gentleman' was to Shaw a term of abuse, and as to 'amateur', who could have been more professional in his methods than Stanford? Indeed, it was this very technical expertness that was an occasional snare to him.

Stanford had none of the clumsiness of his contemporaries. Though a great admirer of Brahms, he did not imitate his awkward execution. Stanford's orchestration, though perhaps unadventurous, is a model of clarity: every stroke tells. It was the fashion, as I have said, among a certain class of journalists about fifty years ago to describe Parry, Stanford, and others who ruled at the Royal College of Music as 'academic', which apparently meant that they founded the emotion of their music on knowledge and not on mere sensation. To these critics, admiration of Brahms was equivalent to dry as dust pedantry. If they are still alive they must feel rather foolish when they see Brahms filling the house at a Promenade Concert.

Stanford was a great teacher, and like all great teachers he was narrow minded. A broad-minded teacher is useless. To say that he was strict was to put it mildly. Everything he disapproved of had no quarter. It was 'damnably ugly' and that was the end of it. Once, when I was his pupil, I showed him what I considered was a world-shaking masterpiece; he looked at it and then said curtly: 'All rot, my boy.' He was quite right. It was. But it took me some time to discover it. The work is now, happily, lost. The only way to get good out of a teacher is to divest yourself entirely of your own personality and do what your teacher wants; only in that way can you get any good out of him. I was hopelessly obstinate. In order to secure a lighter touch in my work he once told me to write a waltz. At that time I was obsessed with the modes. I wrote him a modal waltz!

Stanford as a conductor had no truck with the temperamental orchestral director; his object was to present faithfully what the composer intended. For that reason the silly journalists who labelled him 'academic' complained that he lacked imaginative fancy. Against this let me set the opinion of Eugene Goossens who told me that he was the finest interpreter of Brahms that he had ever heard.

Stanford's misunderstanding with Elgar was unfortunate for both men, but in spite of this, in spite of the fact that he was temperamentally allergic to *Gerontius*, he urged, though in vain, that it be performed in Leeds. He was also instrumental in obtaining for his supposed enemy an honorary Doctorate at Cambridge University.

Stanford's career, after his childhood and youth in Dublin, may be divided into two periods. The first dates from his appointment as organist at Trinity, College Cambridge, and afterwards as Professor in the University; that was in the 'seventies when critics were still talking about 'the unhealthy influence of Wagner and Brahms'. Stanford, fresh from Leipzig, astonished his audiences by playing the Overture to *Die Meistersinger* from the full score on the organ. It was this I suppose that made the Master of Trinity introduce him to a friend as 'Mr. Stanford, whose playing always charms us, and occasionally astonishes; and I may add that the less he astonishes the more he charms.'

Stanford's second period begins when he left Cambridge, about 1893, and lived in London. He was already conductor of the London Bach Choir, and later became conductor of the Leeds Festival: still continuing his immense output of music, often inspired, sometimes less inspired, but keeping always within the bounds of classical beauty.

An artist cannot always control his inspiration, but Stanford saw to it that his tools were bright and sharp and fashioned of tempered steel. His music is educated music, founded on the great traditions by one who was determined to uphold the nobility of his art.

(1952)

10

The Mass in B Minor in English: A Programme Note

The text of Bach's Mass in B minor to be sung tonight is an attempt to adapt the words of the English Liturgy to Bach's music.

Why is such an adaptation desirable?

To many, the Latin text has connotations which are repugnant: again, as a choral singer once said to me, 'We like to sing what we understand.' One might add, what they can pronounce. When Latin has to be represented phonetically by such hideous gibberish as 'Kwee prohptair noce hoh-mee-nace', as given in a well-known book on choral singing, surely it is time something was done.

A third, to my mind, cogent reason for this adaptation is that it will enable this great music to be sung at Anglican services.

The task has been beset with pitfalls; it would indeed have been comparatively easy to have made a translation into the most approved 'libretto English' which would have fitted the music like a glove—e.g. 'Et resurrexit tertia die secundum scripturas' might have become, 'The third bright morn saw his arising as prophets told of eld'. Nor is the English text necessarily a translation; e.g. 'hominibus bonae voluntatis' becomes 'Goodwill towards men'.

The English have a very proper traditional reverence for the incomparable language of their liturgy, and any distortion of this would, I believe, cause offence to many, as have similar distortions of the English Bible in the *St. Matthew Passion* and Mendelssohn's *Elijah*. It seems, therefore, worth while occasionally to alter a crotchet into two quavers, to re-articulate a tied note, or even (occasionally) to add a note, or (very occasionally) to omit one, for the sake of keeping the Prayer Book text unaltered. My principles have generally been as follows:

1. When Bach attaches a particular word to a particular group of notes for expressive purposes, every attempt has been made to keep that marriage intact; where that is impossible, a word with a similar emotional connotation has been used—e.g., in the *Credo* (Novello, page 96, line 1; Peters, page 79, line 3, soprano), where 'Credo' is represented by 'One God'.

Similarly in the *Dona Nobis* I have represented 'Pacem' by 'Grant us', the vowel sounds and the emotional connotation are the same and 'Peace' would have been very awkward.

In many cases, however, the connexion between word and note is obviously fortuitous; in that case it seemed more important to consider the syllabic rather than the emotional connexion, e.g., in the *Gloria* (Novello, page 39, line 1; Peters, page 32, line 2, soprano). Here it must be admitted that the 'Pax, pax' of Bach is rather a mouthful, and 'Peace, peace' would be worse; so I have substituted 'Good will'.

2. The Latin language abounds in feminine endings while the ends of most English sentences are masculine; e.g., how is 'Gloria in excelsis Deo' to be fitted to 'Glory be to God on high'? In this case (Novello, p. 29, line 5; Peters, p. 26, line 5, soprano), I have fitted the complete sentence to the beginning of the musical phrase and repeated the word 'Glory' for 'Deo'. The effect is perhaps rhetorical, but I hope not worse for that.[1]

3. So far as possible the note values have been kept intact. Occasionally it has been necessary to substitute two crotchets for a minim and vice versa; sometimes a tied note has been re-articulated and, as already mentioned, I have been obliged in a few cases to add notes, and in a very few to omit them.

4. Bach repeated the words of his text several times so as to expand each paragraph into a long musical movement. I have been careful to give the text complete at the first statement, but later on in the movement to use only such words as are suitable. The *locus classicus* of this procedure, and also the most thorny problem I

---

[1] *Note:* In other places also I have made rhetorical use of language—e.g. 'crucified' without verb or pronoun.

have had to solve, comes in the *Quoniam* (No. 10) and *Cum Sancto* (No. 11). It was a convention in Bach's time to write a fugue for the *Cum Sancto*. Bach, who never defied convention, but used it for his own great purposes, obeyed the convention here: but in England we have no such convention, and it would sound rather absurd to sing the most jubilant music in the world to 'with the Holy Ghost, in the glory of God the Father'. Moreover, Bach, when setting these words, surely had in his mind not any ecclesiastical dogma, but an expression of the 'Glory of God the Father'. Therefore I feel justified in leaving out any extraneous words in this chorus. Nevertheless, by my rules I was obliged to fit the complete sentence in somewhere. Why not at the end of the *Quoniam*? Here the word 'altissimus' actually occurs, which in English becomes 'Most High', the structure of the Latin sentence being quite different from that of the English; this leaves me free to use the words, 'Thou only art most high in the glory of God the Father. Amen', as a fitting background for what is, to some of us, the greatest musical movement ever written.

(1947 and 1948)

11

Shrubsole

We are told in the text-books that the eighteenth century was the nadir of English music. As a matter of fact it is from the eighteenth century that some of the strongest and most characteristic of our musical invention dates, albeit on a small scale, exemplified, perhaps, by a hymn-tune or a chant; but what does size matter? Who would not rather have drawn eight bars straight from the fountain-head than have compiled whole symphonies strained very thin through the medium of the best foreign models?

It has always been the case in the history of English music that the bright young sparks with dazzling ideas, who imagine the home circle too narrow and the home ideals too low wander off, spiritually if not physically, to foreign countries and return lisping in bad German or Italian, and have left it to the homely people with homely names, who practised their art in their plebeian homes and in the chapels in the local lanes ('Miles Lane Chapel'—what a picture it calls up!), to write what was characteristic and strong and lasting.

The fashionable and learned world knew nothing of these humble folk. The fashionable amateurs were worshipping at the shrine of Handel and Buononcini; the learned, as typified by Burney, travelled round Europe discovering Porpora and Philipp Emmanuel Bach, but not John Sebastian Bach.

To digress a moment. Why did J. S. Bach mean nothing to Burney? Was it because J. S. Bach was too democratic and had to wait for a later generation, who after the Industrial Revolution brought into prominence their ideals of 'Miles Lane'—namely, the people who sang in the local choirs and choral societies to whom music meant scraping on the fiddle and blowing on the clarinet in the parlour behind the shop after business hours?

John Sebastian Bach wrote (of necessity, I admit) for the amateur; that is why Bach's voice parts are so interesting and Handel's so dull. Bach knew that unless he gave his amateurs something interesting to sing they would desert him. Handel knew that the unhappy professional choralist had to sing what he was told or he would lose his fee. The truth is that J. S. Bach is much more akin to Shrubsole than to Burney. Both had the outlook of the 'local musician'—the life bounded by the church choir and the town choral society. The intrigues of the 'Italian' opera and the attitude to art typified by the 'primo uomo' were not for them. It is true that Bach's fame penetrated to Berlin and that Shrubsole was for a short time organist at Bangor Cathedral, but Bach was glad to be home again with Magdalena and the children and Shrubsole had to leave Bangor because he openly preferred the 'conventicle'.

Shrubsole wrote this one superb tune and no more—at least no more of any note. He was a 'one tune' man. There are many such: people who get a glimpse of the eternal glory once in a lifetime for a few moments and, like Gerontius, are blinded by it and turn their faces away for ever; but in that one moment these Shrubsolian composers may have achieved something which neither Beethoven nor Bach could have bettered. It is to be noted that these moments will not be realized without long and careful preparation, so that the interminable oratorios and cantatas of minor composers which are now crowding our salvage heaps are not waste, because without them the moment of inspiration could not have been caught.

It is on these foundations that the music of a nation is built up on this soil, and on this only, that the great artist can come to maturity. It takes a thousand small composers to make one great one—this is some comfort to those of us who feel the urge to 'find out musical tunes', knowing at the same time that our compositions are destined for the lumber-room during our lifetime and eventually for the waste-paper baskets of our executors. At all events our forgotten symphonies and fugues will form the 'humus' which alone can fertilize the great flower which blooms but once in a hundred years.

Of course, 'Miles Lane' owes something to the splendid words to which it is set, which, as Percy Dearmer writes, 'rang the changes on the rhymes to "Lord of All". Immortality was the inevitable result', but it was left to Shrubsole to add the coping-stone to the structure with his threefold repetition of the words 'Crown Him'. I do not suggest that this is a new device; we find it in that other great tune 'Helmsley', where the double repetition of 'Deeply wailing' and 'O come quickly' produces an almost unbearable emotional stress, and we find its reductio ad absurdum in the probably apocryphal 'Come down Sal' and 'O for a man' story.

The composer of 'Miles Lane' realized to the full the dramatic possibilities of this repetition. Great men do not necessarily invent the means which they use, but they see their full possibilities. Bach did not invent the Choral Prelude, but he carried it to its logical conclusion. Beethoven did not invent the sonata form, but he developed it from a precise dance pattern to an epic poem.

This, then, is the history of a tune which Elgar is credibly reported to have pronounced the finest in English hymnody; and, be it noted, the tune is not by Byrd or Purcell, Boyce or Arne, it was not written for Westminster Abbey or York Minster, it was composed by William Shrubsole for Miles Lane Chapel. It is this that gives it the strength which arises direct from the spiritual needs of that great middle class which is the salt of England's earth. What is the moral of all this? Virginia Woolf writes:

Masterpieces are not single and solitary births; they are the outcome of many years' thinking in common, of thinking by the body of the people, so that the experience of the many is behind the single voice.

Without Veit Bach there would never have been John Sebastian. Would the *Magic Flute* ever have existed without the spade-work of Adam Hiller? These lesser people, with their limited but intense vision, can concentrate that vision into sixteen bars better than those great ones whose minds are occupied with symphonies forty minutes long, and it is certainly true that whereas Shrubsole could not have written *Gerontius*, Elgar could not have written 'Miles Lane'.

Immortality plays us strange tricks. Perhaps hundreds of years hence when Byrd and Purcell and Parry and Stanford and Elgar and Walton are mere names in dictionaries, a tune by an obscure composer of Canterbury will still be remembered and loved in 'Quires and places where they sing'.

(1943)

THE MAKING OF MUSIC

1

Why Do We Make Music?

Why do we make music? There can be no doubt that at certain emotional moments most people want to make particular kinds of noises. Indeed, we may say with Carlyle that if we search deep enough there is music everywhere. But why? Neither I, nor anyone else, has been able to solve that problem. But one thing we can be certain of: we do not compose, sing, or play music for any useful purpose. It is not so with the other arts: Milton had to use the medium of words whether he was writing *Paradise Lost* or making out his laundry list; Velasquez had to use paint both for his *Venus* and to cover up the dirty marks on his front door. But music is just music, and that is, to my mind, its great glory. How then do I justify music? There is no need to justify it, it is its own justification; that is all I know and all I need to know.

2

What is Music?

Before we go further we had better have a definition of what we mean by music, and I would define it thus: music is a reaching out to the ultimate realities by means of ordered sound. By 'ordered sound' I mean sounds of a definite pitch in a definite rhythm and, perhaps we should add, with a definite harmony. But it may be asked what does music mean? A lot of nonsense is talked nowadays about the 'meaning' of music. Music indeed has a meaning, though it is not one that can be expressed in words. Mendelssohn used to say that the meaning of music was too precise for words. The hearer may, of course, if he chooses, narrow the meaning of music to fit words or visual impressions, as for example in opera. But this particularization limits the scope of music. The fire on Brünnhilde's rock may have suggested Wagner's music to him; but the music goes further and transports us from the particular to the universal. Liszt used to talk rather foolishly about it being nobler for a piece of music to be about Orpheus than to be a mere pattern in sound, not realizing that it is these great patterns in sound, designed by Beethoven or Bach, which open the magic casements and enable us to understand what is beyond the appearances of life.

There are two theories of how these ordered sounds arose. Some people think that they grew out of excited speech, some that they developed from blowing through a pipe pierced at definite intervals with holes.

I do not want to set up my opinion against that of those learned musicologists who hold the pipe theory. But an ounce of experience is worth a pound of speculation, and I want to describe a personal experience, when I actually heard excited speech grow into melody. I once heard a sermon at an open-air service in the Isle of Skye. As the preacher spoke in Gaelic, which I do not understand, I was able to devote my attention to the actual tones of his voice. The fact that he was out of doors forced him to speak loud, and that, coupled with the emotional excitement which inspired his words, caused him gradually to leave off speaking and actually, unconsciously of course, to sing. At first he was content with a monotone, but as his excitement grew, he gradually evolved the following melodic formulae:

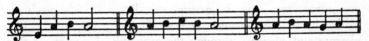

Now these melodic formulae are common to the opening of many Scottish and British folk-songs; here are two examples:

'Bushes and Briars'

'Searching for Lambs'

This experience has convinced me that these melodic formulae come spontaneously to the minds of primitive singers. We can hardly believe that our preacher obtained his notes by blowing through a mathematically measured pipe. I have lately read a book by the Reverend George Chambers in which he describes how in primitive religious services the logical meaning of the words spoken proved inadequate and was supplemented by song, including cantilenas on pure vowel sounds, which were called 'jubilations'; these evidently had a mystical meaning to their singers that words

* From *English Folk Songs*, collected and arranged by Cecil J. Sharp, selected ed. (London: Novello and Co., n.d.), I, 74. By permission.

could not give them. Indeed, as I have already said, the meaning of music is beyond words.

We now come to the question of rhythm. What is rhythm? I have tried various sources for a satisfactory definition and have, so far, failed. Frank Howes, the musical critic of the London *Times*, calls it 'an innate faculty for the apprehension of time'. Here is Professor Carl Seashore's definition: 'An instinctive disposition to group recurrent sense impressions vividly and with precision, mainly by time or intensity, or both, in such a way as to derive pleasure and efficiency through the grouping.' I cannot see that either of these is very helpful. Other writers talk magniloquently about the importance of rhythm, not only in art, but in life, without troubling to explain what they mean when they talk about the rhythm of life. (Incidentally, I much dislike the modern practice of using the technical terms of one art to illustrate another, as when one speaks of the tempo of an essay, or the orchestration of a picture, or the rhythm of a building.) Perhaps the word is indefinable. A French musician is reported to have said to a lady who asked him what rhythm was, 'Madame, if you have already rhythm in your nature, there is no need for me to explain it to you; if you have not, you would not understand my explanation.' Or there is Lord Haldane's famous epigram: 'I cannot define an elephant, but I recognize one when I see it.' In the same way, without being able to explain it, those who are naturally musical can appreciate rhythm, or the want of it, in a piece of music.

Here are one or two examples of the way in which a very slight alteration in rhythm can entirely change the nature of a melody. Compare the opening of Brahms's B flat Pianoforte Concerto with the 'Inter oves' from Verdi's *Requiem*. Both extracts are in the same key, their notes are identical—except for one slight rhythmical change. But how extraordinarily different they sound.

Here is another, stronger example. The well-known English dance-tune, 'Sellenger's Round', apparently crossed over to Germany, and by the ironing out of the rhythm became converted from a lively dance measure to a solemn hymn-tune.

'Sellenger's Round'

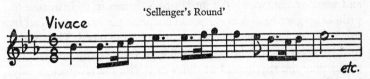

'Valet will Ich'—J. S. Bach, after Teschner

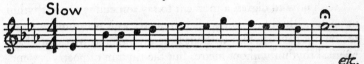

And as a climax I will quote from Edmund Gurney's *The Power of Sound*, in which by rhythmical distortion he converts the magnificent chorale melody, 'Ein' feste Burg', into a vulgar jig tune.

J. S. Bach, after Luther

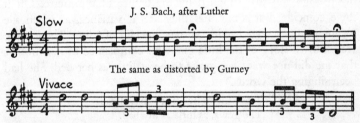

The same as distorted by Gurney

In this connexion it must be confessed that the tune as Martin Luther is supposed to have played it on his flute to his family seems rather a poor affair; it was left to Bach to develop it into magnificence in his Cantata No. 80.

The Greek word *rhythmos* means 'flow'; so flow may be taken to be an essential part of rhythm. An orderly succession of sounds at regular intervals is also a part of rhythm, but it is not, as many people imagine, the whole of rhythm. The ticking of a clock, for example, is not rhythmical, because it has no periodic accents. Some years ago an American, Dr. Thaddeus Lincoln Bolton, made the following experiment: A machine like a clock, with absolutely regular ticks but without any accent, was set going, and several people were asked to give their impression of what they heard.

Almost all said that after a certain number of ticks, usually three or four, the next appeared louder. This was a purely mental illusion and was due to the desire for rhythmical quality implicit in their nature. This gives us another principle of rhythm, that of strong and weak accent, which the monks of Solesmes in their treatise on plainsong describe as *élan et repos*. This principle has been called by other writers 'exertion and rest', or 'impulse and relax'. The Greeks, in their poetry, used the words *arsis* and *thesis*, 'rising and falling', to describe the rhythmical qualities of poetic metres. Incidentally, both these words are derived from dancing.

I wish now to digress a moment to say something about rhythm in poetry. Rhythm is as essential to poetry as it is to music, and as we cannot have rhythm without time in music, so we cannot have poetical rhythm without metre. But the rhythm of poetry is something more than this. Is not the caesura a momentary breaking of the metre for the sake of the larger aspect of rhythm? In poetry there are always two kinds of accent, that supplied by the sense of the passage and that supplied by the nature of the metre. Often these coincide, but sometimes they are at variance, as when the meaning of a passage carries on over the end of a line. There is the well-known story of the little girl who complained to her mother that she did not want her grave to be as little as her bed. She had been singing the words,

> Teach me to live that I may dread
> The grave, as little as my bed.

When she sang it with the tune, it became,

> Teach me to live that I may dread,
> The grave as little as my bed.

Another humorous example of this cross accent is the clown's prologue in *A Midsummer Night's Dream*.

I should like to add one personal experience. I was setting to music one of Gilbert Murray's translations of Euripides, and I came upon these lines:

> Only on them that spurn
> Joy, may his anger burn.[1]

---

[1] From *The Bacchae*, ll. 425–426, in *The Complete Greek Drama*, ed. by Whitney J. Oates and Eugene O'Neill, Jr. (New York: Random House, 1938), II, 241. By permission of George Allen & Unwin.

I pointed out to Professor Murray that if I set the words strictly according to their meaning, it would convert the verse into prose:

Only on them that spurn joy, may his anger burn.

If I set it strictly according to the metre, it would make nonsense of the words:

Only on them that spurn,
Joy may his anger burn.

He solved my difficulties by declaiming the lines to me in a manner which I can describe only by musical notation:

On-ly on them that spurn Joy, may his anger burn

From the question of rhythm we pass naturally to the question of form, which is, after all, nothing more than rhythm on a large scale. We often hear people say, 'I know nothing about musical form, but I like a good tune when I hear it.' They do not realize that to appreciate the simplest tune requires a knowledge of form. The physical ear can hear only one sound, or a vertical group of sounds, at a time; the rest is a question of memory, co-ordination, and anticipation. When the first note passes on to the second, the hearer must not only keep the first note in memory, but co-ordinate it with the second, and so on to the third; and occasionally he has to anticipate what is to come. When community singers are learning a new tune, they often get the tune wrong because they anticipate a different note from what actually comes. If we did not have these powers, the simplest tune would be meaningless. To appreciate the 'Hammerklavier' Sonata or the Ninth Symphony requires exactly the same qualities as the appreciation of the simplest tune—such as 'The Bluebell of Scotland', which any child can learn—only to a greater degree. Musical form is not a series of mysteries or trade secrets but is simply the development of a power natural to the human ear and the human mind. To understand a big symphonic work there is no need to look up text-books or memorize regulations; one need only develop the qualities of attention, memory, and co-ordination to the utmost. One thing, however, is needful: the whole passage, whether it be a folk tune or a symphony, must grow, organically, from its roots.

This leads us on to the question of form and content. These two words are often taken to mean separate and opposite parts of an artistic structure. We talk about the form of a sonata being good and its content poor; but it not the content poor because the form is bad? And so we go on, ad infinitum. It is the content which settles the form of any organic structure.

What, after all, is good content? Is it not a matter of suitability to its purpose? The opening theme of the 'Eroica' Symphony is just an arpeggio, and not original at that, but what a wonderful foundation for a great movement! The famous drum passage at the end of the Scherzo of Beethoven's C minor Symphony would not, without its context, be evidence of the mind of a great composer; but coming where it does, as a sort of resurrection from the abyss, at the end of the Scherzo, and then building up on those reiterated drum taps into the glorious outburst of the finale, does it not reveal the master mind at work? The theme connected with the Rheingold in Wagner's *Ring* is a little flourish such as any boy bugler might have invented. But coming where it does, its dramatic effect is overwhelming. In all these cases there is organic connexion between the whole and the parts. This organic connexion can also exist between symphonic themes which have little physical resemblance. The second subject of the finale of Mozart's G minor Symphony runs as follows:

When it reappears in the recapitulation, it is hardly recognizable, mechanically speaking, as the same theme. But its inevitable rightness in its place and its organic connexion with the original idea make it a true development.

Now comes the question of harmony. It is doubtful whether this should count as a fundamental element of music, because, so far as we can make out, primitive music had no harmony but was purely melodic. This is true, so far as we can tell, of the early Greek music. The word *harmonia* does not mean harmony in our sense of the word, but the relation to each other of the notes in the Greek modes. The same is true of the plainsong of the early Christian church, and folk-song, at all events in western Europe, was sung without harmonic accompaniment. However, it seems almost impossible that harmony should not have occurred to primitive singers and players, if only by accident. A cithara player must occasionally have twanged two strings at the same time; or if two pipe players happened to be playing at the same time within hearing distance of each other, this must have resulted in harmony, or even counterpoint. Why did not the performers carry on with the good work? The only explanation can be that when they heard the result they disliked it. There is no physical reason why an eighteenth-century composer should not have written the whole of Stravinsky and Schönberg, provided he had the pen and paper. We know as a fact that Stanley, an eighteenth-century English composer, experimented with the whole-tone scale about a hundred years before Debussy. Here are two examples, one from Mozart's quartet in C major and one from Haydn's Prelude to *The Creation*, which anticipate Wagner's 'Tristan'.

Introduction to Quartet in C major—Mozart

Representation of chaos in *The Creation*—Haydn

These harmonies were, for these two composers, obviously an experiment; they had no emotional significance for them. For Wagner, an almost identical passage symbolized the height of amorous passion. To Haydn and Mozart they had no such suggestion. When Mozart wanted to be erotic he wrote 'Là ci darem'.

Now let us look at the obverse of the medal. Debussy's strange atmospheric effects still thrill us, though they are by now the common property of every conservatory student. And when these same students write out bits of Debussy, under the impression that they are composing, their efforts fall dead even before the ink is dry. The moral of all this seems to be that any musical phrase, to be a complete artistic whole, must be the result of a personal emotion.

These, then, are the three elements which go to make up music—melody, rhythm, and harmony.

3

How Do We Make Music?

Among the foundations of our art we can count the means by which the singer or player communicates his ideas to others—what we call musical notation. But first I want to try to dispose of a very prevalent fallacy. My old teacher, Max Bruch, used to say to me, 'You must not write eye music, you must write ear music.' He, at all events, had got hold of the truth. But many musical writers who ought to know better think that music is not what we hear with our ears but what we see on the printed or written page; and some of them say with pride that they never want to hear music, it is enough for them to see the score. I suppose I must take them at their word that they can tell exactly what the music will sound like by reading it.

Now music differs from the sister art of poetry in that the emotion of poetry grows out of the meaning of words and can be achieved as well by reading as by hearing. If you listen to a poem recited in a language you do not understand, you get very little of the emotion that the poem is intended to express. Sometimes, indeed, you get something quite different, as in the ludicrous case of the audience at Covent Garden who, when the prisoners in *Fidelio* were whispering 'leise, leise', tittered with amusement because they were reminded of a popular song of the day about a young lady called 'Liza.

Many people imagine that a printed page of music is the equivalent of a painted picture; but the painter has a dual nature, he is both composer and performer. A picture is the finished article; but this is not so with a page of music, which is, at the best, a rough description of what the composer hopes will happen if the sounds he has indicated by certain symbols are produced in actuality. Until this takes place the music does not exist. A page of music should be

H

compared, not to a picture, but to a map, which indicates by certain conventional signs where north and south are, the direction of a road, what sort of road it is, how high the hills are, whether they are steep or gradual, where there are buildings, and so on. The expert map reader, like the expert score reader, may be able to tell fairly exactly what sort of country he may expect to find, but he cannot possibly experience the beauty of the trees, the intense emotion of a wonderful landscape, the exhilaration of rushing down hill on a bicycle, or the delightful relaxation when he reaches the comfortable inn, indicated, in England at all events, by the magic letters 'P.H.' So it is with the score reader. Haydn would never have declared that his great shout, 'Let there be light!' came straight from heaven if he had been content to read the music and not hear it. Nor would Ulysses have been obliged to be tied to the mast if the Sirens, instead of singing to him, had given him a presentation copy of the full score.

In primitive times a written score was unnecessary because the composer and the performer were the same individual, who wanted to touch the heart of those, only, who were within hearing distance. But supposing the musician's fame grew and people far off wanted to hear his music, what was to be done then? He must invent and write out a series of symbols which will say in effect, 'If you sing, blow, scratch, or hit exactly according to the directions here given, you will make the same sound as I have been imagining.' Or, to put it in another way, the composer has a vision and he wants others, out of earshot, to share that vision; so he crystallizes that vision into definite musical sounds. Then he devises a series of black dots, circles, and so on which will explain what sounds must be made in order to realize his vision. This is what is called musical notation. It is notoriously inadequate, so that those who translate these symbols into music are bound by their personal equation and each performs slightly differently. Thus come about what we call the different renderings by great performers or conductors of the same music. Those who are going to translate these black dots into sound must first find out how to use them adequately. Also, they must learn to realize, when the sounds are made, the connexion between the various notes which they produce and the ultimate meaning of it all. Then, and then only, can they realize in sound the vision that has passed through all these stages and back again to arrive once more at the magic casements and the fairyland which lies beyond them.

What are the sources of a composer's inspiration? Now inspiration and originality do not necessarily mean something no one has ever heard before. To my mind the most original of present-day composers is Jean Sibelius. All he says in his great moments seems to me absolutely new; but his actual method of diction is purely traditional. As Hans Sachs said of Walther, 'It was so old, it sounded so new.'

We often find that music which at its first appearance seemed *outré*, to the dismay of the audience and the delight of the composer, becomes quite outmoded after a few years and gives way to a new method of shocking the bourgeois. In Leipzig, in the eighteenth century, Bach was already considered an old fogey, and all the bright young things swore by Telemann. Bach, after a period of eclipse, has come back into his own, while Telemann only bores us.

When Liszt produced his well-known pianoforte concerto, it was hailed by one school of German thought as something new and incomprehensible to the public, while Brahms was condemned as being *routinier* and academic. Now Brahms sounds as fresh as ever, while, to one hearer at least, the music of Liszt seems intolerably old-fashioned.

Therefore I beg all young composers not to try to be original, within the narrow sense of the word. Originality will come of itself if it is in one's nature. This does not mean that the composer must be careless and thoughtless. It is hard, indeed, to find a true expression of one's vision. But the artist must not rest until he has discovered the *mot juste*. If another composer has said the same thing before, so much the worse for the other composer. The originality, or perhaps I should say the personality, of music depends very little on the actual outline of the notes. It derives from something more subtle, which perhaps we cannot define but can recognize at once. Schumann used to say that Beethoven's chromatic scales sounded different from other people's. Here are three fugue subjects, each distinct and individual, but built up on the same phrase:

'And with His stripes'—Handel

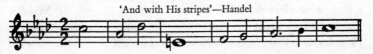

Forty-eight Preludes and Fugues, No. 20, from Book II (transposed)—Bach

Kyrie from the *Requiem* (transposed)—Mozart

One of the most important elements of our art is the craft which must inevitably accompany it—the craft of the composer, the performer, and the instrument maker. These three are inseparably connected. The player must have something to play; the composer is impotent unless there is someone to realize his ideas; and both of them are lost, except of course in the case of vocal music, unless there is someone who can devise and construct a machine to carry out the composer's ideas through the skill of the performer.

In primitive times these three persons were probably merged in one: a man thought of a tune; next he had to cut a reed and pierce it with holes so as to make the noises he needed; then he had to acquire enough skill to make these noises. But perhaps things did not always happen in that order. Perhaps he heard a song tune and, having a sore throat, wanted to realize it in some other way. Or perhaps, like the lady in 'The Lost Chord', his 'fingers wandered idly Over the noisy keys' until he found something that he liked. Or perhaps he made the pipe first and in trying it out hit upon a good tune.

These methods still exist in modern times. We are told in textbooks that a composer must write down his ideas without going near an instrument. Indeed 'composing at the pianoforte' was described by R. O. Morris as 'not quite playing the game'. Nevertheless it is a practice that I hope all young composers will indulge in freely, when they are in the mood and the teacher is out of earshot. Inspiration does not necessarily come from the brain. Unfortunately, one cannot play the pianoforte with one's solar plexus, but I see no reason why ideas should not ooze out of the finger tips. Maurice Ravel used to blame me for trying to compose without using a pianoforte, saying, 'How then can you invent new harmonies?' I do not suggest to composers that they should invent, like the young genius in the films, with one hand holding a pen and the other improvising at the pianoforte, but I can see no moral harm, and great artistic advantage, in making certain of our ideas by trying them over and exploring their possibilities at the pianoforte.

Where does craft end and art begin? When I first heard the Prelude to *Lohengrin*, I wondered how Wagner had devised all those wonderful high string effects. But when I saw the full score I realized that I, or any other composer, would have done the same *if only we had thought of the music*. I was like the schoolboy who said, 'I could easily have written all that Shakespeare stuff myself if I'd only thought of it.'

Craft by itself can do nothing, I admit, and in some ways is a dangerous thing. When a composer of great skill finds his invention at a low ebb, he can still write music which almost deceives the elect, and he himself sometimes cannot tell whether he is inspired or whether he is doing mere routine work. Nevertheless, the most inspired composer is impotent unless his craft keeps pace with his art.

It is now fashionable to teach children painting without any technical training. They are given a paintbox and a brush and told to 'express themselves'. I have seen the results. The children could not draw a straight line and had no idea of anatomy or perspective. When I pointed this out to the drawing mistress, she rebuked me and told me that the 'feeling' was wonderful. Fortunately, in music we still believe, to a certain extent, in technique. But, in England at all events, we are no longer allowed to speak of harmony and counterpoint but must call our theoretic studies 'paper work'. I am glad to say that I was brought up in the traditional manner. I worked right through MacFarren's *Harmony* and the Cherubinic system of counterpoint and have never regretted it. At a recent meeting of modern composers the only thing they all agreed on was that the only sure foundation for musical composition was strict counterpoint.

We now come to a very important factor in our art, the means by which we make the necessary noises. The chief of these is the human voice, which has been called the perfect instrument—perfect in the sense that there is a minimum of mechanism between the initial impulse and the result. The voice in this respect is unlike the oboe or horn, in which the connexion is not so direct between the performer's will and the sound he makes.

The scope of the human voice is, of course, limited. The range of the four main voices, bass, tenor, contralto, and soprano, is not more than four octaves, from C below the bass clef to c''' above the treble clef, except in the case of Russian basses and freak sopranos. On the other hand, the art of singing is nearly universal; most people can sing a bit. Moreover, the technique and the nature of the human voice is very much what it was two thousand years ago. This is why choral music has remained in the straight road much more than has instrumental writing. In *a cappella* singing there are no instrument makers to lure the composer aside with exciting new devices. When Stravinsky writes his *Symphony of Psalms*, one can feel that he is dealing with something fundamental, almost primitive. In the choral music of Copland the tradition of the white spiritual unconsciously affects his music. Music for voices deals with something essential, not with the tricks of presentation.

Whether the instrument or voice came first, there can be very little doubt that the pipe and harp appear very soon in primitive music, and the question arises, Was it the inventions of instrument makers which enticed composers into new styles of music or was it the imperious demands of the composers for fresh means of expression which led the instrument makers to see what they could do to help? We can imagine that Strephon made a pipe for Amaryllis to play the little tunes that she had invented; did Amaryllis say that her new tune demanded an extra hole in the pipe, or did Strephon tell Amaryllis that he had pierced a new hole and expected her, forthwith, to make use of it?

Up to the sixteenth century music was almost entirely vocal, unable to move very fast, but capable of holding a sound for a long time. Then came the development of the lute and virginals, unable to sustain sounds like the voice but able to play very quickly. So composers of virginal music invented a new means of covering the ground by the use of elaborate scales and arpeggios, as we find in the final cadences of almost all virginal music. These limitations and new capabilities led the way from the pure choral counterpoint of Palestrina to the instrumental polyphony of Bach. For the harpsichord, though it could not hold long notes, could play the quick passages and could achieve phrases and intervals which would be unsingable by unaccompanied voices.

Bach's style, even in his vocal works, has an instrumental foundation. I have it on the authority of Tovey that Bach never wrote for unaccompanied chorus. Even in his motets and chorales the voices were doubled by instruments, which enabled them to achieve passages that they could not have sung unaccompanied, with the result that a choral technique developed. Nowadays we often sing these compositions *a cappella*, and to my mind they sound very beautiful that way. We are told that we are wrong to perform them thus because that was not what Bach intended. Are we so sure that he did not so intend them, but was prevented by the inadequacy of the means at his disposal?

Sir George Dyson once said to me that in his opinion Bach never heard a decent performance of one of his cantatas or motets. We know that he complained bitterly of the inferiority of his players and singers. Are we not then justified in modifying his instrumentation where it is obvious that he was buying a pig in a poke? There is good evidence that Bach was prepared to cut his suit according to his cloth, an instance being the beautiful passage for the lute from the *St. John Passion*, to which Bach appended a note that if necessary it could be played on the organ! In Bach's time the pianoforte had only just been invented, and he is reported to have commented unfavourably on the imperfect examples which were shown him by Frederick the Great. Tovey was of the opinion that if Bach had known a modern grand pianoforte he would have preferred its tone to the nasty jangle of the harpsichord to which he was condemned for filling in his continuo.

This question of the continuo, or figured bass, requires a little more consideration. If we look at a full score of an aria from a Bach Passion or the B minor Mass, we find something very different from what appears in the vocal score editions. In the full score we see the voice part and, usually, only the bass, with perhaps a line for an obbligato instrument. The bass sometimes has figures under it to indicate what the inner parts are to be. The director, or his substitute, sat at the harpsichord or organ improvising these inner parts and generally keeping the whole performance together.

What initiated this continuo system? The music of the great

choral period, the sixteenth century, made use of no such device. The figured bass arose from weakness rather than from strength. About the year 1600 some Italian amateurs devised the beginnings of opera. They had very little technical knowledge of music and therefore left the filling in of the harmony, we may suppose, to some professional expert, indicating to him only the bass and the voice parts. This was all very well for a recitative, accompanied by a few chords, but to hear a large choral work thickened out by the continual presence of the harpsichord or organ must have become intolerably monotonous. But it obtained all through the eighteenth century until the advent of the conductor and the increased efficiency of the performers made it unnecessary. But even now, in solo songs of the Bach period, we usually have to use some instrument to fill up the inner parts. A good grand pianoforte does this much less obtrusively and more artistically than the harpsichord. But I am sorry to say that in obedience to the new Bach-as-he-wrote-it fashion this instrument is again raising its unpleasant head.

The clarinet is a good example of the way in which an instrument will stimulate a composer. It was not an inevitable part of the orchestra in the time of Bach and Handel; it belonged chiefly to the open-air wind band and was, I imagine, a coarse and rather loud instrument, as its name, 'little trumpet', suggests. But in the early eighteenth century the conductor of the well-known Mannheim orchestra added what must have been an improved version of the clarinet to his band. It was here that Mozart heard this beautiful instrument, for which he later wrote a concerto. He also added a clarinet part to the score of his G minor Symphony. Haydn followed suit, first using the instrument rather tentatively to fill up the tuttis; but when he wrote the Prelude to *The Creation*, he had fully realized its possibilities. Here then is a case of the instrument maker prompting the composer.

It was just the opposite with Wagner and his tubas: he wanted four of these instruments to suggest Valhalla, in the *Ring*—higher in pitch and rather thinner in tone than the ordinary bass tuba. So he set to work with an instrument maker and together they devised the so-called Wagner tubas.

I fear that it is the mid-nineteenth-century composers who are to blame for the deterioration of the modern horn and trumpet. They were continually demanding from the trumpet higher and higher notes and from the horn more and more agility, with the result that the noble old trumpet in F had to be given up in favour of a tinny little instrument in a higher key and the true French horn, the soul of orchestral poetry, disappeared in favour of an instrument which looks, indeed, like a horn but sounds more like a mixture of a saxophone and a euphonium. All of Richard Strauss's tricks can be played easily on this instrument, and it is said to be quite safe and never to bubble, but its poetry is gone. A few years ago I heard the opening of Schubert's C major Symphony played on a real horn, and all the world beyond the world seemed open to me. Later on I heard it played on a modern instrument; the notes were as certain as if they were being played on an organ, but the magic was no longer there.

Hubert Parry used to say that the beauty of the French horn was partly due to its human fallibility. Is not this true, to a certain extent, of all instrumental playing? Does not the thrill of sixteen violins playing together come from the fact that they are not scientifically in tune with each other? Would not the wonderful surge of the opening of Schubert's 'Unfinished' Symphony be lost if the violoncellos and basses moved from note to note with mathematical exactness at the same moment? An orchestra must not become a perfect machine.

Now comes the question of making the instrument first and finding the music for it afterwards. Berlioz is the great sinner in this respect. He did not, of course, make instruments himself, but he thought out such devices as the four brass bands in the *Messe des morts*, and in the excitement of the invention of the means forgot about the end. When it came to the point, he could think of nothing better for his four brass bands to play than a banal march tune. This was indeed putting the cart before the horse. And so the old problem of form and content crops up again; the idea and its presentation should be simultaneous and indivisible.

I have purposely reserved for special discussion the most important instrument in our modern musical armoury. The pianoforte is a comparatively new invention. It was a long time before it superseded the clavichord as a household instrument and the harpsichord for public use. The famous organ builder, Gottfried

Silbermann, made some experimental pianofortes for Frederick the Great; Bach tried them and, it is reported, did not care for them. Probably these early examples were very imperfect. The early manufacturers made the mistake of trying to make the pianoforte sound like a harpsichord. Even Beethoven's pianoforte was a very different affair from our modern grand.

Gradually the new instrument acquired its own character and atmosphere. The tone of the harpsichord was constant: only by the manipulation of stops and manuals could the player vary from loud to soft, while crescendo and diminuendo were impossible. A good player on a modern pianoforte can pass at will, gradually or quickly, from an almost inaudible softness to a thundering loudness, and this almost entirely by finger pressure, which has no more effect on the harpsichord than it does on the organ. The pianist can pick out a phrase for special prominence in the middle of a contrapuntal web in a manner that was impossible to his predecessor; by the use of the loud pedal he can prolong the sound of a note and thus evoke the idea of a violin or vocal cantabile. A clever pianist can suggest the orchestra, the organ, or even the choir, by his playing and can often get much nearer to the composer's idea than a second-rate orchestra.

Not only can a pianoforte look forward, it can also look back. Music written for the earlier instruments can also be played with good effect on the pianoforte. It may not be exactly what the composer intended, but composers are bound by their means, and I have little doubt that Bach would have thought that his music sounded better on our modern instruments than on those which he had at his disposal. I have heard many of the Forty-Eight Preludes and Fugues played alternately on the pianoforte and harpsichord, and I have no doubt which I prefer. For one thing, on the harpsichord the music sounded like 'period music'. To deprive a composition of its period might be fatal to something which is only of its period. Though Bach belongs superficially to the eighteenth century, spiritually he belongs equally to the twentieth. Therefore we can interpret him by our own minds and means and find that he lives for us, more than for the burghers of Leipzig; for them Bach was indeed the music of the future.

There is a modern fashion, originating, I believe, in Germany, of playing Bach's music 'as he wrote it', which, as I suppose, means that we must, if possible, use the exact instruments which Bach used, presumably at the same pitch, and play them exactly as the eighteenth-century musicians played them—violins with flat bridges and bows held taut by the thumb. We should, of course, substitute the harpsichord for the pianoforte and make use of that atrocious bubble-and-squeak monstrosity, the so-called baroque organ. Our oboes would have to bray like bagpipes and our horns bellow like bulls. Well, we cannot do this even if we wanted to, and if we could, I cannot imagine anyone wanting to substitute the coarse tone and asthmatic phrasing of Bach's oboe for the exquisite cantabile of one of our fine symphonic players in the great watching song from the *Matthew Passion*.

The pianoforte at its best is now the universal provider, and at its worst, the maid of all work in our musical commonwealth. At one moment the pianoforte can be used to realize the most ethereal fancies of Chopin or Debussy and at another, to thump out a comic song in a tavern. The pianoforte is equally at home in the palace or the cottage and has a colossal specialized literature of every degree of goodness or badness. Thus the pianoforte has completed the democratization of our art. The performer's intonation on a pianoforte does not depend on his own musical nature but on the state of his instrument. That is why for every one player on the flute or violin there are probably a hundred who can tap out a tune on the pianoforte. Here, then, is mass-made music for the masses; we must be careful that quantity does not oust quality.

May I put in a word for the pianoforte duet? When I was young and orchestral concerts were few, when full scores were beyond our means and the radio and phonograph were not yet invented, our chief means for studying orchestral music was the pianoforte duet. With all our modern aids to listening, we are too apt to hear music in a daydream, without giving it our real attention. But the pianoforte duet gave us an intimate knowledge of the great classics which we are all too likely to miss if we turn on the radio and the phonograph.

4

When Do We Make Music?

Music has always been part of ceremony, especially religious ceremony. From primitive times both song and dance have made part of religious ritual, which calls forth the desire for music, and especially song, to enhance the excitement and spiritual exaltation of the worshippers. The most important of these ceremonies for the last two thousand years have been those of the Roman church. In early days the priests had to wean their followers from the pagan festivals which they loved; so they built Christian churches on the sites of pagan temples and converted the gods of the Greek and Roman pantheons into companies of saints. Also, it is almost certain, they adapted the songs the people were already singing for use in their own services.

Father Chambers, well supported by quotations from the early fathers, argues that the melismata which are so characteristic of the Roman rite are adapted from the jubilations of primitive folk-song. These were sung without words, which the people found to be inadequate, and they discovered a mystical meaning in these word-less cantilenas. When the church took over the jubilations, they found them difficult to memorize and they added to them words such as 'alleluia' and 'amen' and later whole poems as a sort of aide-mémoire. In the same way a folk-singer will add words without meaning, such as 'hey derry down', to help him remember the melody of a refrain. Not only did the church use these melismata for its own purposes, but it adapted whole ballads to ecclesiastical use, substituting pious words for the unseemly cries of the tavern love song. Father Chambers quotes a story of Brother Henry of Pisa, who, on hearing a servant girl sing a love song as she passed through the cathedral, was at once struck by the idea that the same tune could be set to religious words as a good means of converting the ungodly.

The same kind of thing has happened in modern times; in my own lifetime I have known the Salvation Army choirs to sing

Ta-ra-ra-boom-de-ay
We've saved a soul today.

John Wesley is reported to have said that he did not see why the Devil should have all the pretty tunes. True to his principles he set that superb hymn, 'Lo He comes with clouds descending', to a popular tune known as 'Miss Catley's Hornpipe', which begins, 'Where's the mortal can resist me?' I need hardly add that the original tune is nearly unrecognizable in its present stately form.

In the fifteenth century church composers began to use secular tunes as *canti fermi* on which to build their contrapuntal masses and motets. Almost every composer, including Palestrina, wrote a mass founded on the folk-tune '*l'homme armé*'. One English composer, Taverner, used a ballad tune, 'Westron Wynd', as a *canto fermo* for a mass:

O western wind when wilt thou blow
That the small rain down may rain?
Christ, that my love were in my arms
And I in my bed again.

The congregations in the churches sometimes used to recognize these tunes, hidden though they were in the contrapuntal web (I fear that modern congregations might not be so clever), and having got hold of the tune they sang it, not to the words of the Mass, but to the original words of the folk-song, which were, as we have seen, delightful in themselves but unsuitable for church use.

This state of affairs caused a scandal and led to a reform; Palestrina was called in to help and wrote the famous *Mass of Pope Marcellus*. But as we have seen, he still had a sneaking feeling for the old tunes, and sometimes he introduced a 'tuney bit' into his music, such as the *Noe* from his 'Hodie Christus natus est'. The word *Noe* is not in the office and was probably an importation from a popular song. Perhaps Palestrina used the very tune to which the words were usually sung.

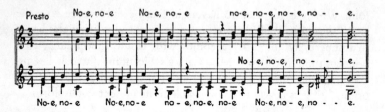

There is also the well-known 'Gloria' from his Magnificat in the Third Mode, which sounds much like a popular tune and is sung, in a slightly modified form, as a hymn-tune to this day.

The same sort of thing was going on in France; in his book on French folk-song Tiersot tells a wonderful tale of how, when Charlemagne brought his French church singers to Rome, the Roman complained of the rough, country character of their singing. What can this mean but that they were singing adapted popular songs? Now one of the psalm-tunes which the French singers almost certainly brought with them is that known as the 'Pilgrim's Tune', or 'Tonus Peregrinus'. Another tune which they almost certainly sang was the famous Easter hymn, 'O filii et filiae'. Tiersot gives two French folk-songs, 'Rossignolet du bois' and 'Voici venir le joli mois';[1] the resemblance between these songs and the two hymns can scarcely be accidental. What can be more likely than that the ecclesiastical musicians should have adapted such songs for their own hymns?

The Lutheran Reformation produced its own corpus of tunes. Some of these were specially composed, even by Luther himself; some were taken over from the Roman rite; and some were adaptations of popular songs, of which not only the tunes but the words were adapted for church use. The latter were called 'spiritual parodies' of the originals. The best known of these is the famous tune 'Innsbruck', which started life as 'Innsbruck, ich muss dich

[1] Julien Tiersot, *Histoire de la chanson populaire en France* (Paris: Plon, Nourrit et Cie., 1889), pp. 73, 361.

lassen' but which became in the parody, 'O Welt, ich muss dich lassen'. The original was probably a nostalgic song by a wandering apprentice, leaving his native town; one can see how easily this could be changed to a spiritual meditation. There is a beautiful setting of the original tune by Heinrich Isaac. Then it found its way into church, where congregational singing caused it to put on a strait waistcoat; it finally achieved immortality in Bach's *St. Matthew Passion*.

Another good example is a love song, 'Flora, meine Freude'. Here is one of the earliest versions of the tune, as given in Johannes Zahn's great collection, *Die Melodien der deutschen evangelischen Kirchenlieder*:

This song became, at the hands of the parodists, 'Jesu, meine Freude'. One version of the tune and the revised words became the basis of Bach's great motet of the same name.

The connexion between music and dance is obvious: dance music is a specialized form of the art, because the nature of the dance demands strong accents, a square pattern, and short phrases. Dance music is really applied art. I do not mean by this that dance is the justification of music; rather, music is the justification of the dance. Who would dream of dancing without music? Would not the dance alone become a series of meaningless antics? On the other hand, dance music is often played without the dance; the waltzes of Johann Strauss can arouse enthusiasm in the concert room until it is difficult to keep one's feet still. So we come to the old conclusion that beauty derives from suitability but often outlives its original purpose.

Miss Maud Karpeles, the well-known authority on folk-song and former assistant of Cecil Sharp, writes as follows:

The folk themselves are very conscious of the intimate connection between music and the dance. Mr. Sharp often had the experience that a dancer would sing him the tune and then be quite surprised if having learned the tune he could not tell how the dance went. One old dancer said to him, 'We used to learn the song and then there was no trouble for the steps are just as the words be.' From that one would imagine that the words were some kind of description of the dance, but usually they were just nonsense rhymes. For instance, the words of Greensleeves, the tune used for the Bacca Pipes Jig, are

> Some say the devil's dead   (three times)
> And buried in Cold Harbour
>
> Some say he's rose again   (three times)
> And married to a barber.

It is certainly a little difficult to see the connection between these words and the steps of the Jig, but the explanation is that the dancer felt that the words enforced the rhythm of the music and helped him to get hold of the tune and sing it himself. And once having got the tune inside him, so to speak, all was plain sailing.[2]

This brings us logically to our next consideration, that of words and music.

How far can we count language as one of the sources of music? Primitive singers, as we know, used music only as a means of memorizing words or dances, but we have seen that, in the jubilus, music often gets beyond words, which then become mere vehicles for punctuating the vowel sounds. The word 'Nowell', for example, which so often comes in the refrains of carols, probably means 'good news', *nouvelles*, but from the singer's point of view, when coupled with the music, it transcends meaning and thus enters a mystical world.

Words when sung are sometimes only the framework for sound. Wagner used to read the libretti of his operas to his friends; I am glad I was not there. One could not fill the Metropolitan or Covent Garden with a spoken recital of the *Ring*. But one can excite an audience to enthusiasm in the concert room with the *Meistersinger* overture, or with the 'Liebestod', though one may not be able to hear, or understand, any of the words sung by Isolde. This may indeed be an advantage, because her words, by themselves, are a very poor exposition of the situation. It is the music that reaches the sublimity of passion. Of course words are necessary in opera;

[2] From a letter to the author. By permission.

the singers are there singing, and it would never do for them to declaim 'la, la, la', all the time. However, in his lyrical moments Wagner was very clever in using words such as *Liebe, Nacht, ewig*, or even the names of the two protagonists, all of which have a strong emotional connotation and help the music to rise to the heights.

The names of places and people can give emotional intensity to a poem, even a mere recital of them. Here are the lines of 'Thyrsis', in which Matthew Arnold gives a list of the places he loved near Oxford:

> Runs it not here, the track by Childsworth Farm,
> Past the high wood, to where the elm-tree crowns
> The hill behind whose ridge the sunset flames?
> The signal-elm, that looks on Ilsley Downs,
> The Vale, the three lone weirs, the youthful Thames?

The emotional value is enhanced, as if by music, by the singing quality of such words as 'the three lone weirs'.

5

What are the Social Foundations of Music?

We must not suppose that composers invent their music out of the blue, without forerunners or surroundings. The innovators are the small men who set the ball rolling. The big men come at the end of a period and sum it up. Thus it was with Bach. The period of Haydn and Mozart, not to speak of the smaller people like Cherubini and Hummel, led the way to the supreme master, Beethoven. We can trace the art of Wagner through the early *Singspiele* of Adam Hiller and his contemporaries in the eighteenth century, through Weber and Marschner, to find its culmination in *Die Meistersinger* and 'Tristan'. These were the right men coming at the right time and under the right circumstances; that is what enabled them to be great. Sometimes the potentially right man comes at the wrong time. Purcell, for example, was a bit too early for his flower to bloom fully; Sullivan, who in other circumstances might have written a *Figaro*, was thwarted by mid-Victorian inhibitions: the public thought that great music must be portentous and solemn, an oratorio, or a sacred cantata at the least, and that comic opera was beneath notice as a work of art.

The great example of the right man, at the right time, in the right place, is John Sebastian Bach. He was not a biological sport: he came from a long line of musical ancestors. And what is more, the musical gift did not die out with him, for he had several sons who would have shone brightly in the musical firmament if they had not been partly eclipsed by their great father. John Sebastian's first musical ancestor appears to have been Veit Bach, by profession a baker and miller, who used to spend his spare time playing on his beloved zither. Veit had a son who became a *Spielmann*, or professional musician; and from that time onward the tribe of family musicians grew until nearly every town in Thuringia had a Bach as its 'town piper', as the official musicians were called. They held a humble enough position; their duty was to provide music for all civic occasions as well as for weddings, banquets, and funerals. Doubtless some little thing of their own was often played on these occasions. Then came 1685: the time was ready, the place was ready, and the circumstances were ready for the man who, to my mind, is the greatest musician of all time. J. S. Bach's position was, nominally, not much more important than that of his numerous cousins and uncles. True, Leipzig is a comparatively large town, and he was dignified by the name of 'cantor', but his duties included teaching, not only music, but also Latin, to the boys at the public school. He had to play the organ, either himself or by deputy, in two churches and to conduct the services. Every week he had to provide a little thing of his own for performance on Sunday. It happened that these compositions included the *St. Matthew Passion* and the B minor Mass.

6

The Folk-song Movement

Hubert Parry, in his great book *The Evolution of the Art of Music*, has shown that a Beethoven symphony, for instance, is not a unique phenomenon but that its whole structure can be traced back, stage by stage, to the art of the primitive folk-singer.

The early nineteenth century started a movement among composers to short-circuit all the intervening evolutionary process and cut straight back to the origin of things. These nationalist composers tried to found their style on the folk-songs of their own countries. I think the movement started in Russia when Glinka began using street songs in his operas: the idea was taken up, *con amore*, by his successors, Moussorgsky and Borodin, who not only used traditional melodies in their compositions, but built up their original work on the same basis. Even Tchaikovsky and Rachmaninov, though they were frowned on by the ultra-nationalists as not being true Russians, often showed the influence of Russian folk-songs in their compositions.

Members of the fashionable Russian world were shocked at anything national, as we know from Tolstoi's and Turgenev's novels, and habitually talked French to each other, reserving their native Russian for peasants and droshky drivers; therefore it is not surprising that they labelled this nationalist style as 'coachman's music'. But the coachman's music has survived, while the sham classical style of Rubinstein has almost disappeared.

I have just used the word 'classical'; anti-national musical critics are in the habit of declaring that the so-called classical style is the only true path, and that the nationalist music of the Russians, of Dvořák, and of Grieg is mere affectation or cliquishness. But what is the classical style? It is nothing more or less than the Teutonic style. It so happened that for nearly a hundred years, in the eighteenth and early nineteenth centuries, the great composers, with the possible exception of Haydn, were all German or Austrian. So the Teutonic style became accepted as the classical model. But what is the Teutonic style? When people hear a German or Austrian folk-song, they say, 'This is just like Mozart or Beethoven in their simpler moods; it is not a folk-song at all, but was probably composed by Michael Haydn or Leopold Mozart.' It never occurs to these good people that Mozart, Beethoven, and Schubert came from the humbler classes and were doubtless imbued from childhood with the popular music of their country. The truth, I believe, is not that Teutonic folk-songs are like the melodies of classical composers but that the simpler melodies of classical composers are like Teutonic folk-songs, and that we can claim Mozart and Beethoven as nationalists as much as Dvořák and Grieg.

Music, like language, derives ultimately from its basic beginnings. May I give an instance from my own country? About fifty years ago Cecil Sharp made his epoch-making discovery of English folk-song. We young musicians were intoxicated by these tunes. We said to ourselves, 'Here are beautiful melodies of which, until lately, we knew nothing. We must emulate Grieg and Smetana, and build up, on the basis of these tunes, a corpus of compositions arising out of our own country and character.' And we proceeded to pour out Overtures and Rhapsodies and Ballad Operas to show the world that we were no longer a land without music. We had our critics, who took the curious line that, though it was perfectly right and proper for a Russian or a Norwegian to build up his style on his own national melodies, if an Englishman tried to do so, he was being what they described by that appalling, invented word 'folky'.

Of course the movement has had its camp followers: composers have thought that if they pitchforked one or two of Sharp's discoveries into a ready-made mixture imported from Russia or France they were inventing a national style. This was the bad side of the movement, and none of the more level-headed of us imagined that because Beethoven quoted a Russian tune in one of his Rasumovsky quartets he thereby became a Russian composer; or that because Delius used an English folk-song in one of his compositions it made him into an Englishman. Those who claim

England as the birthplace of Delius's art must base their argument on more valid premises than this. The movement is now fifty years old, the tunes are again common property, and every English child must know them as well as he knows his own language, whether he likes it or not. Composers of the younger generation emphatically do not like it, but they cannot help being influenced by these beautiful tunes. As Gilbert Murray says, 'The original genius is at once the child of tradition and a rebel against it.'

EPILOGUE

Making Your Own Music

All vital art is creative art; and musical appreciation especially demands active participation rather than passive acceptance on the part of the hearer. When we listen to a symphony as we should do, we are actually taking part, with the composer and the performers, in the creation of that symphony.

Shakespeare wrote some very beautiful lines about letting music creep in our ears, but this is not a true picture of real, creative listening, which cannot exist except as a counterpart of active participation by the hearer. Therefore, before we truly listen we must be able also to create.

When I write about the creation of music, I do not mean merely putting black dots on a piece of paper. The humblest member of a choral society, the shy beginner who takes his place at the back desk of the second violins in an amateur orchestra, the child who plays a triangle in a percussion band, if he sings or plays with understanding and purpose, is a creator.

I have great admiration for the wonderful revolution in the status of music achieved in our time by the radio and the phonograph. These inventions have given to millions the opportunity to hear great music greatly played or sung. They have also set a standard for many amateurs and students of what to imitate, and occasionally, it must be confessed, of what to avoid—if they will only profit by it.

But will they so profit? Will not all this listening to superb, expert performances bring on a counsel of despair in the mind of the humble amateur, who, for example, plays the flute a little for his own amusement? Will he not feel inclined to say, 'With my limited capacities, my small opportunities for practice, I cannot hope to approach the perfection which I hear. Better give up the struggle and become a merely passive listener.' If our amateur flautist thinks thus, he will have lost one of the greatest assets of his spiritual life, the vision of the ultimate realities through the making of music.

Gustav Holst used to say that if a thing was worth doing at all, it was worth doing badly. I entirely agree, with this proviso—that this 'doing' must be a sincere attempt towards self-expression. Superficiality, half-heartedness, sham, and swagger must have no part in the scheme. Granted this sincerity of purpose, we may well say with Calverley:

> Play, play your sonatas in A
> Heedless of what your next neighbour may say!

Music is, first and foremost, self-expression; without that it is a falsehood. I feel sure that a man marooned for life on a desert island would continue to make music for his own spiritual exaltation even though there were no one to hear him. Sometimes these spiritual exercises spread beyond the individual; the neighbours may, after all, like the results. And so we go on till we come to the famous expert whose music is for all the world. But first he must to his own self be true; he cannot then be false to any man. Wordsworth's Solitary Reaper sang for herself alone, little thinking that she was being indirectly responsible for one of the world's greatest poems.

Supposing we all became passive listeners? Whom should we find to listen to? For a time the great virtuosi who are still with us will satisfy our needs. But voices fail, fingers become stiff, vision grows dim, even in the greatest of us. Our beloved art will die of inanition unless there are young men and women to seize the torch from the faltering hands of their elders. Where are these young men and women to be found? Surely among those who are attempting to make music for themselves. How are we to discover among these the private soldier who bears the marshal's baton in his knapsack? Only by trial and error.

Music must be offered to all, though it will not be accepted by all. We must speak the password to everybody; only in that way can we find out who will respond. The many must be called so that the few may be chosen. Virginia Woolf has written: 'Master-pieces are not single and solitary births, they are the outcome of many years of thinking in common, of thinking by the body of the people, so that the experience of the mass is behind the single voice.'

I am not trying to exalt the dilettante at the expense of the expert. The virtuoso is essential to our musical life. The world-famous musician is like a pinnacle, shining for all to see; but unless the pinnacle rests on a solid foundation, it will totter and fall. The musical life of a community may be compared to a pyramid. At the apex are the great and famous; below, in rank after rank, stand the general practitioners of our art, competent and enthusiastic, and often endowed with a musical insight which their more famous but more specialized fellows do not possess. Here are the hard-working and unassuming men and women who are the musical salt of the earth. They wish for neither fame nor fortune; their one desire is to spread the gospel of music by precept and practice; but, like Chaucer's Poor Parson who preached the gospel of goodness, first they follow it themselves. Lastly we come to the great army of humble music makers, who, as Hubert Parry says, 'make what they like and like what they make'. These are the foundations of the pyramid, sustaining those above them and at the same time depending upon them for strength and inspiration. So, by laying stone on stone, we build up a great structure of music, reaching higher and higher into the empyrean but with its foundations firmly set on the great traditions of our art. Thus the humblest and the highest join in the service of music.

There is another side to this question of self-made music; as the Preacher discovered years ago, it is the business of some men to find out musical tunes. Surely if anyone ever made his own music, it was these men. But some people who ought to know better think otherwise. A foolish fellow once labelled music as the universal language. Whistler was equally foolish when he said that it was as wrong to talk about national art as national chemistry. As a climax we have Rossini's epigram, 'I know only two kinds of music, good and bad.'

Music, it is true, has a universal vocabulary, but each composer uses this vocabulary as his own nature and the circumstances of his surroundings dictate. We may say to Whistler that chemistry is a science whose business it is to discover and co-ordinate facts; art is the means by which one man communicates spiritually with another. As for Rossini, let me quote an example. Verdi's *Requiem* is a work which defies all the canons of good taste. It is melodramatic, sentimental, sometimes almost cheap; it employs without shame such well-worn means to excitement as the diminished seventh and the chromatic scale. Yet it is one of the greatest works of art and gained the reluctant admiration of a composer with a much different artistic philosophy, Brahms. Now, Mr. Rossini, is this good music or bad?

All young composers long to be individual and are inclined to defy the tradition in which they were brought up. This is very right and proper, but when they plunge into unknown waters, let them hold fast to the life-line of their own national tradition; otherwise the siren voices from foreign shores will lure them to destruction. Musical invention has been described as an individual flowering on a common stem. Now, young composers, do not try to be original; originality will come of itself if it is there. However individual your flowering may be, unless it is firmly grafted on the common stem, it will wither and die. I have all honour for those adventurous spirits who explore unknown regions; I cannot always follow them, but I admire their courage. Sometimes, however, I ask myself whether those composers have not even more courage who find new and unheard-of beauties along the beaten track. Try the beaten track first; if an irresistible impulse leads you into the jungle, be sure that you know the way back.

You in America have a fine literary and scholastic tradition; why not add to this a musical tradition? It is to be found in unexpected corners in this country. Do not rest until you have found it, and when it is found, do not deny your birthright. Remember what Walt Whitman said to the American poets of his time:

Come muse migrate from Greece and Ionia,
Cross out please those immensely overpaid accounts,
That matter of Troy and Achilles' wrath, and Æneas', Odysseus' wanderings.
Placard 'removed' and 'to let' on the rocks of your snowy Parnassus,
Repeat at Jerusalem, place the notice high on Jaffa's gate and on Mount Moriah,
The same on the walls of your German, French and Spanish castles, and Italian collections,

For know a better, fresher, busier sphere,
A wide, untried domain awaits, demands you.

American architects could find no classical models for their dams, grain elevators, and oil refineries; the need created the means, and now it is these buildings which are the glory of American architecture. Whitman, Lowell, and Longfellow found their best inspiration, not in classical models, but in American life and American traditions. How about American music? Until lately that was dominated by foreign influences, but a change has come over the scene. It is not for me to suggest in detail how that has come about. John Powell has experimented with a folk-song symphony; others have tried jazz. We must not make the mistake of thinking lightly of the very characteristic art of Gershwin or, to go further back, the beautiful melodies of Stephen Foster. Great things grow out of small beginnings. The American composers who wrote symphonic poems, for which they were not emotionally ready, are forgotten, while the work of those who attempted less but achieved more has become the foundation on which a great art can rise.

As a suitable ending let me quote a passage from G. M. Trevelyan's *History of England*:

One outcome of the Norman Conquest was the making of the English language. As a result of Hastings, the Anglo-Saxon tongue, the speech of Alfred and Bede, was exiled from hall and bower, from court and cloister, and was despised as a peasants' jargon, the talk of ignorant serfs. It ceased almost, though not quite, to be a written language. The learned and the pedantic lost all interest in its forms, for the clergy talked Latin and the gentry talked French. Now when a language is seldom written and is not an object of interest to scholars, it quickly adapts itself in the mouths of plain people to the needs and uses of life. This may be either good or evil, according to circumstances. If the grammar is clumsy and ungraceful, it can be altered much more easily when there are no grammarians to protest. And so it fell out in England. During the three centuries when our native language was a peasants' dialect, it lost its clumsy inflections and elaborate genders, and acquired the grace, suppleness and adaptability which are among its chief merits. At the same time it was enriched by many French words and ideas. . . . Thus improved, our native tongue re-entered polite and learned society as the English of Chaucer's Tales and Wycliffe's Bible, to be still further enriched into the English of Shakespeare and of Milton. There is no more romantic episode in the history of man than this underground growth and unconscious self-preparation of the despised island *patois*, destined ere long to 'burst forth into sudden blaze,' to be spoken in every quarter of the globe, and to produce a literature with which only that of ancient Hellas is comparable.[1]

Could not this fable be told also of our music in America and England? I will not weary you with English sins against light, but Americans have not been blameless. What did you know of the music germinating in underground growth while the so-called educated classes, if they considered music at all, thought of it in terms of Wagner and the world's worst Festival March and of highly paid European performers showing off their fine feathers, while the real foundations of your art were neglected, with the result that for years American music consisted of watered-down imitations of European models? Even that American of all Americans, Walt Whitman, seemed to think that music consisted of nothing but Italian coloratura singers and cornets playing Verdi.

I think that both our countries are now returning to the true path. I do not wish to advocate a back-to-folk-song policy. Chaucer, Shakespeare, and Milton enriched our language with cullings from France and Italy, Rome and Greece. Our music can also be enriched from foreign models, but it must be an enrichment of our native impulse and not a swamping of it. We have been too apt to think that though we could beat the foreigner at business and sport, the foreigner must necessarily beat us in questions of art. We thought that if we imitated his tricks of diction, we should achieve his inspiration, forgetting that these are only an outward and visible sign of an inward and spiritual grace, rooted in an age-old tradition.

[1] London: Longmans, Green and Co., 1926, pp. 131–132. By permission.

Index